Surviving the Trading Shark Tank

Detecting HFT, Spoofing, and Predatory Algorithms

Noble Trex

Published by NobleTrex Press

For permissions and other inquiries, write to:
P.O. Box 3132, Framingham, MA 01701, USA

Contents

Contents

Introduction

The popular imagination of the stock market is still dominated by the sepia-toned imagery of the twentieth century: a chaotic floor filled with shouting men in colorful jackets, frantically waving scraps of paper to signal intent. It was a visceral, human arena where aggression was visible, and the pace of the game was dictated by the speed of a human voice. That world is gone. It has been replaced by a silent, sterile, and infinitely faster reality-a digital ecosystem housed in windowless data centers, where fiber-optic cables pulse with light and algorithms compete for dominance in the span of microseconds.

For the casual investor or the retail trader, the screen acts as a deceptive interface. It presents a sanitized view of the market: a ticker symbol, a bid price, an ask price, and a chart that seemingly tells the history of value. However, this interface hides the violent turbulence of the modern market microstructure. When you press "buy," you are not simply exchanging capital for equity; you are stepping into a shark tank. You are entering a domain where your intentions are scrutinized, your latency is exploited, and your predictable behaviors are monetized by entities you will never see.

This book, *Surviving the Trading Shark Tank: Detecting HFT, Spoofing, and Predatory Algorithms*, is born from a necessity to bridge the widening chasm between institutional reality and retail perception. The democratization of finance has granted millions access to the markets, yet it has not granted them access to the playbook used by the dominant players. As execution speeds accelerate and artificial intelligence becomes more pervasive, the playing field has tilted aggressively against the uninitiated. The water you swim in is no longer neutral; it is teeming with predatory logic designed to extract value from the slow, the emotional, and the uninformed.

To navigate this environment, one must first dismantle the myths of traditional investing education. Most trading literature focuses on technical analysis-reading charts-or fundamental analysis-reading balance sheets. While these disciplines are vital for deciding *what* to trade, they are woefully inadequate for understanding *how* trading occurs. In the modern era, the "how" creates the edge. The mechanics of price discovery, the nuance of order types, and the hidden architecture of the limit order book are the variables that determine whether you are the predator or the prey.

We begin our journey by examining the foundations of this liquidity landscape. We must distinguish between the act of investing, which is a bet on economic value, and the act of trading, which is often a battle for liquidity. We will strip away the abstractions of the "stock market" to reveal the fragmented network of exchanges and dark pools where prices are actually formed. Understanding the friction costs-slippage, spreads, and market impact-is the first step in realizing that the price you see is rarely the price you get.

Once the stage is set, we will lift the hood to examine the engine of the market: microstructure. This is the realm of the order book, a dynamic stack of buying and selling interest that shifts faster than the human eye can register. We will explore the matching engines that prioritize orders, the routing protocols that fragment liquidity across dozens of venues, and the concept of "toxic flow" that terrifies market makers. It is here that we encounter the High-Frequency Trader (HFT). We will move past the sensationalism and conspiracy theories to understand the economics of speed. HFT is not inherently evil, but it creates an asymmetry of information and time that can leave the casual trader exposed. By understanding how speed is monetized, you learn to spot when you are outmatched.

However, not all participants are merely fast; some are deceptive. A core objective of this text is to provide a taxonomy of manipulation. We will delve into the darker arts of the electronic frontier, such as spoofing, where large orders are placed with no intent of execution, serving only to create the illusion of demand and lure other traders into a trap. We will dissect layering, quote stuffing, and momentum ignition-strategies designed to exploit the emotional reactions of human traders and the programmed logic of other algorithms. You will learn to see the "ghosts" in the machine, recognizing when the depth of the market is a mirage.

Detection, however, is useless without defense. The ultimate goal of this book is to help you build a defensive playbook. We do not promise to teach you how to beat the HFT firms in a race; that is a race you cannot win. Instead, we teach you how to step out of the race entirely. We will discuss the art of "building your cage"-constructing a trading methodology that prioritizes capital preservation. This involves selecting the right order types to control your risk, timing your entry to avoid periods of high volatility and thin liquidity, and configuring your brokerage tools to prevent you from becoming low-hanging fruit for an algorithm.

We will also traverse the complex regulatory landscape, understanding why enforcement lags behind innovation. The definition of manipulation is often contingent on intent, a quality that is notoriously difficult to prove in a court of law when the defendant is a distinct line of code. We will examine the ethical boundaries of the market and the "cat-and-mouse" game played between regulators and those who seek to bend the rules of market integrity.

Finally, we will ground these concepts in reality through narrative case studies. We will walk through the anatomy of a spoofing event, the chaos of a stop-loss cascade, and the frustration of latency arbitrage. By analyzing these scenarios, we transform abstract theory into recognizable patterns.

The modern market is a marvel of efficiency, but it is also a ruthless mechanism for transferring wealth from the impatient to the disciplined. It is a Shark Tank, yes, but it need not be a slaughterhouse for the individual trader. The sharks hunt based on movement, blood, and vibration. They look for the panic of the market order and the predictability of the stop loss. By understanding their nature, their incentives, and their hunting grounds, you can learn to swim among them untouched. This book is your survival guide. Welcome to the deep end.

Chapter 1

The Water You Swim In: Market Foundations

To the casual observer, the stock market looks like a single, unified stream of ticking numbers-a digital ticker tape that moves up or down based on news and corporate performance. But beneath that surface lies a fragmented, high-speed ocean where prices aren't just 'set' but fought over in microseconds. Before you can spot the sharks-the high-frequency algorithms and predatory strategies-you must understand the water itself: how orders travel, why prices flicker, and the hidden currents of liquidity and leverage that can pull you under even when the market seems calm.

1.1 Understanding the Trading Landscape

Most people speak about *"the stock market"* as if it were a single place with a single price—like a giant public bulletin board where everyone sees the same thing and trades the same way.

That mental model is comforting, but it is not how modern markets work.

To survive the "trading shark tank" (the fast, competitive world where professional algorithms operate), you need two foundation ideas:

1. **Trading and investing are not the same activity**, even when they involve the same ticker symbol.
2. **"The market" is not one place.** It is a network of many venues (exchanges and off-exchange systems) connected by brokers and routing rules.

These points may sound philosophical, but they lead directly to practical consequences: what your broker does with your order, why you might not get the price you expected, and why short-term trading is uniquely exposed to fast, aggressive strategies.

Investing vs. trading: same instrument, different game

A share of stock is a single financial instrument. But the *reason* you buy or sell it determines the game you are playing.

Investing: buying ownership and letting time do the work

When you invest, you are primarily trying to capture returns that come from **business performance over time**. You are closer to the mindset of an owner:

- You care about **cash flows** (dividends today, potential dividends later, reinvestment into growth).
- You care about **fundamentals** (revenue, margins, competition, management, balance sheet strength).
- Your main advantage is **time horizon**. You can wait through short-term noise.

In plain language: investing is often about being right *eventually*. If a company compounds earnings over years, temporary price swings are mostly a distraction rather than the main event.

Trading: managing exposure to price changes

When you trade, your return depends far more on **price movement** over your holding period than on business performance over the next decade. Traders focus on:

- **timing** (entering and exiting at favorable prices),
- **liquidity and execution** (how easily you can trade without paying too much to do it),
- **risk control** (position size, stop rules, and avoiding catastrophic drawdowns).

In plain language: trading is often about being right *now enough*—and paying close attention to how you get in and out.

The key difference: your biggest opponent changes

Both investors and traders can lose money, but they tend to lose money for different reasons:

- **Investors** often lose to **bad businesses**, overpaying, or impatience.
- **Traders** often lose to **friction and microstructure**: spreads, slippage, sudden liquidity gaps, and adverse selection (getting filled when it is bad for you and not filled when it is good for you).

This book focuses on threats that disproportionately affect *trading*: fast strategies that react to order flow, exploit fragmented venues, and profit from the small mechanical weaknesses that casual participants rarely notice.

A practical self-check: what must be true for you to win?

A simple way to tell whether you are investing or trading is to ask:

> If I am correct, **what must be true** for me to make money?

- If your answer is "the company must grow over years" or "earnings must compound," you are investing.
- If your answer is "the price must move up in the next week" or "momentum must continue through tomorrow," you are trading.

Neither approach is morally better. But mixing the two is a common failure mode: people *trade* (short horizon, frequent action) while telling themselves they are *investing* (long horizon, patient ownership). That mismatch creates rushed decisions in the exact environment where speed and structure favor professionals.

The "single market" myth: where you think your order goes

Many casual traders imagine a straight line:

You click Buy → The Stock Market → You get "the" price

In reality, your click does not go to "the market." It goes to a **broker**, and the broker (often through automated routing logic) chooses **where** and **how** to attempt the execution.

That matters because price is not a magical universal label. Price is an outcome of **matching** buyers and sellers somewhere, under specific rules, at a specific moment.

The real landscape: a web of venues, not one marketplace

Modern equity trading is fragmented. Instead of one central place, there are many different venues where trading can occur. At a high level, they fall into two buckets:

1. **Lit exchanges (public)**: orders contribute to visible quotes (the displayed bid and ask).
2. **Off-exchange venues (less visible)**: various systems where trades can occur with limited or no public display of the full order book.

This fragmentation is not a conspiracy; it is the result of regulation, competition among venues, and technology. But it creates complexity that fast traders can exploit, especially when they can react to changes across venues quicker than a human can blink.

What is an "exchange" in modern markets?

An exchange is a regulated trading venue with:

- a rulebook for matching orders,
- certain order types it accepts,
- fees and rebates that can influence behavior,
- and a public display of the best bids and offers it hosts ("lit" liquidity).

When you hear names like NYSE or Nasdaq, you are hearing brand labels for major exchange groups, but the key point is simpler: **there are multiple places where the same stock can trade at nearly the same time**.

What is "off-exchange" trading?

Off-exchange trading is a broad label for executions that occur away from public exchanges. This includes:

- broker internalization (a broker or its affiliate fills your order against its own inventory or against another client's order),
- alternative trading systems (often described as "dark pools" in casual conversation),

- other mechanisms that may not display quotes the same way a lit exchange does.

Off-exchange does *not* automatically mean unfair. Sometimes it can reduce market impact for large orders or offer price improvement. But it does mean: **the path from your click to your fill is less straightforward than most people assume.**

Why fragmentation exists (and why you should care)

Fragmentation exists because:

- venues compete for order flow (by fees, rebates, and execution quality),
- different participants want different things (speed, anonymity, size, price improvement),
- technology makes it possible to connect many venues quickly.

You should care because fragmentation creates:

1. **Multiple near-simultaneous prices.** Quotes may differ slightly across venues.
2. **Routing decisions.** Your broker chooses where to send your order, sometimes splitting it.
3. **Information leakage risk.** When an order "touches" multiple venues, it can reveal intentions in pieces.
4. **An arms race for speed.** Fast firms compete to react across venues before others can.

This is the environment in which high-frequency trading and predatory strategies live. They do not need you to be "dumb." They only need you to be **slower** and to interact with the market in predictable ways.

From a single click to many possible paths

When you submit an order, several decisions happen quickly, often invisibly:

1. **Order intent**: Are you saying "get me in now" (market order) or "only at this price or better" (limit order)?
2. **Venue choice**: Which exchange or off-exchange venue should attempt the execution?
3. **Order slicing**: If the order is large, should it be broken into smaller pieces?
4. **Timing**: Should the router go immediately to one place, or scan multiple places in sequence?

For a long-term investor buying a small number of shares occasionally, these details may not dominate outcomes. For a frequent trader, they can be the difference between a reasonable fill and a frustrating one.

A simple mental model: you are negotiating with a distributed crowd

The most useful way to think about modern markets is:

> You are not trading "with the market." You are negotiating with many other participants across many venues, and your broker is the messenger deciding which rooms to walk into first.

Sometimes the messenger gets you a great result. Sometimes the messenger walks into a room where the fastest participants can react to your presence.

Either way, the key takeaway is the same: **the trading landscape is a network.** To understand predatory behavior later (spoofing, stop-hunting dynamics, adverse selection, and latency-based strategies), you first need to accept that your order does not enter one central pool of liquidity. It travels through a fragmented ecosystem.

What this means for the rest of the chapter

This section sets up the two pillars you will build on next:

- **Microstructure basics**: how bids, asks, and the order book translate intentions into prices.
- **Trading frictions**: why even "small" costs (spread and slippage) matter more when you trade frequently.

Once you understand (1) what you are trying to accomplish (trading vs. investing) and (2) where your orders actually go (a fragmented network, not a single place), the mechanics of price discovery will feel less mysterious—and the behavior of predatory algorithms will become easier to recognize as pattern, not magic.

1.2 The Mechanics of Price Discovery

In the previous section, we replaced the comforting myth of a single, centralized "stock market" with a more accurate picture: a network of venues where your broker routes your order. Now we zoom in on what actually happens *inside* those venues when buyers and sellers meet.

This section has one goal: make the displayed price feel less like a mystical number and more like a **mechanical outcome** of a continuous negotiation.

Price is not a label; it is the last agreement

When you look up a stock and see something like $50.12, it is tempting to think:

"That is the price of the stock."

A more accurate statement is:

That was the price of the last trade (the most recent agreement between a buyer and a seller).

At any moment, many participants may be willing to buy, but only at certain prices. Many participants may be willing to sell, but only at certain prices. The trading venue's job is to keep track of these intentions and match them when compatible.

The core object: the order book

An **order book** is a live list of standing offers:

- **Bids** (buy orders): "I want to buy, and the most I'll pay is ..."
- **Asks** (sell orders): "I want to sell, and the least I'll accept is ..."

Think of the order book as two queues facing each other:

- On the left: buyers lined up from *highest bid* (most eager) down to lower bids.
- On the right: sellers lined up from *lowest ask* (most eager) up to higher asks.

The top of each queue is special:

- The **best bid** is the highest price currently offered by any buyer.
- The **best ask** is the lowest price currently offered by any seller.

Those two numbers form the market's front line. They are the closest the two sides have come to agreeing *right now*.

Bid and ask as competing intentions

A crucial mindset shift is to treat bid and ask not as "two prices" but as **two intentions**:

- A bid is a buyer saying: "If someone wants to sell immediately, I will take shares at this price."
- An ask is a seller saying: "If someone wants to buy immediately, I will provide shares at this price."

So when you see a quote like:

50.10 bid / 50.12 ask

it is not the market being indecisive. It is the market honestly revealing that:

- buyers are willing to pay up to $50.10 *right now*, and
- sellers are willing to accept as low as $50.12 *right now*.

Until one side "crosses" the other (by accepting the other side's price), no trade occurs at the top of the book.

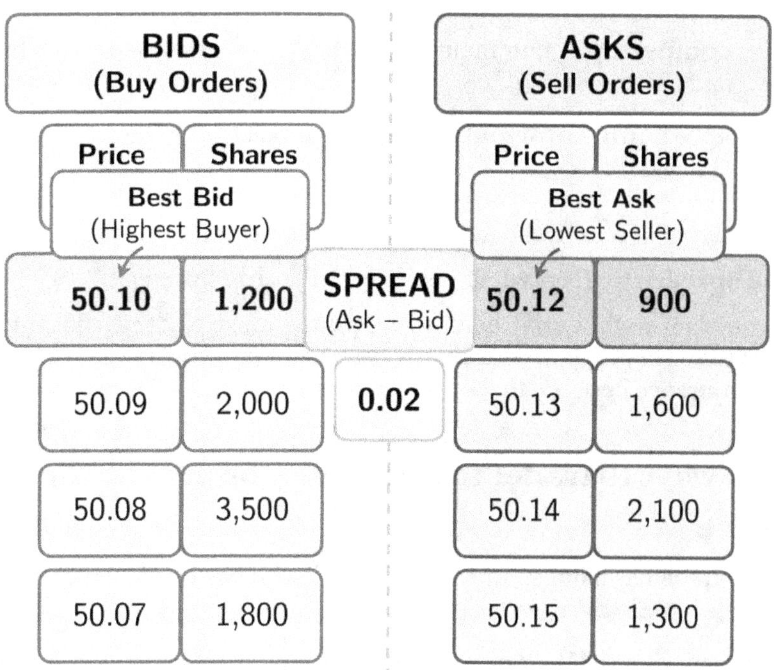

Orders "queue" by price (and then time). Trades occur when a buyer accepts the ask or a seller accepts the bid.

The bid-ask spread: the market's "toll" for immediacy

The **bid-ask spread** is the gap between the best ask and the best bid:

$$\text{Spread} = \text{Best Ask} - \text{Best Bid}.$$

If the best bid is $50.10 and the best ask is $50.12, then the spread is $0.02.

That two-cent gap is not random. It reflects a combination of:

- **liquidity**: how many shares are available near the current price,
- **uncertainty**: how risky it is to stand ready to trade,
- **competition**: how many other traders are trying to provide bids and asks,
- **speed and information**: who can react first when the world changes.

For the casual trader, the most important interpretation is this:

The spread is often what you pay for being "urgent."

If you want to buy *right now*, you typically must pay the ask. If you want to sell *right now*, you typically must accept the bid. The spread is the difference between those two "right now" prices.

Two ways to trade: take liquidity or provide liquidity

Every trade has a buyer and a seller, but it also has a *role* structure:

Taking liquidity (crossing the spread)

If you submit a **market order** (or an aggressively priced limit order) you are usually **taking liquidity**: you are consuming existing bids or asks.

- Buy now $\Rightarrow$ you hit the ask.
- Sell now $\Rightarrow$ you hit the bid.

This is the simplest way to get filled, and the most common way casual traders experience the market. It is also the most exposed to spreads and slippage (more on slippage later).

Providing liquidity (waiting in the book)

If you submit a **limit order** that sits on the bid or ask, you are **providing liquidity**: you are offering to trade with someone else who becomes urgent later.

- Place a buy limit at the bid $\Rightarrow$ you are saying "I will buy if a seller comes to me."
- Place a sell limit at the ask $\Rightarrow$ you are saying "I will sell if a buyer comes to me."

Providing liquidity can reduce costs (you may avoid paying the spread), but it introduces a different risk: you may not get filled, and if you do get filled, it might be because the market moved against you (a concept called **adverse selection**).

At this stage, you do not need the jargon. The intuition is enough:

If you offer a good deal to strangers, you should ask why they accepted it.

How a single trade happens (a concrete walk-through)

Imagine the top of the book is:

$$50.10 \text{ bid} \quad / \quad 50.12 \text{ ask.}$$

Now consider three events:

Event 1: A buyer becomes urgent

A trader submits a market order to buy 500 shares. That order will immediately match against the best ask, because that is the cheapest available seller.

- Execution occurs at (roughly) $50.12 for those 500 shares (assuming at least 500 shares are available at the best ask).
- The last traded price becomes $50.12.

Event 2: The best ask may move

If that buy order consumed all 900 shares at $50.12, then the best ask becomes the next ask level (say $50.13). If it consumed only part of it, the best ask stays $50.12 but with fewer shares available.

This is a key idea: **price levels are not just numbers; they have sizes.**

Event 3: A seller becomes urgent

A seller submits a market order to sell 1,000 shares. That order matches against the best bid, because that is the highest-paying buyer currently waiting.

- Execution occurs at (roughly) $50.10 for those shares (again, assuming enough shares are available at $50.10).
- The last traded price may tick down to $50.10.

The market did not "decide" to move. The market simply matched whoever showed up urgently with whoever was already waiting.

Why the price you see is not always the price you get

Casual traders are often surprised by execution outcomes because they confuse three related but different concepts:

- **Last price**: the most recent execution.
- **Quoted prices**: the current best bid and best ask.
- **Your execution price**: what you actually receive when your order matches.

The last price is backward-looking. Quotes are present-looking. Your execution is *interaction*-looking: it depends on what you asked for (market vs. limit), what size you requested, and what liquidity was available when your order arrived at the venue(s).

In fast markets, those can diverge in ways that feel unfair if you are expecting a single, stable "price."

Why this matters for detecting predatory behavior later

Predatory and manipulative strategies often revolve around one central fact:

The order book is a public signal of intentions.

If you can influence what the book *appears* to say (for example, by briefly displaying large orders you do not intend to execute), you may be able to influence how others react. That is the conceptual doorway to spoofing, layering, and other behaviors we will discuss later.

For now, keep the foundation simple and firm:

- Prices are produced by matching orders.
- The order book is the live map of those orders.
- The spread is the measurable gap between the most eager buyer and the most eager seller.

Once you can "see" the order book as a negotiation queue rather than a mysterious price oracle, the next section's message will land naturally: even when nothing dishonest is happening, trading carries **hidden costs** that accumulate quickly when you trade often.

1.3 The Hidden Costs of Trading

> Even if you predict direction correctly, **trading still has a built-in "tax"** that quietly drains returns.

This section breaks down the three biggest components of that tax—**the spread**, **slippage**, and **market impact**—in plain language, with simple arithmetic that you can reuse on your own trades.

Two kinds of costs: explicit vs. hidden

Most traders can name their **explicit** costs:

- commissions (if any),
- regulatory fees,
- platform subscription costs.

The problem is that the most important costs for frequent traders are often **implicit**:

- you pay them *inside the price*,
- they do not show up as a line item on your statement,
- they compound with activity.

A useful way to think about it is:

> **Your broker statement shows what you paid. The market microstructure determines what you *gave up*.**

We will focus on what you gave up.

Cost #1: The bid-ask spread (the "pay-to-play" fee)

Recall the quote:

$$\text{Bid } 50.10 \quad / \quad \text{Ask } 50.12$$

If you buy immediately (you take liquidity), you typically buy at $50.12. If you then sell immediately, you typically sell at $50.10.

Nothing "bad" happened. No one cheated you. Yet you lost:

$$50.12 - 50.10 = 0.02$$

per share.

That is the spread cost in its purest form: the cost of immediacy.

A simple spread-cost formula

For small, retail-sized trades, a practical approximation is:

Spread cost (round trip) $\approx$ (Ask - Bid) $\times$ Shares.

Example (small spread, small trade). You trade 200 shares with a $0.02 spread:

$$0.02 \times 200 = \$4$$

per round trip, before commissions and before any slippage.

Why it matters. A few dollars sounds trivial, until you repeat it:

- 5 round trips per day $\Rightarrow$ roughly $20/day,
- 20 trading days per month $\Rightarrow$ roughly $400/month,

and that is for a *two-cent* spread and a *modest* share count.

The point is not the exact number. The point is the structure:

> **The spread punishes frequent in-and-out behavior.**

Spread is wider when the water is rough

Spreads are not fixed. They tend to widen when:

- the stock is illiquid (fewer shares waiting at each price),
- the market is volatile (greater risk for liquidity providers),
- news hits (uncertainty spikes),
- the time is awkward (open/close, lunchtime lulls, after-hours).

This is a key reason casual traders often get the worst experience precisely when they feel the most urgency. In stressful moments, the market's "toll" rises.

Cost #2: Slippage (the difference between the price you expected and the price you got)

Slippage is the gap between an expected execution price and the actual execution price.

It commonly shows up in two ways:

Type A: "Quote-to-fill" slippage

You see a quote, you click, and you assume you will trade at that displayed price. But between your click and your fill:

- the best bid/ask can move,
- available shares at the top price can disappear,
- your order can be routed to a venue with a slightly different top-of-book.

Example. You hit buy when the ask displays $50.12. You get filled at $50.13. That $0.01 is slippage.

Notice what makes this psychologically tricky:

- You did not *choose* $50.13.
- You accepted it because you chose *immediacy*.

Type B: "Partial fill" slippage (walking the book)

If you submit an order that is large relative to available shares at the best price, your order may fill across multiple price levels. This is sometimes called **walking the book**.

Example. At the ask side:

- 300 shares offered at $50.12,
- 500 shares offered at $50.13,
- 700 shares offered at $50.14.

If you submit a market order to buy 1,000 shares, you might fill:

- 300 at $50.12,
- 500 at $50.13,
- 200 at $50.14.

Your **average** execution is above the best ask you first saw. That difference is slippage, and it is not a malfunction—it is the book doing exactly what it is designed to do.

A practical slippage definition you can compute from your trade history

For a buy order, define:

Slippage (buy) = (Average fill price - Reference price) × Shares.

For a sell order:

Slippage (sell) = (Reference price - Average fill price) × Shares.

The only "judgment call" is the **reference price**. Common choices are:

- the midpoint: $\frac{\text{Bid}+\text{Ask}}{2}$ at the time you sent the order,
- the displayed best ask (for buys) or best bid (for sells) at the time you clicked,
- the last traded price at the time you clicked (less ideal, but common psychologically).

For learning, midpoint is often the cleanest because it splits the spread.

Cost #3: Market impact (your trade moves the market against you)

Slippage can happen even if you are "small." **Market impact** is what happens when *your own trading* changes the price you receive.

A simple intuition:

> If you show up demanding a lot of shares *right now*, you may have to pay up through multiple price levels—and your buying pressure can push the market up while you are still buying.

This can occur even if no one is predatory. It is a natural outcome of limited liquidity.

Temporary vs. permanent impact

Market impact is often discussed in two flavors:

Temporary impact. Price moves while you trade (because you consume liquidity), and may partially revert after you finish. This is common when you "push through" the book.

Permanent impact. Price moves because the market interprets your activity as information ("someone wants in" or "someone needs out") and others adjust their quotes. This can be stronger in smaller names, during news, or when the order flow is one-sided.

For the casual trader, the exact decomposition is less important than the practical consequence:

The faster and larger you trade, the more you tend to pay.

Why impact makes frequent trading structurally harder

When you trade frequently, you repeatedly:

- pay the spread,
- suffer occasional slippage,
- risk creating impact (especially in less liquid markets or during volatile periods).

In contrast, a patient investor might trade only a few times per year, so these frictions have fewer chances to compound.

This is one reason professionals with superior execution technology can appear "better at trading" even if their directional predictions are not magical. They are often simply paying less tax per trade.

Putting it together: the "all-in" friction estimate

A practical way to estimate your hidden costs on a round trip (buy then sell) is:

$$\text{Total friction} \approx \text{Spread cost} + \text{Slippage} + \text{Impact} + \text{Fees/commissions}$$

You rarely observe impact cleanly as a separate number, but you can observe the outcome: your average fill price is worse than you expected, and the market moves while you trade.

A worked example (the tax shows up even when you are "right")

Suppose:

- You buy 500 shares.
- At the time you click, quote is 50.10/50.12 (spread $0.02).
- You get filled at an average $50.125 (half a cent of slippage relative to the ask).
- Later you sell when the quote is 50.20/50.22.
- You get filled at $50.195 (slippage relative to the bid).

Your *directional* story is right: the market moved up (from about $50.11 midpoint to about $50.21 midpoint). But your realized per-share profit is:

$$50.195 - 50.125 = 0.070$$

per share = $35 on 500 shares.

Now compare that to the midpoint-to-midpoint move:

$$\left(\frac{50.20 + 50.22}{2}\right) - \left(\frac{50.10 + 50.12}{2}\right) = 50.21 - 50.11 = 0.10$$

per share = $50.

The difference, $15, is a rough measure of your **friction** (spread plus slippage plus any impact). You were "right," but the microstructure tax took a cut.

Why these costs favor fast professionals

This book is not arguing that casual traders cannot trade. It is arguing that casual traders should understand the playing field.

Friction costs favor professionals because many professional strategies are built around:

- capturing fractions of spreads repeatedly,
- reacting fast enough to avoid stale quotes,
- earning rebates or optimizing venue selection,

- minimizing their own slippage via smarter execution.

Retail traders, by contrast, often:

- use market orders under stress,
- trade at the most volatile times (open, close, news),
- focus on being correct about direction while underestimating execution quality.

This gap in execution quality is one reason predatory behavior is even possible: if you can anticipate or influence retail-style urgency, you can trade against it.

A defensive takeaway (without "tactics")

You do not need to memorize jargon. You need a habit of mind:

> Before you celebrate a trade idea, ask: **How much does the market charge me to be wrong briefly, and how much does it charge me just to participate?**

As you move forward in this book, keep these three invisible costs in your pocket:

- **Spread**: the toll for immediacy.
- **Slippage**: the gap between the price you expected and your actual fills.
- **Impact**: the price movement you cause by demanding liquidity.

1.4 Risk Principles for the Casual Trader

The last two sections established two uncomfortable facts:

1. Prices are produced by an order book—a fast-moving negotiation between bids and asks.
2. Every trade pays hidden frictions (spread, slippage, and sometimes market impact) that compound with activity.

This section adds the missing piece: **risk**. Not the dramatic kind ("the stock might go to zero"), but the everyday kind that quietly ruins casual traders:

- getting chopped up by noise,
- overreacting to short-term moves,
- taking losses that are small individually but frequent and demoralizing,
- and, crucially for this book, **playing a short-horizon game in a world dominated by fast algorithms**.

The central claim is simple and practical.

Your time horizon is a risk control. It determines which opponents you face and how much microstructure "tax" you pay.

What risk management really means (for non-professionals)

In everyday language, risk management answers three questions:

1. **How much can I lose on this idea?**
2. **How quickly can I lose it?**
3. **If I am wrong a few times in a row, do I survive emotionally and financially?**

Casual traders often focus on being right about direction. Risk management focuses on something more important.

Survival. You do not need one perfect trade. You need a process that can absorb normal bad luck and normal market randomness.

The market has "weather" and "climate"

A useful analogy is to separate market movement into two layers:

- **Weather (short term):** minute-to-minute and day-to-day fluctuations driven by order flow, headlines, positioning, and microstructure dynamics.
- **Climate (long term):** broader forces like earnings growth, macroeconomic trends, and long-run valuation changes.

Casual traders often underestimate how violent the market's weather can be, and how little it tells you about climate. This is where many stop-outs, panic sells, and revenge trades are born.

Time horizon as a natural defense

Time horizon is a defense because it changes what matters.

Short horizons are "microstructure-heavy"

If your holding period is very short (minutes, hours, a day or two), then your outcome is heavily influenced by:

- the bid-ask spread you pay,
- small execution differences (slippage),
- order book dynamics (liquidity appearing and disappearing),
- other participants reacting to order flow.

This is the environment where high-frequency and other fast strategies thrive. They do not need to predict where the company will be in five years. They benefit from the fact that **many participants must trade now**, and that trading now creates exploitable patterns.

Longer horizons dilute the "noise tax"

If your holding period is longer (weeks, months, years), then:

- spreads and slippage occur fewer times (fewer entries/exits),
- short-term random swings matter less,
- it becomes harder for predatory microsecond tactics to directly target your decision-making.

This does *not* mean longer horizon eliminates risk. It means it shifts risk away from the most microstructure-sensitive layer of the market.

A blunt but accurate summary

If you insist on playing a short-horizon game, you are voluntarily entering the fastest part of the pool.

The "three clocks" you are trading against

To make time horizon concrete, picture three clocks ticking simultaneously:

1. **The algorithm clock** (microseconds to seconds): reacts to quote changes, order flow, and venue-by-venue information.
2. **The human trader clock** (minutes to days): reacts to chart patterns, news, and emotions.
3. **The business clock** (quarters to years): earnings, product cycles, competition, and strategy.

Where you choose to operate determines which clock dominates your results. A casual trader cannot win the algorithm clock on speed. The defensive move is not to "get faster"; it is to **stop requiring speed as a condition of success**.

Core risk principles (built for the casual trader)

The following principles are intentionally simple. Simplicity is a feature: complex rules are abandoned under stress.

Principle 1: Position size is your primary safety mechanism

Most blow-ups are not caused by a single bad idea. They are caused by a bad idea that was *too large*.

Position sizing answers: *"If this goes wrong, will I care a little or will I panic?"*

If a normal bad day would cause you to abandon your plan, the position is too big.

This matters for predatory environments because oversized positions create urgency. Urgency turns into market orders, chasing, forced exits, and visible behavior that faster players can exploit.

Principle 2: Define your exit before you enter

An exit rule is not a prediction. It is a seatbelt.

For casual traders, the biggest risk is not lack of intelligence. It is decision-making under pressure:

- holding and hoping,
- selling in fear,
- doubling down to "get back to even."

Defining an exit in advance reduces the chance that a fast, noisy move forces you into improvisation.

Principle 3: Avoid turning normal noise into a forced decision

Markets routinely move against you *a little* even when your overall thesis is fine. If your plan cannot tolerate normal fluctuation, you will be repeatedly forced to act.

This is where time horizon becomes risk management:

- A longer horizon generally implies more tolerance for wiggles.
- More tolerance reduces urgency.
- Less urgency reduces the microstructure tax and your exposure to fast predatory dynamics.

Principle 4: Respect "event risk" and scheduled volatility

Even casual traders should know that certain times are structurally different:

- earnings announcements,
- major economic releases,
- market open and close.

Spreads can widen, liquidity can thin, and prices can gap. If you trade through these periods without acknowledging the higher "weather," you may confuse randomness with a broken thesis.

In shark-tank terms: these are the moments when the water churns and visibility drops.

Principle 5: Minimize the number of "tolls" you pay

From the hidden-cost section, you learned that every entry and exit is a toll booth:

- spreads,
- slippage,
- impact.

Risk management for the casual trader is partly about **reducing the number of tolls you encounter**. The easiest way to do that is not a secret order type or a faster platform. It is **fewer, more deliberate decisions**.

A quick diagnostic: are you living in "shark territory"?

You are likely operating in the highest-noise, most predatory-sensitive zone if most of these are true:

- You feel compelled to act quickly after a price move.
- You frequently use market orders to "make sure" you get filled.
- Small price moves regularly trigger emotional responses (relief, panic, anger).
- You check the price so often that it changes your decision-making.
- A tiny adverse move forces you to close, because the position is too large or the plan is too tight.

None of this is a moral failing. It is a signal that your horizon and sizing are pulling you into the part of the market where speed and microstructure dominate.

The most underappreciated edge: patience

Patience is often described as a personality trait. In markets, it is also a structural advantage.

When you are patient:

- you can use limit prices more often (reducing spread costs),
- you can avoid trading during peak turbulence,
- you are less likely to become predictable "urgent flow",
- you give your thesis time to be tested by more than noise.

In the context of this book, patience is not passive. It is defensive positioning.

Time horizon is camouflage. The less urgent you are, the harder it is for fast strategies to reliably extract edge from your behavior.

Where we go next

Risk management is not separate from microstructure; it is built on it.

Now that you understand:

- how prices are formed (order book, bid/ask, spread),
- why trading has hidden taxes (spread, slippage, impact),
- and how time horizon changes which forces dominate your results,

we are ready to discuss a major amplifier of harm: **leverage**. Leverage compresses your room for error and turns ordinary market weather into forced liquidations—exactly the kind of urgency that predatory dynamics feed on.

1.5 Why Leverage Magnifies Mistakes

Up to this point, the book has been building one idea brick by brick:

- Markets are not a single place; they are a fragmented network of venues.

- Prices are formed by an order book, where bids and asks represent competing intentions.
- Trading has hidden taxes (spread, slippage, and market impact) that punish frequent urgency.
- Time horizon is a form of risk management because it changes how much short-term noise and microstructure you must endure.

Leverage is where these ideas stop being academic and start being dangerous.

Leverage does not just increase potential return. It compresses your margin for error.

For a casual trader, that compressed margin for error is the real problem. It turns ordinary price "weather" into forced decisions, and forced decisions are exactly the kind of predictable, urgent behavior that predatory strategies can exploit.

What leverage is (in plain language)

Leverage means using borrowed money (or leverage-like exposure) to control more assets than your cash alone would allow.

You can get leverage through:

- **margin** in a brokerage account (borrowing against your equity),
- **options** (small premium controlling a larger notional exposure),
- **leveraged ETFs** (built-in leverage inside the product),
- **futures** and other derivatives (high notional exposure with a smaller margin deposit).

This section focuses on the shared mechanics. The wrapper differs, but the risk geometry is similar.

The core math: leverage scales both gains and losses

If you buy $10,000 of stock with $10,000 of your own cash, your leverage is 1:1 (no leverage). A 1% move in the stock roughly creates a 1% move in your position value.

If you instead control $10,000 of stock with only $2,000 of your own equity, your leverage is 5:1. Now a 1% move in the stock creates about a 5% move in your equity *before* fees and financing costs.

A simple approximation:

$$E \approx L \times P$$

where E is Equity % change, L is Leverage, and P is Price % change.

So leverage is not mysterious. It is a multiplier.

What casual traders miss is that risk is not just "how much can I lose in theory." Risk is also **how much normal fluctuation your account can tolerate before you are forced to act**.

Room for error: the most important concept in leveraged trading

Every trade needs breathing room. Markets do not move in straight lines. Even when you are "right," price often moves against you first.

Unleveraged example: you can wait out noise

Suppose you buy a stock at $100 and you think it will go to $120 over the next few months. It is common for a stock to wiggle 2–5% in the short term, sometimes more.

If you are unleveraged and properly sized, a dip from $100 to $97 is uncomfortable but survivable. You are not forced to sell. You can let the thesis play out.

Leveraged example: the same wiggle becomes an emergency

Now suppose you take high leverage so that a 3% adverse move becomes a 15% hit to your equity (because of the multiplier). That same dip from $100 to $97 can trigger:

- a margin call,
- a forced liquidation by the broker,
- a discretionary panic sell because the loss feels catastrophic,
- or a stop-loss order being hit prematurely.

The market did not do anything unusual. **Your leverage setting converted normal noise into a crisis.**

Leverage and the microstructure "tax" interact

Earlier, we discussed friction costs: spread, slippage, and impact. Leverage makes these more harmful in two ways.

First: leverage magnifies all frictions measured in dollars

If you trade bigger (which is often the point of leverage), the same spread and slippage cost more in dollars:

- more shares ⇒ more spread paid per entry/exit,
- larger orders ⇒ more chance of walking the book (slippage),
- higher urgency ⇒ worse fills.

Second: leverage creates urgency, and urgency increases frictions

When your account is tight, you cannot "wait for a better price." You feel compelled to:

- hit the market to get in,
- hit the market to get out,
- chase,
- or exit at the worst possible moment.

This creates a feedback loop:

Leverage → Less room for error → More urgency → Higher friction costs → F

In the shark-tank metaphor: leverage makes you bleed faster, and bleeding attracts sharks.

Why leverage increases vulnerability to stop-hunting dynamics

This book is careful about language: "stop-hunting" is often used loosely, and not every stop-out is the result of manipulation. Many stop cascades occur simply because:

- lots of traders cluster stops at obvious levels (round numbers, recent lows/highs),
- a burst of selling or buying can push price into those levels,
- stop orders convert into market orders, adding fuel to the move,
- liquidity temporarily thins as others back away.

Whether or not a malicious actor "targets" you personally, the structure is real:

Leverage forces stops to be close. Close stops are easier to trigger. Triggered stops can create cascades.

The clustering problem: predictable exits are exploitable

Casual traders often place stops where they feel "safe":

- just below a recent low,
- just below a round number,
- just below a widely watched moving average.

Those levels become crowded. Crowded levels are not secret. They are inferred from public price behavior and common human habits.

Fast traders do not need to know *your* stop. They only need to know where *many* stops are likely to be.

Leverage worsens the situation because it tends to force:

- tighter risk limits (small adverse moves are intolerable),
- more frequent use of hard stops (automated exits),
- faster capitulation (panic selling).

Stop orders and liquidity: why execution can be worse than you expect

A stop-loss order is not a magic escape hatch. Once triggered, it often becomes a market order (depending on the type), meaning it will fill at available prices.

In a fast move, available prices can gap:

- You expected to exit near $97.00.
- The trigger occurs at $97.00.
- The actual fill occurs at $96.70 or $96.40 because liquidity at $97.00 vanished.

That is slippage—and with leverage, that slippage hits your equity harder.

Margin calls: the broker's risk management, not yours

A margin account has a second risk manager: your broker.

This is a common misunderstanding. Many casual traders think:

"I will decide when to exit."

With leverage, the more accurate statement is:

"I will decide when to exit *unless the broker exits me first.*"

When equity falls below maintenance requirements, the broker may require additional funds or liquidate positions. This liquidation can happen:

- quickly,
- at unfavorable prices,
- during volatile conditions (precisely when liquidity is thin).

So leverage changes the nature of control. You are no longer fully steering the vehicle.

Leverage shrinks your time horizon (whether you want it to or not)

Remember the earlier principle: time horizon is a defense. Leverage undermines that defense by forcing you onto the short clock.

Even if your idea is "long-term," high leverage can turn it into a short-term trade because:

- you cannot tolerate temporary drawdowns,
- you cannot hold through normal volatility,
- you must react to short-term fluctuations to avoid liquidation.

In other words, leverage often *converts* investing-like ideas into trading-like behavior, which drops you back into the microstructure-heavy environment where speed and predation matter most.

The casual trader's leverage checklist

If you choose to use leverage, the defensive mindset is to assume that anything which forces urgency is hazardous.

Before using leverage, ask:

- **What is "normal" volatility for this asset?** (Not the best-case day. The typical wiggle.)
- **Can my position survive that wiggle without forcing me to act?**
- **If my stop triggers in a fast move, can I tolerate slippage?**
- **What happens if I am wrong three times in a row?** (Not because you're bad, but because randomness clusters.)
- **Who controls the exit: me or the broker?**

If these questions feel uncomfortable, that is the correct signal. Leverage is not dangerous because it is complicated. It is dangerous because it is **unforgiving.**

A closing principle: leverage is a bet against noise

The market produces noise. Noise is not an error; it is part of the system. Leverage is effectively a bet that:

- the market will move your way soon enough,
- and it will not wiggle against you first by more than your thin margin can tolerate.

That is a fragile bet for a casual participant, especially in an ecosystem where speed, fragmentation, and order-flow dynamics can create short, sharp moves.

If you want to survive the shark tank, prioritize staying afloat over swimming faster.

In the chapters ahead, we will examine specific fast and manipulative behaviors (including spoofing) and, more importantly, the defensive thinking that reduces your exposure. But the foundation remains this: **risk management is about avoiding forced decisions**, and leverage is one of the fastest ways to manufacture them.

Chapter 2

Under the Hood: Market Microstructure Mechanics

When you click 'buy', you aren't handing cash to another person; you are feeding instructions into a complex, high-speed machine. To the casual observer, the market looks like a stream of ticker prices. To the predatory algorithm, it is a rigid system of queues, routing protocols, and priority rules. This chapter lifts the hood on that engine. We will explore how the 'Order Book' actually works, why being fast effectively means cutting the line, and how your order travels through a fragmented landscape of exchanges. Understanding these mechanics is the first step in realizing why the price you see isn't always the price you get.

2.1 Mastering Order Types: The Inputs

Markets look complicated on the surface-candlesticks, headlines, indicators, and constant motion. Under the hood, though, modern electronic markets run on something much simpler: *instructions*. Every participant, from a long-term retirement saver to a high-frequency trading (HFT) firm, interacts with the market by sending an order that tells the exchange (or broker) what you want to do.

In this chapter, we are going to treat order types the way an engineer treats the controls of a machine. If you don't understand the controls, you can't predict the machine's behavior-especially when the machine is being pushed by faster, more aggressive players.

This section focuses on the two foundational order types that power almost everything else:

- **Market orders** (aggressive): "Get me in or out *now*."
- **Limit orders** (passive): "Only trade if I can get *this price or better*."

Understanding the trade-off between them-**execution certainty vs. price control**-is one of the simplest ways to reduce the odds of being the "easy liquidity" that predatory algorithms prefer to trade against.

Every trade has two roles: maker and taker

A crucial microstructure idea is that *every executed trade involves two sides with two different behaviors*:

- The **maker** posts a resting order (almost always a limit order). This order *adds* liquidity to the order book because it sits there waiting.
- The **taker** submits an order that *removes* liquidity (commonly a market order, or a marketable limit order). This order "hits" available liquidity immediately.

You do not need to memorize jargon, but you *do* want the mental model:

> *Makers wait. Takers demand.*

This distinction matters because the market tends to *reward* makers (with slightly better prices and sometimes exchange rebates) and *charge* takers (with the spread and sometimes higher fees). More importantly for this book, many predatory strategies are designed to detect and exploit the behavior of takers-because "demanding immediacy" often reveals urgency, fear, or a lack of patience.

Market orders: the command for certainty (but not for price)

A **market order** tells the venue:

> Buy or sell *immediately* at the best available prices.

If you submit a market **buy**, you will purchase from the lowest-priced sellers currently available (starting at the best ask, then the next ask, and so on). If you submit a market **sell**, you will sell to the highest-priced buyers currently available (starting at the best bid, then lower bids, and so on).

What market orders guarantee-and what they do not

A market order usually offers:

- **High execution certainty**: you are very likely to get filled quickly.

But it does *not* guarantee:

- **Your price**: you accept whatever prices are available at that instant.
- **A single clean fill**: a larger market order can be filled across multiple price levels.

This is where everyday traders get surprised. They think, "The stock is at $100." Then they place a market buy and end up with an average fill price of $100.12, $100.25, or worse. Nothing "illegal" happened. The market simply did what you asked: *buy now*, not *buy at $100*.

Slippage: the hidden price of urgency

The gap between the price you *expected* and the price you *actually receive* is commonly called **slippage**. Slippage is not a mysterious fee; it is a mechanical consequence of how orders consume liquidity.

A clean way to think about it:

> *Slippage is what you pay when the market has to "search upward" (for a buy) or "search downward" (for a sell) to find enough opposite-side orders to fill you.*

Slippage tends to grow when:

- the **spread** widens,
- the visible **depth** at the best price is thin,
- volatility increases (prices jump between updates),
- many other traders are trying to do the same thing at once (news, open/close).

These are exactly the conditions where predatory fast strategies thrive: rapid movement, stressed liquidity, and participants who feel forced to act immediately.

Limit orders: the command for price control (but not for certainty)

A **limit order** tells the venue:

> Buy or sell *only* at my price (the limit) or better.

Examples:

- A **limit buy at $100.00** means: "Buy at $100.00 or lower."
- A **limit sell at $100.00** means: "Sell at $100.00 or higher."

Limit orders give you **price control**. If your order fills, it will not fill at a worse price than your limit (ignoring rare edge cases like certain extreme market dislocations, venue-specific rules, or special order instructions). The trade-off is that you may not get filled at all.

The limit order trade-off: avoiding bad fills by accepting non-fills

A limit order offers:

- **Price protection**: you decide the worst acceptable price.
- **Potentially better execution**: you may capture part of the spread if you provide liquidity at the bid (buy) or ask (sell).

But it comes with:

- **Execution risk**: the market can move away and leave you unfilled.
- **Queue risk**: even if the market touches your price, other orders at the same price may be ahead of you.

That second bullet is not academic. In an electronic order book, "same price" does not mean "same priority." If many traders want to buy at $100.00, the exchange fills them in a defined order (typically price first, then time). A fast participant can reach the front of that line more often.

Even so, for many casual traders, *choosing price protection over speed* is a sensible default-especially in fast markets.

Market order vs. limit order: the core decision

You can reduce most order-type confusion to a single question:

> **Which risk can you live with right now: price risk or execution risk?**

- If you use a **market order**, you reduce execution risk but accept price risk (slippage).
- If you use a **limit order**, you reduce price risk but accept execution risk (no fill or partial fill).

For the everyday participant, this decision is not about outsmarting the market. It is about *not accidentally giving away an edge.*

Predatory algorithms do not need you to be "wrong." They often only need you to be **urgent**. A market order is one of the clearest mechanical expressions of urgency because it says: "I am willing to pay the spread and whatever comes next to be done immediately."

A practical mental model: "Am I crossing the spread?"

When you place a market buy, you **cross the spread** (you pay the ask). When you place a market sell, you also cross the spread (you hit the bid). Crossing the spread is not "bad"-it is simply the cost of immediacy.

A limit order placed *outside* the spread (buy below the ask, sell above the bid) typically **does not cross** the spread; it waits. This is why limit orders are associated with *patience* and market orders with *immediacy.*

Two clarifications keep this accurate:

- A limit order can be **marketable** (e.g., a buy limit set above the current ask). In that case it will execute immediately, behaving like a market order *up to your limit.*
- A market order can be **small and safe** in a deep, stable market, but can be **dangerous** in a thin, fast market.

So the real issue is not "market orders are always bad." The issue is that market orders *remove your price brake*. In calm conditions, that may cost pennies. In stressed conditions, it can cost far more than you intended.

Flowchart: choosing between market and limit during a price spike

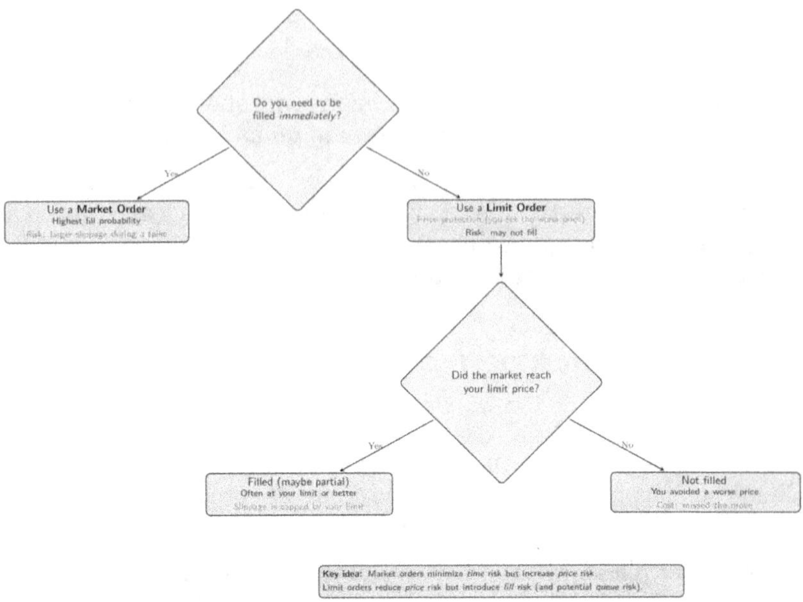

Defensive thinking: why predatory algorithms prefer your market order

In a fast, fragmented, electronic market, a market order is attractive "food" for sophisticated participants for three straightforward reasons:

- **It is information-rich.** It signals urgency: you are willing to accept the best available price *right now*.

- **It is mechanically vulnerable to thin depth.** If liquidity is briefly scarce, your order can be forced up or down the book.
- **It pays the spread by design.** Even if nothing predatory happens, the taker typically gives up the bid-ask spread.

This does *not* mean every market order is being "hunted." It means that when conditions become jumpy-news releases, the open, the close, sudden volatility-the combination of urgency and thin liquidity creates an environment where fast strategies can consistently obtain favorable executions *against* slower orders.

The objective in this book is not to turn you into a low-latency competitor. It is to help you stop sending the market an unnecessary message: "I don't care what price I get, just fill me."

Concrete rules of thumb (that keep you out of trouble)

For casual traders, the following rules are intentionally simple. They are about reducing avoidable microstructure risk, not optimizing every execution:

- **Default to limit orders when you can tolerate waiting.** If your trade idea is not time-critical, you usually gain more from price protection than you lose from waiting.
- **Be most suspicious of market orders in exactly the moments you feel most emotional.** Fear and excitement often coincide with widened spreads and thin depth.
- **If you must use a market order, reduce its size and avoid stressed moments.** Smaller orders are less likely to "walk the book."
- **Remember the real choice:** do you want to control *price* or control *time*? You rarely get both.

Bridge to the next section

So far we have treated the market as if there were a single "price." That is the illusion most screens present: one last trade, one quote, one chart.

Next, we will replace that illusion with the real object that your orders interact with: **the order book**-a stacked set of bids and offers at many prices. Once you can *visualize* that stack, slippage and "mysterious fills" stop being mysterious. They become a predictable consequence of how aggressively you chose to interact with the queue.

2.2 Visualizing the Order Book

In the previous section, we reduced the confusing idea of "the market" to two simple inputs you control: **market orders** (demand immediate execution) and **limit orders** (demand a specific price). Now we need to answer a natural follow-up question:

If a market order is willing to trade at the "best available" price, where does that best price come from?

The answer is the object that quietly runs most modern electronic trading: the **central limit order book (CLOB)**. Think of the CLOB as a continuously updated list of standing intentions-people (and algorithms) publicly offering to buy or sell at specific prices.

From "one price" to a stack of prices

Most casual investors experience the market as a single number: the last traded price, or a quote that looks like:

Last: $100.03 Bid: $100.02 Ask: $100.04

That's useful, but it is a *compressed* view. It hides the more important truth:

There is not one price. There is a ***ladder*** *of prices, with quantities waiting at each rung.*

In other words, the market is not a single point—it is **depth**.

Level I vs. Level II: what you see (and what exists)

Level I data is the simplified view most screens default to:

- best bid price and size (highest buy offer currently resting),
- best ask price and size (lowest sell offer currently resting),
- last traded price (where a recent match occurred).

Level II data (often called *market depth* or *Depth of Market*) expands that view into multiple price levels on both sides:

- many bid prices below the best bid, each with a displayed quantity,
- many ask prices above the best ask, each with a displayed quantity.

Level II is where the CLOB becomes visible: a **stack of bids** and a **stack of offers**.

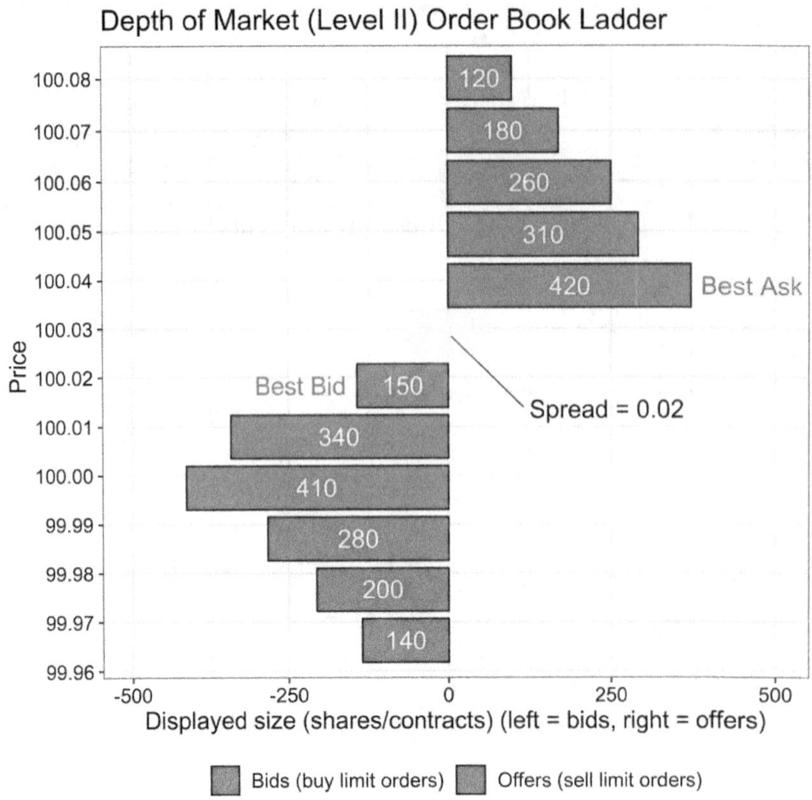

Reading the ladder: bids, offers, and "who is willing to do what"

A Depth of Market ladder is simply a structured answer to two questions:

1. **How many shares are waiting to buy at each price?** (the *bid* side)

2. **How many shares are waiting to sell at each price?** (the *offer/ask* side)

Each horizontal row is one price level. The size shown is the amount of *displayed* liquidity-limit orders that are currently resting and available to be matched.

When you see a thick bar on the bid side at (say) $100.00, that means there is a meaningful amount of buying interest *waiting* there. But notice the word "waiting." A bid does not push the price upward by itself; it is a standing invitation: "If someone sells to me at $100.00, I'll buy."

Likewise, a thick bar on the offer side at $100.05 is a standing invitation to sell: "If someone buys from me at $100.05, I'll sell."

The spread: the market's "gap" you must cross to trade immediately

The **spread** is the distance between:

$$\text{Best Ask} - \text{Best Bid}$$

Conceptually, the spread is the market's small no-man's-land:

- Buyers are currently willing to pay up to the best bid.
- Sellers are currently willing to accept down to the best ask.
- If you want an *immediate* trade, you must cross that gap by taking the other side.

This connects directly to the previous section's maker/taker idea:

- If you place a **market buy**, you become the **taker** and you cross the spread to hit the best ask (and possibly higher asks if size is thin).
- If you place a **limit buy at or below the best bid**, you are trying to be a **maker**; you wait in line for someone else to cross to you.

For everyday traders, this is the first major "aha" moment: the spread is not a vague concept-it is a *visible gap in the book*. Paying it is the cost of immediacy.

Liquidity is not a feeling; it is resting limit orders

People often say a market is "liquid" or "illiquid" as if it were an opinion. In microstructure, liquidity has a practical meaning:

Liquidity is the availability of resting limit orders to trade with, at many price levels, in meaningful size.

A highly liquid market tends to have:

- a tight spread (best bid close to best ask),
- deeper size at each level (thicker bars),
- less slippage for a given market order size (because there is more to trade against nearby).

An illiquid or stressed market tends to have:

- a wide spread,
- thin depth at the top levels,
- higher slippage (market orders "walk" up or down the ladder).

This is why the order book is not just "interesting." It is the mechanism that translates your urgency into your execution price.

A small thought experiment: why size matters more than you think

Imagine the best ask is $100.04 with only 50 shares available, and the next ask is $100.08 with 300 shares.

If you submit a market buy for 200 shares, the exchange can only fill:

- 50 shares at $100.04,
- then the remaining 150 shares at $100.08.

Your average fill price becomes something like:

$$\frac{50 \cdot 100.04 + 150 \cdot 100.08}{200} = 100.07$$

Nothing mystical happened. Your order simply climbed the visible ladder to find enough sellers. The order book is the map that tells you whether your "small" order is actually small relative to nearby depth.

Why the order book perspective matters for detecting predatory conditions

This book is not about turning you into a professional tape reader. But you *do* want to train a defensive instinct: when the visible book looks thin and jumpy, your risk rises.

Three practical observations follow naturally from the CLOB view:

1. **Thin top-of-book depth makes market orders fragile.** If the first rung is small, your market order is more likely to "spill" into worse prices.

2. **A widening spread is a warning light.** It is the market openly saying: "Immediacy just got more expensive."

3. **Displayed depth can change faster than your eyes can track.** In later sections we will connect this to speed advantages and why some liquidity can appear and disappear rapidly.

For now, keep it simple: when you stop thinking in terms of "the price" and start thinking in terms of "the ladder," you naturally begin to ask better questions before you trade:

- How wide is the spread right now?
- How much size is really sitting at the best prices?
- If I demand immediacy, how many rungs might I consume?

Bridge to the next section

The CLOB is a **queue** of intentions organized by price levels. But within a single price level, there can be many orders competing for priority. That raises the next mechanical question:

If you and I both post the same price, who gets filled first?

Next we will examine the exchange's matching and priority rules-the digital version of standing in line-and why "being early by a microsecond" can matter.

2.3 Matching and Priority Rules: The Digital Queue

Once you start seeing the market as an order book—a stacked ladder of bids and offers—the next question becomes unavoidable:

> If many people want to trade at the same price, who gets served first?

The answer is not "who deserves it" or "who has the best broker." It is a set of **matching and priority rules**: deterministic procedures an exchange uses to decide which resting orders get executed when an incoming order arrives.

This section is about those rules. They sound technical, but the core idea is simple:

> The order book is a **digital queue**. Exchanges need a fair, mechanical way to decide who is at the front of the line.

Understanding this queue is essential for two reasons:

1. It clarifies why **speed** can have real economic value (even at the same displayed price).
2. It explains a common retail frustration: "The price touched my limit, but I didn't get filled."

Two jobs the exchange must do: match and prioritize

When an exchange receives orders, it must do two distinct things:

1. **Matching:** Determine whether an incoming order can trade immediately against existing orders on the opposite side.
2. **Priority:** If there are multiple eligible resting orders, decide which one(s) receive the fill first.

Matching is the "does a trade happen?" question. Priority is the "which trade happens first?" question.

The second question is where the digital queue lives.

Price–time priority (FIFO): the most important baseline rule

The most common baseline priority rule in modern electronic markets is **price–time priority**, often described as **FIFO** (First-In, First-Out) *at a given price level.*

It works like this:

1. **Best price wins.** Orders at a better price have priority over orders at a worse price.
2. **Earlier time wins (within the same price).** If multiple orders are at the same price, the order that arrived first gets filled first.

This is straightforward when you translate it into the order book ladder you saw in the prior section:

- On the **bid** side, higher bid prices are "better" (more aggressive) and therefore have higher priority.
- On the **ask** side, lower ask prices are "better" (more aggressive) and therefore have higher priority.

Within each row of that ladder, the exchange maintains a time-stamped line: earliest orders at the front, newest orders at the back.

A concrete example: one price level, many buyers

Suppose the best bid is \$100.00 and the order book at that price contains three separate buy limit orders:

09:30:00.100	Buy 200 @ \$100.00
09:30:00.102	Buy 100 @ \$100.00
09:30:00.105	Buy 300 @ \$100.00

Now a seller arrives with a market sell for 250 shares. Under FIFO at \$100.00, the fills are allocated like a line at a ticket counter:

- The first buyer (200 shares) gets filled completely.
- The second buyer gets the remaining 50 shares (partial fill).
- The third buyer gets nothing *yet*, even though they posted the same price.

The key takeaway is subtle but powerful:

> A limit order is not just a *price*. It is a *place in line* at that price.

Why "my limit was touched" does not guarantee a fill

Many casual traders place a limit order and then watch the market trade at (or even through) their price without getting executed. This feels unfair until you apply the queue model.

Here are the most common, non-mysterious reasons:

Reason 1: you were too far back in the queue

If thousands of shares are already waiting ahead of you at the same price, the market can trade there briefly, fill some of the earlier orders, and move away before it reaches yours.

In queue terms: the store opened, the line moved a little, but it didn't get to you before the rush ended.

Reason 2: displayed liquidity is not the whole story

Even in a standard CLOB environment, not all liquidity is equally visible or equally "simple." Some venues and order types can interact in ways that mean the displayed quantity at a price level is not the full set of competing interest.

You do not need to master every special order type yet (we will discuss hidden liquidity later), but you should internalize the defensive lesson:

> The order book is a map, not the territory. It is useful, but it is not a guarantee.

Reason 3: the market traded *elsewhere* first

Modern equities trading is fragmented across multiple venues. Your screen may show the consolidated best bid/ask, but trades can execute across different exchanges and pools. A "touch" on one feed does not always imply your specific venue/order had priority at that instant.

We will tackle fragmentation and routing in a later section; for now, it is enough to understand that "the market" can be a network, not a single room.

Priority is a design choice: different markets, different rules

Price–time priority is common, but it is not universal. Exchanges choose rules to balance fairness, liquidity provision, and speed incentives.

Without diving into venue-by-venue details, it helps to know the broad categories you may encounter:

- **Price–time (FIFO):** rewards being early at a price; speed matters at the margin.
- **Pro-rata (size priority):** at a given price, fills are distributed proportionally to order size; size matters more than arrival time.
- **Hybrid rules:** combinations that may use price–time for some participants or size/other logic for others.

For a casual trader, the actionable point is not memorizing every system. It is recognizing the general implication:

> Whatever the rule, **something** determines who is first. If you are slower, you are more often later in that ordering.

Why speed is valuable even when the price is the same

At first, "speed" sounds like a vanity metric. If everyone can place a limit order at $100.00, why should microseconds matter?

Because in a price–time queue, speed determines:

- whether you get near the **front** of a desirable price level,
- whether you can **cancel** and re-post quickly when conditions change (which can help avoid being adversely selected),
- whether you can react to new information before slower participants can update their orders.

This is where the link to predatory behavior begins to form—without needing conspiracy theories.

A fast participant does not need to "predict" the market perfectly. They can pursue a simpler edge:

> *Be first in line when it is good to be first, and step out of line when it is dangerous to be first.*

Slower participants are less able to step out of line in time, which can turn their resting limit orders into easy targets during rapid price moves.

Cancellations and re-posting: the queue is constantly rearranged

One of the most unintuitive features of modern electronic markets is how frequently orders are modified or canceled. From the outside, it can look like liquidity "appears" and "vanishes."

From the queue perspective, this is exactly what is happening:

- Posting a new limit order is joining the back of a line at a price.
- Canceling is leaving the line.
- Re-posting at the same price is often rejoining at the back (depending on venue rules).
- Improving price by one tick is like moving to a better line entirely.

This matters to retail traders because it changes what "patience" means. Patience is not just waiting; it is waiting in a line where others may be repeatedly entering, exiting, and repositioning at high speed.

What this means for your order choices (defensive, not tactical)

The goal here is not to encourage you to race. As a casual participant, you generally cannot and should not compete on latency. But you can avoid misunderstandings that lead to costly decisions.

Three defensively useful conclusions follow from the digital queue model:

1. **A limit order is a request, not a promise.** It is conditional on price *and* on your place in line.
2. **Market orders skip the line (and pay for it).** You become the taker, cross the spread, and accept the best available liquidity *now*.
3. **Queue risk is real.** Even if the market reaches your price, you may not be served if you are late in the line or if liquidity shifts.

You can now interpret a common experience more accurately:

> "I didn't get filled" often means "I was not at the front of the queue when the opposite-side demand arrived."

Bridge to the next section

So far we have described a single order book that matches and prioritizes orders with clear rules. Real markets add one more layer of complexity: **fragmentation**.

In the next section, we will address a misconception many investors carry for years:

> *A stock does not trade in one place. It trades across many venues at the same time.*

Once you understand that, you can see how routing, venue selection, and split orders create opportunities for fast participants to react to pieces of your activity—sometimes before the full order has finished executing.

2.4 Fragmentation and Order Routing

Up to this point, we have built a clean mental model:

- Orders rest in an order book as bids and offers (the CLOB).

- When an incoming order arrives, an exchange matches it.
- If multiple orders are eligible at the same price, **priority rules** decide who is first in line.

That model is correct-but incomplete. It describes what happens *inside one venue*. The next layer of modern market reality is that, for most widely traded stocks, there is not one venue. There are many.

> **Fragmentation** means the same stock is traded across multiple exchanges and multiple off-exchange venues at the same time.

This is not a small detail. Fragmentation changes how prices form, how quickly information travels, and how easily fast traders can exploit tiny timing differences.

The misconception: "The stock trades on the exchange"

Many casual investors imagine a stock as living in a single place:

> "I'm buying Apple *on the NYSE*," or "Tesla trades *on Nasdaq*."

A stock may be *listed* on one primary exchange, but its trading is typically *distributed* across:

- multiple lit exchanges (public order books),
- alternative trading systems (ATS) and dark pools (limited or no pre-trade display),
- internalizers/wholesalers and other off-exchange mechanisms for retail flow (in some markets),
- other specialized venues with their own microstructure rules.

So the practical reality is better stated as:

> A stock is a **networked market**, not a single order book.

What fragmentation looks like in everyday terms

Think of a popular concert where tickets are sold through many websites at once. The "true" price of a ticket is not a single number; it is the best available offer across all sites *at that moment*. If one site briefly posts a cheaper ticket, buyers rush there until it is gone.

Stocks behave similarly:

- Each venue has its own order book (or matching mechanism).
- Each venue can momentarily have a slightly better bid or ask.
- Competition and arbitrage tend to keep prices aligned-but not perfectly, and not instantaneously.

Those tiny, fleeting differences are where speed becomes valuable, and where slower participants can experience "ghost liquidity" (a quote you see but cannot actually trade) or unexpected partial fills.

NBBO: one "best" quote assembled from many venues

Because trading is fragmented, many markets publish a consolidated view of the best available prices:

- the best bid across venues, and
- the best ask across venues.

In U.S. equity market language, this idea is often discussed as the **National Best Bid and Offer (NBBO)**-a composite of the best publicly displayed prices.

For a casual trader, the key point is conceptual, not regulatory:

> What you see as "the" bid and ask is often a **summary of many books**, not a single book.

This matters because your order is not automatically matched against the entire market everywhere at once. Your order is routed somewhere, and routing decisions can change your outcome.

Order routing: how your broker chooses where to send the order

When you click Buy or Sell, your order does not magically touch every venue simultaneously. Your broker (or your broker's routing technology) chooses a path.

That choice is called **order routing**. In many broker and institutional systems, the routing logic is implemented by a **Smart Order Router (SOR)**.

You can think of an SOR as a GPS for orders:

- It tries to find where liquidity is available.
- It tries to achieve a good execution price.
- It may try to minimize fees, reduce market impact, or satisfy venue-specific rules.
- It may split the order into pieces and send them to multiple venues.

The reason splitting exists is simple. If you want to buy 10,000 shares and only 2,000 are available at the best ask on one venue, you can either:

- take worse and worse prices on that single venue (walking the book), or
- simultaneously search other venues for additional shares at good prices.

Splitting reduces visible footprint and can reduce slippage-*but* it creates timing and information problems that faster participants may exploit.

Lit venues vs. dark pools: why some liquidity is visible and some is not

Fragmentation also involves different *types* of venues.

Lit exchanges (public books)

A **lit** exchange displays at least some of its resting orders to the public. This is the classic CLOB image from the previous section: a ladder of bids and offers.

Advantages for the public market:

- Price discovery is transparent.
- The order book provides information about depth and spread.

Trade-off:

- Displayed orders can be targeted. If you show your hand, others can react.

Dark pools and other non-displayed venues

A **dark pool** (or more generally, a non-displayed liquidity venue) does not show the full order book publicly before trades occur.

Why would anyone trade in the dark?

- Large institutions may want to reduce information leakage.
- Displaying a large buy order can invite front-running behavior and worsen execution.

But the trade-offs are real:

- Less transparency for everyone watching the market.
- More complexity in understanding where trading is happening.
- Potential for sophisticated participants to specialize in predicting and interacting with routed flow.

You do not need to take a moral stance on dark pools to protect yourself. You simply need to know they exist and that they contribute to a market where "the visible book" is only part of total liquidity.

Why fragmentation creates an opening for fast strategies

In a single-venue world, the matching engine sees everything at once. In a fragmented world, there is a coordination problem:

> If Venue A updates first and Venue B updates a few milliseconds later, there is a brief window where prices are **out of sync**.

That window is often tiny, but it is enough for a fast participant to:

- buy at a stale, cheaper ask in one venue while the broader market has already moved up,
- sell at a stale, higher bid in one venue while the broader market has already moved down,
- reposition quotes across venues as soon as one venue reveals a shift in supply/demand.

This is not yet "spoofing" or an explicitly manipulative act. It is a structural consequence of a distributed system:

- multiple venues,
- different feed speeds,
- different matching rules,
- and different routing paths.

In the next section on information speed, we will name and unpack the most important version of this phenomenon: **latency arbitrage**. For now, the groundwork is that fragmentation is the *map*, and latency is the *time delay* that makes the map exploitable.

The practical consequence for casual traders: your order may be "in motion"

A helpful way to update your mental model is to stop picturing your order as placed "into the market" as a single event. Instead, picture your order as a message traveling through a network:

- Your click → broker systems → router decision → one or more venues.
- If it is split, each child order has its own path, timing, and queue position.
- Partial fills can occur across venues at slightly different prices.

This network journey explains several common experiences:

- **Partial fills:** you get some shares now and the rest later (or not at all).
- **Multiple fill prices:** different venues provide different liquidity at different moments.
- **A quote you could not hit:** the best price was real somewhere, but vanished by the time your routed order reached it.

None of this requires anyone to "cheat." It is what happens when a fast-moving system is distributed.

Defensive takeaways (without turning this into a routing manual)

As a non-professional trader, your edge is not choosing the perfect route. Your edge is choosing behaviors that are robust to complexity.

A few defensively oriented lessons follow from fragmentation:

- **Treat the top-of-book as fragile during fast markets.** In a fragmented system, the best displayed quote can disappear quickly because it was small or because it was hit elsewhere first.

- **Prefer price protection when immediacy is not essential.** A well-chosen limit order can cap your worst outcome even if routing and venue conditions are messy.
- **Expect more slippage and less predictability around news and open/close.** Those are moments when routing systems are busiest and when books across venues can desynchronize.

These are not “advanced tactics.” They are mindset adjustments that keep you from assuming the market is a single orderly room when it is actually a crowded building with many doors.

Bridge to the next section

Fragmentation explains *where* prices can differ: across venues. The next question is *how* those differences persist long enough to matter.

To answer that, we have to confront the physical side of markets: the speed of data, the difference between fast and slow feeds, and why the quote on a retail screen can be a stale snapshot-a ghost of a market that has already moved.

That is the subject of the next section: **The Speed of Information**.

2.5 The Speed of Information

In the previous section, we replaced the comforting idea of “one market” with the real picture: **fragmentation**. The same stock trades across many venues at once. That immediately creates a new question:

> If the market is a network of venues, how do those venues (and their participants) learn what just happened elsewhere?

The answer is **information transmission**. And the uncomfortable truth is that information does not arrive everywhere at the same time. It travels through physical infrastructure—fiber, microwave links, switches, matching engine connections, and software pipelines. Even when the delays are "only" milliseconds, they can be economically meaningful because modern electronic markets can change multiple times within a single millisecond.

This section explains, in plain language, why the quote on a typical retail screen can be a *slightly stale snapshot* and how professional firms pay for faster, cleaner views of the market.

Prices are messages, not facts

A useful mental shift is to stop thinking of price as a static fact ("the stock *is* $100.03") and start thinking of it as a message ("a trade *just happened* around $100.03, and that information is being broadcast").

Every important market event is turned into data:

- a trade occurs,
- a limit order is posted, modified, or canceled,
- the best bid/ask changes,
- the spread widens or tightens,
- depth at a price level appears or vanishes.

Those data must travel from where they occur (a venue's matching engine) to:

- other market participants,
- other venues and routers,
- market data consolidators,
- and your broker's systems and app.

Once you see price as a message, it becomes obvious that a "fast" participant is often just someone who receives, processes, and reacts to the message sooner.

Latency: the small delay that changes outcomes

Latency is the time delay between an event happening and someone else observing it (and being able to act on it).

Latency comes from several sources:

- **Propagation delay:** signals take time to travel through cables or the air.
- **Processing delay:** computers must parse data, update books, run risk checks, and make decisions.
- **Queuing delay:** data and orders can wait briefly behind other traffic in network equipment or software pipelines.

You do not need to know the exact millisecond count to understand the consequence. The consequence is structural:

> If two participants see the same market event at different times, they are not trading in the same reality.

This is why speed is valuable: it buys you a more current picture of the order book and lets you act before others have even seen the change.

Public feeds vs. professional feeds: why screens disagree

Most casual investors see market data through a **public or retail-oriented feed** that is optimized for broad distribution and stability, not for being the absolute fastest.

Professional firms often pay for:

- **direct exchange feeds** (often called proprietary feeds),
- **co-location** (placing servers physically near an exchange's matching engine),
- low-latency network routes and specialized hardware/software stacks.

The important contrast is not "retail is blind" versus "pros are omniscient." The contrast is:

- **Retail view:** slightly delayed and sometimes aggregated.
- **HFT/pro view:** earlier, more granular, and engineered for reaction speed.

When the market is calm, these differences may not matter much. When the market is moving quickly, they can change who gets filled and at what price—especially for market orders (urgent takers) and for limit orders sitting in fragile top-of-book positions.

Latency arbitrage: "picking off" stale quotes in plain English

Now we can name the most important phenomenon created by fragmentation + latency:

> **Latency arbitrage** is profiting from the fact that different participants (and venues) momentarily disagree about the current best price because information arrives at different times.

Here is the plain-English storyline:

1. A price change happens on Venue A (say, the best ask jumps up because someone bought the available shares).
2. Fast firms learn about this change almost immediately via direct feeds and close proximity.
3. Slower feeds and slower participants update a bit later.
4. During that delay, there may still be resting sell orders at the *old*, now-too-cheap price on Venue B (or displayed on a slower screen).
5. A fast firm buys those stale offers before they are canceled or repriced.

To a casual trader watching a retail quote, it can feel like this:

> "The price was there, but when I tried to trade, it vanished."

Often, it did not "vanish." It was **consumed** by someone who saw the change earlier, or it was **canceled** by someone who realized they were about to be picked off.

This is why fast markets frequently show a widening spread and thinning visible depth: liquidity providers protect themselves when their risk of being "last to know" increases.

The quote on your screen can be a "ghost"

A retail screen is not lying. It is just showing you a picture that may be slightly out of date by the time you react. In a slow environment, that is harmless. In a fast environment, it becomes a practical hazard.

A helpful metaphor is video streaming:

- The game is happening live.
- Your stream is delayed.
- You are making decisions based on a feed that is real, but not current.

In microstructure terms, your screen can display a best bid/ask that is already gone, because:

- it was executed by someone faster,
- it was canceled by someone faster,
- or it never existed on the venue your routed order will reach first.

This matters most when you are using **urgent order types** (market orders, marketable limit orders) because you are asking to trade *now*, in whatever reality exists when your order arrives.

Timeline: how HFT and retail can observe the same event at different times

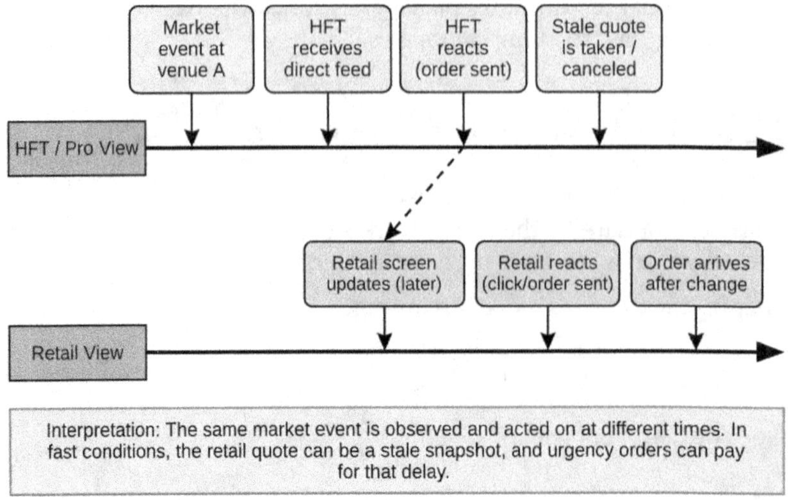

Why this matters for spreads, slippage, and your choice of order type

You can now connect the dots across the chapter:

- **Order types:** Market orders demand immediacy; limit orders demand price control.

- **Order book:** Liquidity is resting limit orders at many price levels.
- **Priority:** Being earlier in the queue matters at a given price.
- **Fragmentation:** There are many venues, not one.
- **Speed:** Information arrives at different times; reactions are staggered.

When speed differences become important, two market-wide symptoms often appear:

Symptom 1: spreads widen

Liquidity providers protect themselves against being picked off. One way to do that is to quote less aggressively, which widens the bid–ask spread. A wider spread is the market's way of increasing the "toll" for immediacy when the environment feels dangerous.

Symptom 2: slippage increases

When top-of-book liquidity becomes thin or flickery, market orders are more likely to walk the book and get worse average prices. Slippage is not just about "volatility" in the abstract; it is often about **how quickly the book changes relative to how quickly you can see and respond**.

This ties back to a practical defensive idea:

> In fast markets, the cost of urgency rises.

A defensive checklist for casual traders

This book is not asking you to out-speed professionals. It is asking you to avoid being unintentionally predictable and mechanically vulnerable.

Here are simple, robust habits that align with what we just learned:

1. **Be cautious with market orders during news, the open, and the close.** These are exactly the moments when feeds and venues can desynchronize and top-of-book liquidity can evaporate.

2. **Use limit orders when you can tolerate not being filled.** A limit order acts like a circuit breaker on price.

3. **Interpret sudden spread widening as an information-speed warning.** It often means liquidity providers are defending against adverse selection.

4. **Mentally separate "what you saw" from "what was tradable."** Your screen is an observation, not a guarantee.

These habits do not require special tools. They require a realistic understanding of the time dimension of markets.

Bridge to the next section

Once you accept that information arrives at different times, the next logical question is how sophisticated traders hide their intentions in the order book to avoid being exploited.

In the next section, we will look at **hidden liquidity** and **iceberg orders**: methods institutions use to avoid advertising size, and the cat-and-mouse game that emerges when fast algorithms try to detect what is hidden beneath the surface.

2.6 Hidden Liquidity and Icebergs

The last section introduced an uncomfortable but essential idea: in modern markets, **speed is an informational advantage**. Some participants see changes sooner, react sooner, and can avoid being "picked off" while slower participants are still looking at yesterday's snapshot.

That creates a natural next question:

If showing your intentions in the public order book can make you a target, why would a large institution ever display a big order at all?

Often, they don't.

This section explains **hidden liquidity**—ways traders can provide or seek liquidity without fully revealing their size—and the most intuitive example of all: the **iceberg order**. We will keep the focus on practical understanding: what these orders are, why they exist, and how they connect to predatory detection behavior.

Why institutions try to hide: information leakage is expensive

A large institution (mutual fund, pension fund, insurer, ETF market maker, etc.) might need to buy or sell hundreds of thousands of shares. If they simply post:

"Buy 500,000 shares @ $100.00"

they reveal three pieces of valuable information to the market:

- **Direction:** they are a buyer (or seller).
- **Urgency:** if the order is large and persistent, it may signal a real need rather than a casual idea.
- **Magnitude:** the market learns that a lot of shares need to be absorbed.

This information can move prices against them. If other participants believe a large buyer is present, sellers may raise their offers. If a large seller is present, buyers may lower bids. Either way, the institution pays more (when buying) or receives less (when selling). This is **market impact**, and it is one of the largest hidden costs of trading.

So institutions face a trade-off that resembles the one you already learned with order types:

- Show your hand and risk worse prices (information leakage).
- Hide your hand and risk slower execution or less certainty.

Hidden liquidity tools exist because the cost of revealing intentions can be enormous.

Displayed vs. hidden: what the public book can (and cannot) tell you

In the earlier section on the order book, we used Level II depth to visualize bids and offers. That picture shows **displayed** limit orders—orders that are visible to the market.

But in many markets and venues, there can also be:

- orders (or portions of orders) that are not displayed,
- midpoint or pegged interest that only becomes visible at execution,
- conditional liquidity that appears only when certain criteria are met.

The main lesson is not to memorize venue features. It is to adjust your expectations:

The visible order book is an important signal, but it is not the full inventory of supply and demand.

This is one reason you can sometimes see price move "through" a thick-looking level, or conversely, see surprising support/resistance that was not obvious in displayed depth.

Iceberg orders: the simplest way to understand hidden liquidity

An **iceberg order** is a large limit order that displays only a small portion of its total size to the public order book.

The metaphor is deliberate:

- The **displayed quantity** is the tip of the iceberg.
- The **hidden quantity** is the submerged mass.

A typical iceberg has two key parameters:

- **Total size** (the true intended quantity).
- **Display size** (the "clip" size that is shown at any one time).

Example:

- Total: Buy 50,000 shares at $100.00
- Display: Show only 500 shares at a time

On Level II, other traders may only see "Bid 500 @ $100.00" even though far more buying interest is actually available at that price.

How an iceberg replenishes

When the displayed portion (the tip) is executed, the exchange can automatically refresh the visible tip by exposing another slice of the hidden remainder—again and again—until the full size is filled or canceled.

Mechanically, this creates a distinctive footprint:

- The displayed size at a price level may appear to "refill" repeatedly.
- The market may have difficulty pushing through that price, because new liquidity keeps appearing.

From the institution's perspective, this accomplishes the goal: trade patiently at a chosen price without advertising the full size to the entire market at once.

The hidden cost of hiding: queue position and execution uncertainty

Hiding size is not free. It changes how you interact with priority rules.

Recall the digital queue:

- At a given price, orders are typically filled in time order.
- Being first matters.

With an iceberg, the displayed tip participates in that queue. But when it refreshes, the refreshed portion may:

- keep its priority under certain rules, or
- lose priority and go to the back of the line (depending on venue and how the refresh is implemented).

You do not need to know every implementation detail to understand the consequence:

Icebergs trade transparency risk for execution risk: they can reduce information leakage, but they may fill more slowly or less predictably than a fully displayed aggressive order.

That trade-off makes sense for large institutions because the cost of moving the market against themselves can dwarf the cost of waiting.

The cat-and-mouse game: detection and "pinging"

Hidden liquidity creates incentives for other participants to *discover* what is hidden.

If you are a fast trader and you suspect there is a large iceberg buyer at $100.00, that is valuable information. It tells you:

- there may be a durable source of demand at that level,
- short-term downward moves might be cushioned,
- price may revert upward after dipping toward the iceberg level.

This is where predatory and semi-predatory behavior can emerge, even without any overtly illegal action.

What it means to "ping" the book

Pinging is a broad term for using small, often rapid orders to probe for hidden liquidity. Conceptually, it resembles tapping a wall to find a hollow spot. The goal is to learn:

- Is there more liquidity here than is displayed?
- Does the displayed size replenish after being hit?
- How quickly does it replenish?

A simple intuition:

If a price level keeps refilling after small trades, someone may be hiding size there.

Not all probing is manipulative; some of it is ordinary information gathering in a competitive market. But the line between "learning" and "predation" is crossed when a strategy is designed to:

- force another participant to reveal information,
- exploit that revealed information in a way that predictably worsens their execution,
- or create deceptive signals to induce others to trade at worse prices.

Later chapters will discuss clearly abusive tactics (including spoofing). For now, the important point is that hidden liquidity exists *because* information can be weaponized, and once hidden liquidity exists, there is an incentive to hunt for it.

Why hidden liquidity matters to everyday traders (even if you never use it)

Many casual traders assume hidden liquidity is a niche institutional feature that does not affect them. In reality, it affects the "feel" of the market you trade in.

Implication 1: displayed depth can be misleading in both directions

- A thin-looking book might actually have hidden size behind it (making slippage less severe than expected).
- A thick-looking level might evaporate if much of it was fleeting or cancels quickly (making slippage worse than expected).

So Level II is still useful, but you should treat it like a dashboard instrument: informative, not infallible.

Implication 2: price levels can behave "sticky"

You may observe certain prices acting like they have "support" or "resistance" even when the visible book does not look extraordinary. One reason can be hidden liquidity that absorbs flow repeatedly.

This is not magic. It is just the iceberg mechanism doing what it was designed to do.

Implication 3: sudden "bursts" of volume can be a clue

When an iceberg is being executed, the tape can show repeated prints at the same price (or tight range) as the hidden order repeatedly refreshes. This can create volume patterns that are hard to interpret if you assume every order is fully displayed.

Connecting the dots: why this belongs in a chapter about predatory algorithms

Let us link this section back to the broader theme of surviving a predatory environment.

- **Order types** determine whether you are demanding immediacy or offering liquidity.

- **The order book** is the battlefield where those intentions rest.
- **Priority rules** determine who gets served first.
- **Fragmentation** means activity is dispersed across venues.
- **Speed differences** mean not everyone sees the same state at the same time.
- **Hidden liquidity** exists because revealing intentions can be exploited.

In other words, hidden liquidity is not an exotic add-on. It is a rational adaptation to a market where information moves fast and where being predictable can be costly.

Defensive takeaways for casual traders

You do not need special access to protect yourself from the most common misinterpretations. The following ideas are simple but powerful:

- **Do not assume visible depth is the full truth.** It is a partial picture, and it can change quickly.
- **Be cautious about interpreting "walls" as permanent.** A large displayed level can be real, hidden, or fleeting.
- **When volatility rises, prioritize price protection.** If the book becomes unreliable, limit orders help cap your worst-case execution.
- **Expect sophisticated participants to search for information edges.** Institutions hide size because others try to detect it; that arms race is part of the terrain.

Where we go from here

With hidden liquidity, you have now seen a complete microstructure loop:

- liquidity providers display (or hide) orders,
- fast traders observe and react,
- slower traders interact through delayed views and routed orders,
- and the market's visible shape (spread, depth, volatility) changes as participants defend themselves.

In later chapters, we will build on this foundation to discuss how certain strategies cross the line from competitive to deceptive—especially tactics that intentionally create false signals in the order book.

Chapter 3

The Players and Their Incentives

When you click 'buy,' you aren't just sending an order into a void; you are stepping into a crowded room filled with highly specialized participants. Some want to help you trade for a fee, while others want to trade against you for a profit. To survive the shark tank, you must first recognize the species swimming next to you. This chapter peels back the curtain on the market's cast of characters-from the helpful-seeming broker to the lightning-fast market maker-and exposes the hidden economic incentives that dictate their every move.

3.1 Who is on the Other Side?

If you have ever clicked *Buy* or *Sell* and gotten a fill instantly, it can feel as if the market is a single, friendly machine that simply *gives you a price*. But markets are not vending machines. Every trade is an interaction among participants with different goals, different speeds, and different information. This book is about surviving a "shark tank," and the first survival skill is basic orientation: knowing who is in the water with you, and what they are trying to do.

In the previous material, we established a key idea that will keep returning throughout this book:

> **Your order is not an isolated action.** The moment it leaves your screen, it becomes an event in a competitive ecosystem.

So when you ask, "Who is on the other side?" the most accurate answer is: *it depends on where your order goes, what type of order you used, and what the market is doing at that instant.* Still, we can map the ecosystem into a few understandable groups and then build intuition about incentives.

At a high level, there are two broad roles in any market interaction:

- **Service providers** who make the market usable (brokers, exchanges, many market makers). They earn fees, rebates, or spreads for providing access and immediacy.

- **Profit hunters** who try to earn money from predicting, detecting, or reacting to short-term price changes (some high-frequency traders, some institutional strategies, and yes, sometimes other retail traders).

Crucially, a single firm can be both. A participant can provide liquidity *and* attempt to extract informational advantage. This is why the "friend vs. enemy" framing is often misleading. The better framing is:

> **Everyone has an objective. Your job is to understand which objectives are advantaged by your particular order.**

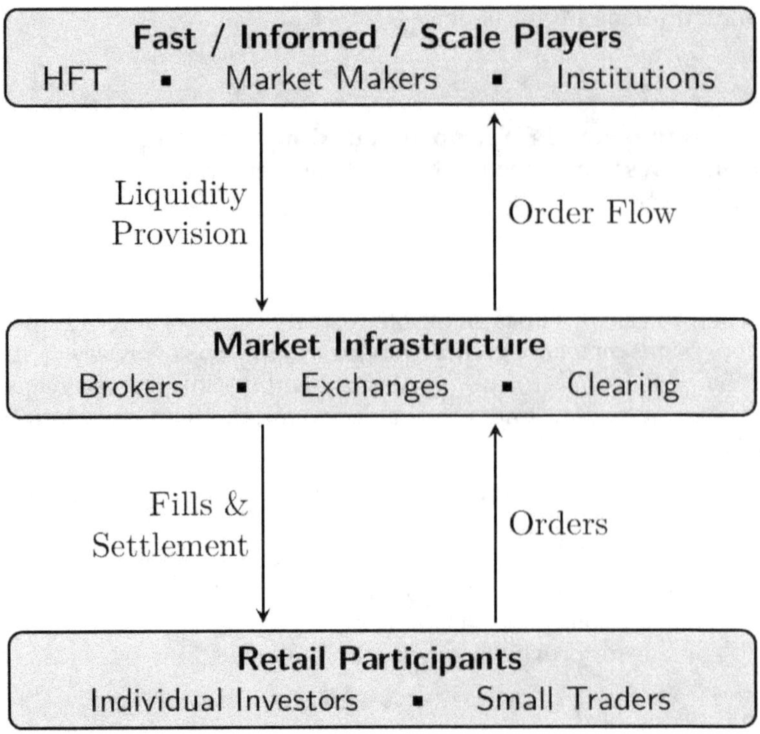
Fast / Informed / Scale Players
HFT ▪ Market Makers ▪ Institutions
Liquidity Provision
Order Flow
Market Infrastructure
Brokers ▪ Exchanges ▪ Clearing
Fills & Settlement
Orders
Retail Participants
Individual Investors ▪ Small Traders

The ecosystem, translated into plain language

The diagram above is not a moral ranking ("good at the bottom, bad at the top"). It is a *power and incentive map.* Participants near the top typically have:

- **Lower latency** (they react faster),
- **More data** (they see richer market information, sometimes from more venues),
- **More scale** (they can transact in size and repeatedly),
- **More optionality** (they can choose *when* and *where* to trade).

Participants near the bottom tend to have something else:

- **Real-world motives** (investing, hedging, saving, rebalancing),
- **Less time sensitivity** (you usually do not *need* the next tick),
- **Smaller size** (which can be an advantage *if* you avoid broadcasting urgency).

This section will define the main groups in the simplest useful way and connect each group to a single question: *what do they get paid for?*

Retail ("the casuals"): the motive-driven trader

Retail investors include individuals placing trades through apps and online brokers. Their defining feature is not account size; it is **purpose**. Retail activity is often linked to:

- saving and long-term investing,

- reacting to news or social sentiment,
- expressing a directional view ("I think this will go up"),
- managing life events (income, taxes, rebalancing).

Retail traders tend to be at an informational disadvantage about the *micro* state of the market: the shape of the order book, the hidden liquidity, the routing logic, and the speed competition. That does not mean retail cannot succeed. It means retail success relies on a different edge:

> **Patience and selectivity.** If you are not forced to trade right now, you can refuse bad terms.

A theme we will return to is that predatory strategies often feed on one thing: **observable urgency**. A market order, a stop order near the current price, or repeated chasing behavior can advertise urgency. Your best defense begins with recognizing that your *order type* and *timing* are forms of communication.

Institutions ("the whales"): scale, constraints, and footprints

Institutional investors include mutual funds, pension funds, insurance companies, endowments, and many hedge funds. They may manage huge portfolios and rebalance under constraints:

- tracking an index,
- controlling risk exposures (sector, duration, volatility),
- meeting inflows/outflows,
- executing mandates with compliance rules.

Institutions are not necessarily "smarter" on short-term price direction. Their advantage is often **resources and scale**: better tools, specialized execution teams, and the ability to pay for high-quality market data and infrastructure.

Their weakness is the flip side of scale: **they leave footprints**. If a large institution needs to buy a meaningful amount, it cannot do so invisibly all at once without moving the price. As a result, institutions often break orders into smaller pieces and use execution algorithms designed to reduce market impact.

From the perspective of a predatory trader, institutional flow is attractive because it is:

- **large** (more profit potential),
- **persistent** (a program may last minutes or hours),
- **constrained** (the institution must complete the trade).

Understanding this matters to you because retail sometimes gets caught in the turbulence created by institutional execution: spreads widen, prices jump between venues, and liquidity becomes "thin" near obvious levels.

Market makers ("the digital middlemen"): selling immediacy

Market makers and other liquidity providers post prices at which they are willing to buy (bid) and sell (ask). Their ideal business is not to guess the market's next move. Their ideal business is closer to running a store:

- quote two-sided prices,
- trade frequently,
- keep inventory risk controlled,
- earn small amounts per trade (spread and/or rebates).

In a calm market, this can feel beneficial to retail: you click and get filled. But remember: the market maker is not providing liquidity out of kindness. They provide it because they believe, on average, they can manage the risks and get compensated.

That compensation is fragile. When market makers fear they are trading against someone better informed (a concept we will later call *adverse selection*), they widen spreads or pull back. To the casual trader, this feels like the market becoming "slippery" exactly when you want it to be stable. That is not an accident; it is a rational defensive response.

High-frequency traders ("the sharks"): competing on speed and micro-edges

High-frequency trading (HFT) is not one strategy; it is a *style of competition*. The shared feature is using automation to react extremely quickly to short-lived opportunities: tiny price discrepancies, queue position, and fleeting patterns in order flow.

Some HFT firms are essentially modern market makers. Others are aggressive liquidity takers. Some practices are widely considered legitimate; others cross ethical or regulatory lines. Because this book focuses on survival rather than sensationalism, we will use a practical rule:

> **If a strategy profits from your predictable behavior rather than from a fundamental view of value, treat it as predatory for defensive purposes.**

The reason speed matters is that it can convert public events into private advantage. For example, when a large order hits one venue, a fast trader might infer information and adjust quotes elsewhere before slower participants can respond. You do not need to know the engineering to understand the outcome: **the fastest players often get first choice.**

Brokers and exchanges ("the infrastructure"): the hidden decision layer

Most casual traders think the trade goes "to the stock market." In reality, it goes through:

1. your broker (who receives the order and decides how to route it),

2. a venue (exchange, off-exchange market maker, internalizer, or other trading facility),
3. a matching process (rules that determine execution and priority).

Brokers and venues are often described as neutral plumbing. But neutrality is complicated by **business models**:

- Brokers may monetize order flow, spreads, interest on cash balances, or routing arrangements.
- Venues may charge fees or pay rebates depending on whether you *provide* liquidity (post a limit order) or *take* liquidity (hit an existing quote).

This matters because incentives shape behavior. If you want one mental model for the rest of this chapter, use this:

> **Your broker chooses a path; the path changes who sees your order, how fast they see it, and what they can do in response.**

We will later discuss execution quality in a way that does not require jargon. For now, the key point is simply that "commission-free" does not mean "cost-free." Costs can be paid in less visible ways: slightly worse prices, partial fills, or lost opportunities when the market moves.

A simple incentive checklist: "What are they trying to be paid for?"

When you are uncertain who is on the other side, stop trying to identify a specific villain. Instead, classify the likely counterpart by incentive. The following checklist is deliberately simple:

- **If they earn the spread,** they prefer frequent trades and controlled risk (market making / liquidity provision).
- **If they earn fees or rebates,** they care about where the trade happens and how it is tagged (venue economics and routing incentives).

- **If they earn from predicting short-term moves,** they care about information, timing, and your order's signals (alpha and order-flow inference).
- **If they must complete a large trade,** they care about minimizing footprint and impact (institutional execution constraints).

This checklist is a defensive lens. It pushes you away from the fantasy that your order goes into a neutral pool and toward the reality that your order enters a competitive environment.

Why this matters for the rest of the book

The central tension of modern electronic markets is that the same mechanism that makes trading easy for you—automation, fast matching, and continuous quoting—also creates opportunities for participants who specialize in being faster, more informed, or more strategically positioned.

Everything that follows in this chapter builds on one foundational idea introduced here:

> **The market is an ecosystem.** Some participants earn money by providing services; others earn money by detecting and exploiting patterns in others' behavior. Often, the same participant does both.

In the next sections, we will zoom in on the most important service provider you routinely interact with (often without noticing): the modern market maker, how they quote prices, and what causes them to retreat when the flow becomes "toxic."

3.2 Market Makers and Liquidity Provision

In the previous section, we mapped the market ecosystem and emphasized a practical truth: your order enters an environment where different players are paid for different things. Now we zoom in on one of the most important (and most misunderstood) roles in that ecosystem: the **market maker**.

A market maker is the modern digital middleman. They do not primarily get paid for being "right" about whether a stock will be higher tomorrow. They get paid for something much more mechanical:

They get paid for standing ready to trade with you *right now*.

That readiness is called **liquidity provision**. And the basic paycheck for liquidity provision is the **bid–ask spread**.

Liquidity, translated: "Can I trade without moving the price?"

Liquidity is one of those words that sounds academic until you attach it to an everyday feeling.

- In a **liquid** market, you can buy or sell quickly at a price close to the last traded price. You do not feel like you are "pushing" the market.
- In an **illiquid** market, trades feel sticky: spreads are wider, fills are uncertain, and the price can jump when you try to trade.

Market makers are firms (often algorithmic) that try to keep markets liquid by continuously posting **two-sided quotes**: a price they will pay to buy from you and a price at which they will sell to you.

Those two prices are the bid and the ask.

The two-sided quote: Bid, Ask, Spread

At any moment, you will typically see two prices:

- **Bid**: the best price available to *sell* into (someone is willing to buy from you).

- **Ask** (or **Offer**): the best price available to *buy* at (someone is willing to sell to you).

The **spread** is simply:

$$\text{Spread} = \text{Ask} - \text{Bid}.$$

A spread is not a moral failing or a trick; it is the market's way of pricing immediacy and risk. If you want to trade *now*, you often pay (or receive) the spread.

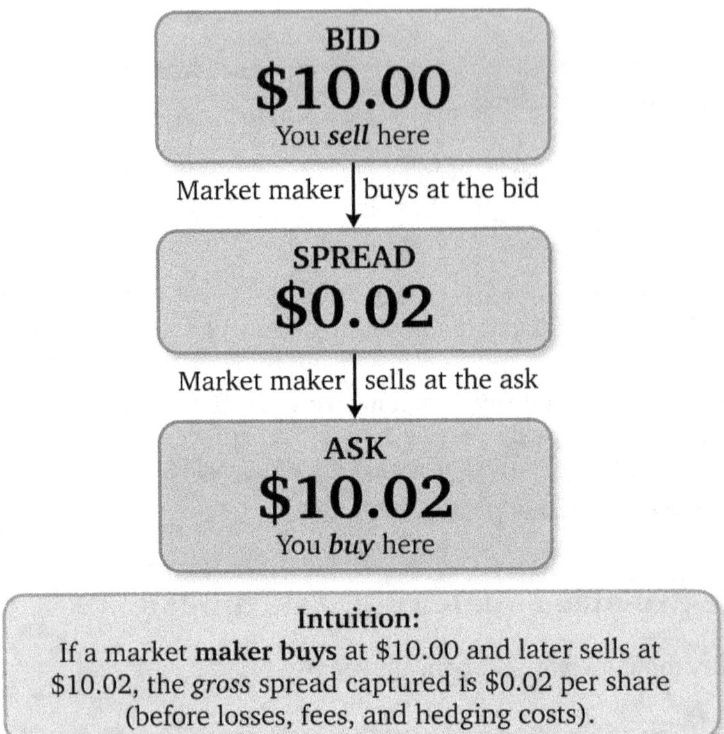

A concrete example: who pays whom?

Suppose the best displayed prices are:

$$\text{Bid} = \$10.00 \qquad \text{Ask} = \$10.02.$$

- If you place a **market buy**, you will typically trade at the **ask** ($10.02). You are paying for immediacy.
- If you place a **market sell**, you will typically trade at the **bid** ($10.00). You are also paying for immediacy (in the sense that you accept the best available buyer).

The spread is $0.02. A beginner-friendly way to interpret the spread is:

The spread is the "toll" for crossing the gap between buyers and sellers instantly.

This is also why costs can exist even in "commission-free" trading. You may not pay a visible commission, but if you frequently cross the spread with market orders, you are still paying a transaction cost.

Why spreads exist at all (and why they change)

A market maker is not simply matching buyers and sellers. They are often taking the other side of your trade *before* an opposite customer arrives. That creates risks they must be compensated for. The spread can be viewed as payment for several bundled risks:

1) Inventory risk (holding the "wrong" thing).

If the market maker buys from you, they may now hold shares. If the price falls before they can sell, they lose money. If they sell to you and the price rises before they can buy back, they lose money. In both cases, speed helps but does not eliminate risk.

2) Adverse selection risk (trading against someone informed).

Sometimes, the trader hitting the quote is not random. They may be reacting to news, a correlated move in another market, or an information signal. If the market maker sells at $10.02 right before the "true" price jumps to $10.20, the market maker just sold too cheaply. This is one of the deepest reasons spreads widen during fast markets. (We will treat this carefully in the next section.)

3) Operational and fee frictions.

Market makers pay exchange fees (or receive rebates), incur technology costs, and manage risk systems. Even if the spread looks like "free money," real-world frictions are constantly eating at it.

So spreads are not fixed. They tend to be:

- **tighter** in high-volume, calm markets with lots of competing liquidity providers,
- **wider** in stressed, jumpy markets where being picked off is more likely,
- **wider** in thinly traded names where inventory is harder to unwind.

The market maker's business model: turnover, not prediction

Many casual traders imagine a market maker as someone taking a strong directional view:

"They bought because they think it will go up."

"They sold because they think it will go down."

That is often the wrong mental model.

A market maker's core objective is usually closer to:

Keep trading, keep spreads small enough to win flow, and keep inventory controlled enough to survive.

This implies three important practical points for the everyday trader:

- **Market makers like predictable, two-way activity.** If buys and sells arrive in a roughly balanced way, they can recycle inventory and capture small spreads repeatedly.
- **Market makers dislike one-way pressure.** If the flow is heavily buy-only or sell-only, they accumulate inventory and become vulnerable to price moves.
- **Market makers adjust their quotes dynamically.** When risk rises, they protect themselves by widening spreads, moving quotes, or stepping back.

You do not need to hate market makers to defend yourself. You just need to understand their incentives so you can anticipate how the "toll" (the spread) will behave when conditions change.

Service provider or shark? A careful distinction

In the ecosystem map, we placed market making near the "shark" tier because market makers are fast, automated, and structurally advantaged in microsecond competition. But this does not mean all market making is predatory.

A useful distinction is:

- **Liquidity provision** is generally about earning the spread for being willing to trade.
- **Predation** is about extracting profit from *your* vulnerability (your urgency, your predictable triggers, or your information disadvantage).

A market maker can be a genuine service provider *most of the time* and still behave defensively in ways that feel hostile when volatility spikes. This is not hypocrisy; it is risk management.

What to remember before we move on

If you remember only a few lines from this section, make them these:

- **Bid** is where you sell; **ask** is where you buy.
- The **spread** is a real cost of immediacy, even when commissions are zero.
- Market makers are not paid mainly to predict direction; they are paid to **provide liquidity while managing risk**.
- When markets feel "slippery," it is often because liquidity providers are protecting themselves from being traded against by someone better informed.

That last point is the bridge to the next section. To understand why spreads suddenly widen, why quotes disappear, and why fast markets can feel unfair, we need to introduce the market maker's greatest fear: **adverse selection** and the idea of **toxic flow**.

3.3 Adverse Selection and Toxic Flow

In the last section we explained the market maker's basic bargain: *quote two prices, trade frequently, and try to earn the bid–ask spread as compensation for providing immediacy.* That story is true—but incomplete. It leaves out the market maker's biggest fear: not volatility in general, but **being systematically traded against by someone who knows more than they do**.

That fear has a name in market microstructure:

> **Adverse selection** is the risk that the person trading with you is doing so because they have information (or speed) that makes your quoted price stale.

When adverse selection risk rises, market makers do not politely continue offering the same tight prices. They defend themselves. And the defense mechanisms are exactly what everyday traders experience as a market that suddenly feels hostile:

- spreads widen,

- displayed size shrinks,
- quotes flicker or disappear,
- fills get worse or more uncertain.

This section will build your intuition for *why* that happens, using plain language and concrete examples.

A market maker is quoting a price in the dark

Even with fast computers and rich data, a market maker is always a little bit in the dark. They do not know:

- whether a breaking news headline is about to hit,
- whether a large institution is starting a multi-minute buying program,
- whether a correlated market (index futures, options, FX) just moved first,
- whether an incoming order is "random" or "informed."

Yet they must still quote a bid and an ask. In effect, they are posting a standing offer:

> "If you want to trade right now, I will take the other side at these prices."

The market maker's problem is that the people who choose to trade *right now* are not a random sample of the world. They are self-selected. And self-selection is where the "adverse" part comes from.

Adverse selection in one sentence

Here is the one-sentence version you should remember:

> **Adverse selection means your trade arrives precisely when my price is wrong.**

If you are a liquidity provider, you lose money when:

- you sell just before the price rises (you sold too cheaply),
- you buy just before the price falls (you bought too expensively).

Notice what that implies: the market maker can lose money *even if they capture the spread.* If the price moves against them immediately after the trade, a small spread is not enough to pay for that loss.

A simple numerical example: spread captured, but still losing

Assume the market maker is quoting:

$$\text{Bid} = \$10.00 \qquad \text{Ask} = \$10.02.$$

Case A: "normal" (uninformed) flow. A buyer hits the ask at \$10.02. A minute later, a seller hits the bid at \$10.00. The market maker has (roughly) completed a round trip: sell then buy back, earning about \$0.02 per share *before* costs.

Case B: adverse selection (informed or fast flow). A buyer hits the ask at \$10.02, but this happens because the "real" price is about to jump. Immediately after the fill, the best prices update to:

$$\text{Bid} = \$10.18 \qquad \text{Ask} = \$10.20.$$

The market maker sold at \$10.02 and now would have to buy back around \$10.20 to flatten inventory. That is a loss of about \$0.18 per share—far larger than the \$0.02 spread they hoped to earn.

In other words, the market maker did not lose because they misunderstood the spread. They lost because they got *picked off.*

What "toxic flow" means (and what it does *not* mean)

The phrase **toxic flow** is market slang. It does not mean the counterparty is evil. It means the flow is *dangerous to stand in front of* as a liquidity provider.

> **Toxic flow** is order flow that is statistically likely to be followed by adverse price movement against the liquidity provider.

Think of it like this: if you are a shopkeeper selling umbrellas, you love steady customer traffic. But if every customer who walks in seems to do so seconds before a storm starts, you would suspect they know something you do not. You might raise prices or close the shop until the storm information is fully reflected.

Markets are similar. Market makers react to patterns. If the incoming trades tend to be "right" (the price keeps moving in the same direction after the trade), then the flow is toxic to the party providing quotes.

Where does toxic flow come from? (Three common sources)

You do not need to memorize these categories, but they help make the concept concrete.

1) News and information shocks. Earnings surprises, macro announcements, analyst reports, geopolitical headlines—anything that causes a rapid reassessment of value creates a window where posted quotes can be stale.

2) Large, persistent institutional execution. When a big fund begins buying (or selling) over time, the flow can be one-directional and persistent. Even if the institution is not "informed" in a news sense, the market maker's inventory and hedging risk rises because the pressure does not quickly mean-revert.

3) Speed advantages and cross-venue/cross-asset signals. Sometimes the information is not a headline; it is a *lead-lag*. Index futures move first, options implied volatility jumps, or another exchange updates a fraction of a second earlier. Fast traders may respond by taking liquidity from stale quotes elsewhere. To the market maker who is being hit, it still looks like: "trades arrive when my quote is wrong."

These sources can overlap. The important point is not the label but the consequence: **the market maker sees a higher probability of losing immediately after filling your trade.**

Why market makers retreat: the logic of widening spreads

When toxic flow rises, market makers have only a few levers. All of them are defensive:

- **1) Widen the spread.** If risk is higher, the "toll" for immediacy must be higher. A wider spread increases the compensation per trade and reduces how often they get hit.
- **2) Reduce displayed size.** Quote fewer shares/contracts so that if they are wrong, they are wrong on less inventory.
- **3) Move quotes away from the market.** They may keep quoting but at less competitive prices, effectively stepping back.
- **4) Cancel quotes (pull liquidity).** In extreme cases, they temporarily stop providing liquidity until uncertainty resolves.

This is why liquidity can appear plentiful in calm periods and vanish during stress. The market maker is not obligated to subsidize your urgency. They are obligated (to themselves) to survive.

What it feels like to you: "Why did my fill get so bad?"

To a retail trader, the defensive actions above show up as practical annoyances:

You see worse prices. A wider spread means you pay more to buy and receive less to sell. Even if the mid-price (the midpoint between bid and ask) has not moved much, your *transaction price* deteriorates.

You get partial fills or no fill. If displayed size shrinks, your order may fill only in part, or it may chase the market as quotes move.

The price seems to run away from you. In fast conditions, quotes update rapidly. A market order can "walk the book" across multiple price levels. Even limit orders can be left behind if the market jumps.

The key mental shift is this:

> **During stress, your main opponent is not a particular firm. It is the market's collective attempt to avoid trading at stale prices.**

Some participants profit from that stress. But the immediate cause of bad trading conditions is often simple self-defense by liquidity providers.

A practical distinction: volatility vs. toxic flow

Many beginners think, "The spread widened because volatility increased." That is often directionally right, but it is more precise to say:

> **Spreads widen when volatility is likely to harm a liquidity provider *right after* they trade.**

Two markets can be equally volatile in the everyday sense (prices move around), but one can be more toxic if the moves are:

- sudden (jumps rather than wiggles),
- one-directional (persistent pressure),
- predictable to a subset of fast/informed traders (creating systematic picking-off).

That is why some periods feel "fair" even with big swings, while other periods feel predatory even with smaller moves.

Why this concept matters for detecting predatory behavior

This book focuses on detection and defensive thinking. Adverse selection and toxic flow are not just academic vocabulary; they are a lens for interpreting what you see on your screen.

When you observe:

- spreads suddenly widening in one symbol while the rest of the market looks calm,
- liquidity vanishing right as you try to trade,
- repeated small quote changes that make you feel "chased" or "front-run,"

you should at least consider that the market has classified the moment as high-risk for liquidity providers.

Sometimes that classification is justified (real information is moving the market). Sometimes it is amplified by fast, aggressive strategies that exploit predictable order placement. The rest of this book will help you tell the difference *as a practical matter*, without needing to see the full order book or decode nanosecond data.

Takeaways: the market maker's fear becomes your trading cost

- **Adverse selection** is the risk that you trade at a price that becomes immediately wrong.
- **Toxic flow** is order flow that tends to be followed by adverse price movement for liquidity providers.
- When toxic flow rises, market makers defend themselves by **widening spreads, shrinking size, moving quotes, or pulling liquidity**.
- The everyday symptom is simple: **trading gets more expensive and less predictable exactly when you most want certainty.**

3.4 The Broker's Role and Execution Quality

In the previous sections, we built a simple picture of the trading ecosystem: market makers provide immediacy and earn the spread, but they fear adverse selection and will widen spreads or pull back when the flow becomes toxic. Now we focus on the participant who sits between you and that ecosystem: **your broker**.

For most everyday traders, the broker feels like a neutral messenger—a mailbox that forwards your order to "the market." In reality, the broker is better understood as a **traffic controller**. Your broker decides, within rules and constraints, *where* your order goes and *how* it is handled.

That decision matters because the modern market is not a single place. It is a network of venues and counterparties. Changing the path can change:

- who gets to trade with you,
- the price you receive,
- how quickly you get filled,
- whether you get price improvement (or not),
- what information your order reveals along the way.

This section explains the broker's incentives and the core conflict: **your objective is best execution; the broker's objective may include revenue from routing choices.**

What brokers do (beyond the app)

A retail broker typically provides:

- account custody and recordkeeping,
- access to trading venues,

- order entry and order type handling,
- risk checks (e.g., buying power, short-sale locate rules),
- routing logic: the "where does it go?" decision.

The first four are mostly visible and intuitive. The last one—routing—is where conflicts can hide, because you usually cannot see the alternatives your broker could have chosen *at the moment you clicked.*

Order routing: the hidden fork in the road

When you submit an order, it rarely goes in a straight line to a single, obvious destination. Your broker may route it to:

- an **exchange** (a lit, public order book),
- an **internalizer / wholesaler** (a market maker or dealer that fills retail orders off-exchange),
- another venue that the broker believes will provide a good execution (sometimes via smart order routing).

This choice is often summarized as **"lit" vs. "off-exchange"** execution. Both can be legal. Both can be beneficial under some conditions. The important point is that *the path is a choice.*

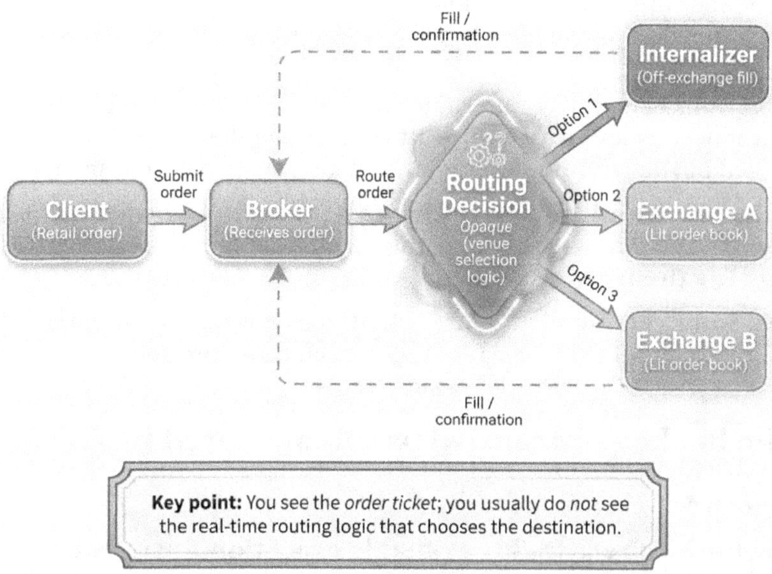

Internalization (wholesalers): what it is and why it exists

When a retail order is **internalized**, it is filled by a dealer/market maker (often called a **wholesaler**) rather than being sent directly to an exchange's public order book.

Why would this happen?

- The wholesaler may be willing to fill you at a price at or slightly better than the best displayed quote.

- The broker may receive compensation connected to sending orders to that wholesaler (in many market structures this is discussed as **payment for order flow**, though details vary by jurisdiction and broker arrangement).
- The wholesaler may value retail flow because it is often smaller and, on average, may be less "toxic" than other types of flow.

From your perspective, internalization can sometimes be beneficial if it produces **price improvement** (executions slightly better than the quoted bid or ask). But internalization also raises a hard question:

If there are multiple places my order could go, how do I know my broker chose the place that was best for me rather than best for them?

That is the core conflict of interest. It does not require anyone to behave illegally. It exists because routing can be monetized.

The broker's incentive problem, stated plainly

Your objective is simple:

Get the best reasonably available execution for my order.

Your broker may have additional objectives:

- minimize their own costs of execution,
- earn routing-related revenue,
- manage relationships with venues and liquidity providers,
- reduce operational risk (e.g., avoid odd-lot complexity, reduce rejects),
- deliver a smooth user experience (fast fills that feel good).

These can overlap with your interests, but they can also diverge.

A particularly important divergence is between:

- **fast fill** (psychologically satisfying, often good),

- **best price** (economically best, sometimes harder),
- **best overall execution quality** (includes price, speed, fill probability, and market impact).

When a broker advertises "zero commission" and "instant execution," that is not necessarily bad. But it should trigger a healthy follow-up question: *How is the broker paid, and does that payment depend on where my order is sent?*

Execution quality: what it means for everyday traders

Execution quality is often discussed with intimidating metrics. You do not need to become a statistician to think clearly about it. For a casual trader, execution quality can be understood through four practical dimensions:

1) Price: did you get a good fill relative to what was available?

A common reference point is the **NBBO** in U.S. equities: the best displayed bid and ask across exchanges at that instant. You can ask:

- Did my buy fill at or below the best ask?
- Did my sell fill at or above the best bid?
- Did I receive any price improvement?

2) Speed: how long did the order take to fill?

Speed matters more for marketable orders (market orders and aggressive limit orders) and less for patient limit orders. But speed can be a double-edged sword: very fast execution is not automatically best execution if it consistently sacrifices price.

3) Certainty: did it fill completely, partially, or not at all?

A partial fill can be fine, but it can also create hidden costs if the remainder fills at worse prices or if you are forced to resubmit.

4) Slippage and re-quotes (in effect): did the market move away as you traded?

In fast markets, slippage increases. But routing can affect how much of that slippage you experience.

These dimensions interact. For example, you might accept slightly slower execution if it tends to deliver better prices, especially when trading is not time-critical.

The hidden cost of "free": spread capture vs. price improvement

Recall from the market maker section that the spread is the toll for immediacy. Here is the subtle connection:

- If your order is routed to a liquidity provider who can capture the spread efficiently, they may be willing to give you a fraction of that spread back as **price improvement**.
- If routing decisions prioritize broker revenue or venue economics over price improvement, you may receive less of that benefit.

In other words, execution quality is partly about *who captures the spread and how it is shared.*

This is why two brokers can both advertise "zero commission" yet deliver systematically different results in real trading, especially for small, frequent orders.

Why routing affects exposure to predatory behavior

Routing is not only about price; it is also about information. Different venues reveal different amounts about your order, and different counterparties react differently.

From a defensive standpoint, remember the ecosystem logic:

- Toxic flow makes liquidity providers defensive.
- Defensive liquidity provision leads to wider spreads, smaller size, and more fragile quotes.

- Routing determines which liquidity pool you interact with *and* which participants get to see and respond to your activity.

This does not mean that exchanges are always better or wholesalers are always worse. It means the path matters, and the incentives behind the path matter.

Practical questions a retail trader can ask (without needing insider data)

You may not be able to see the broker's full routing logic in real time, but you can adopt a sharper mindset. Here are questions that keep you focused on incentives:

- **Where do my orders typically execute?** (exchange vs. off-exchange)
- **Do I receive measurable price improvement on average?**
- **How often do I experience partial fills or worse-than-expected prices in fast markets?**
- **What does my broker disclose about routing arrangements and execution quality reports?**

Even reading these disclosures once changes your posture: you stop treating routing as magic and start treating it as a design choice with economic consequences.

Takeaways: the broker is not just a messenger

- Your broker is a **gatekeeper** that decides where your order interacts with the market ecosystem.
- Routing choices can create a **conflict of interest** when broker revenue depends on destination.

- **Execution quality** is more than commission: it includes price, speed, certainty, and slippage.
- Understanding routing is a core defensive skill because the path shapes both **your costs** (spread/price improvement) and your **exposure** to fast, strategic counterparties.

With the broker's role clarified, we are ready to examine another incentive layer that shapes routing and algorithmic behavior: **exchange fee models**, especially maker–taker economics and the rebate-driven competition for queue position.

3.5 Exchange Fee Models and Behavior

> **Exchange fees and rebates create a second economy layered on top of prices.** Some participants trade not just to earn from price movement, but also to earn (or avoid) fees.

Maker vs. taker: who provided liquidity?

When you trade on an exchange, your order either:

- **makes** liquidity (it posts to the order book and waits), or
- **takes** liquidity (it immediately matches against an existing order).

A limit order that rests on the book is usually a **maker** order. A market order is almost always a **taker** order. A marketable limit order (a limit order priced aggressively enough to execute immediately) is also usually a **taker** order because it consumes displayed liquidity.

This distinction matters because many exchanges charge different fees depending on whether you were a maker or a taker.

The maker–taker model: a rebate for posting, a fee for consuming

Under a common structure known as **maker–taker**, the exchange:

- **pays a rebate** to the *maker* (the party whose order was resting on the book), and
- **charges a fee** to the *taker* (the party whose order removed that liquidity).

So even if two traders interact at the same price, the exchange can collect money from one side and pay money to the other side. The exchange then makes money on the net economics plus other services.

The crucial point is not the exact cents-per-share numbers (they differ by venue and product). The crucial point is that:

> **Queue position can become a source of revenue.** If you can consistently be the maker that gets hit, you may collect rebates over and over.

This is one reason you see intense competition among fast trading firms to post and cancel orders rapidly: they are not only competing on spread, they are competing on *who gets paid the rebate*.

How rebates change behavior: the "liquidity mirage" problem

To a casual observer, a deep order book looks like safety: lots of shares posted at the bid and ask. But fee models can create a kind of optical illusion:

> **Not all displayed liquidity is equally committed.** Some of it is posted because it is economically attractive to post, not because the trader truly wants to buy or sell at that price.

When the rebate is meaningful to a high-volume participant, they may post orders to earn rebates *as long as they can manage the risk.* In calm conditions, this can improve liquidity and tighten spreads. In stressed conditions, the same participants may cancel quickly, because the adverse selection risk overwhelms the rebate benefit.

This leads to a common retail experience:

- In normal times, the book looks thick and fills seem easy.
- In fast times, the book thins and the price seems to jump through levels.

It is not that the exchange "broke." It is that the participants supplying liquidity were responding rationally to changing economics: the small rebate is not worth getting run over by toxic flow.

Why queue position becomes a battleground

On an exchange, if multiple traders post the same price, the exchange usually executes based on **price–time priority**: best price first, and within a price level, earliest order first.

If the rebate is attractive, and the spread is tight, then being *first in line* at the bid or ask can be valuable. It can mean:

- you collect the rebate when someone trades against that level,
- you capture the spread (if you later unwind on the other side),
- you gain information (because being hit can itself be a signal).

The result is an arms race for queue position:

- faster order placement,
- rapid order cancellation and replacement,
- tiny price improvements ("stepping ahead" by a minimal increment),

- fragmentation across venues to maximize the chance of being at the front somewhere.

For retail traders, you do not need to compete in this arms race. But you should recognize its side effects: flickering quotes, sudden changes in displayed size, and fills that depend on microseconds you cannot see.

Why brokers care: routing is partly economics

Now connect this to the broker section. A broker routing an order to an exchange is not only thinking about:

- displayed price (bid/ask),
- likelihood of execution,
- speed.

They may also be thinking about:

- **fees paid** if the order takes liquidity,
- **rebates earned** if the order provides liquidity,
- net execution cost for the broker's execution pipeline.

This is one reason routing decisions can be complex and opaque. Two venues can show the same best price to you, but have different economic outcomes for the broker and different liquidity dynamics under stress.

A critical subtlety is that **the venue that is cheapest for the broker is not automatically the venue that is best for you**. It might be, but the incentives are not perfectly aligned, which is why execution quality measurement exists at all.

The retail trader's view: how fee models show up on your screen

You do not see the fee schedule directly when you place a trade. You see effects. Here are common ones:

1) "Why did my limit order not get filled even though the price touched my level?"

If you posted a limit order at a popular price level, there may have been a long queue in front of you. Rebate-driven posting can increase queue length. The market can trade at your price without reaching your position in line.

2) "Why do quotes disappear when the market gets fast?"

In toxic conditions, the adverse selection risk rises. Liquidity providers who were happy to post for rebates in calm markets may cancel to avoid being picked off. The rebate does not compensate for the jump risk.

3) "Why does the best price seem to be on a venue that I never get?"

Because markets are fragmented, the best displayed quote might be fleeting or available in small size on a particular venue. Routing, queue position, and competition among fast participants can make that quote hard to access consistently.

4) "Why do spreads sometimes stay tight, yet I still feel like I'm paying a lot?"

Because your total cost is not only the visible spread. It can include:

- slippage (price moves while you trade),
- partial fills that force you to trade again,
- opportunity cost if your order sits behind a queue,
- indirect effects of routing incentives.

Maker–taker does not mean "bad"—it means "incentive-shaped"

It is tempting to conclude that maker–taker is inherently predatory. That conclusion is too simple. Maker–taker can:

- attract liquidity providers,
- narrow spreads in competitive products,

- improve visible price discovery on lit venues.

But it also creates predictable behaviors that sophisticated algorithms can exploit:

- fighting for queue position to harvest rebates,
- posting liquidity that vanishes quickly when risk rises,
- routing and re-routing based on micro-economics rather than investor-friendly simplicity.

For this book's purpose, the practical takeaway is:

> **Fee models shape the behavior of fast traders and brokers, and that behavior can change the quality and reliability of the liquidity you think you see.**

What an everyday trader should remember

- Exchanges are marketplaces *and* businesses; fee schedules influence behavior.
- Under maker–taker, posting liquidity can be rewarded (rebates) and taking liquidity can be charged (fees).
- Rebates can intensify competition for queue position, producing flickering quotes and long queues at popular prices.
- In fast or uncertain markets, rebate-motivated liquidity can disappear quickly because adverse selection risk dominates.
- Your execution outcome is shaped not only by the quote you see, but also by routing, queue priority, and the micro-economics of the venue.

Chapter 4

The Speed Race: High-Frequency Trading Fundamentals

Imagine a poker game where one player can see the cards a fraction of a second before everyone else. In modern finance, speed isn't just an advantage; it is the entire game. This chapter pulls back the curtain on the invisible machinery of the market, explaining how algorithms trade faster than a human blink and why physical distance from Wall Street servers has become the most valuable real estate in the world.

4.1 Defining High-Frequency Trading

High-Frequency Trading (HFT) is best understood as a *way of trading* rather than a single, specific strategy. The defining feature is **speed**— not just "fast computers," but **extremely short holding periods** and **extremely high turnover**. In plain language: an HFT system may buy and sell the *same* stock (or futures contract, or ETF) over and over again, sometimes holding it for only **milliseconds** or even **microseconds**, aiming to capture tiny, repeated price differences.

A casual investor might hold a stock for months or years. A day trader might hold for minutes or hours. Many ordinary computer-driven trading systems ("algorithmic trading") might hold for days, hours, or minutes, using software mainly to automate a plan a human could still describe and execute more slowly. HFT, by contrast, is built around **the idea that being early by a sliver of time changes what prices you see and what prices you can get**. If you remember only one distinction, remember this:

> **Algorithmic trading** means "a computer helps execute a strategy."
>
> **High-frequency trading** means "the strategy *depends on* being extremely fast, with very short holding periods and very high turnover."

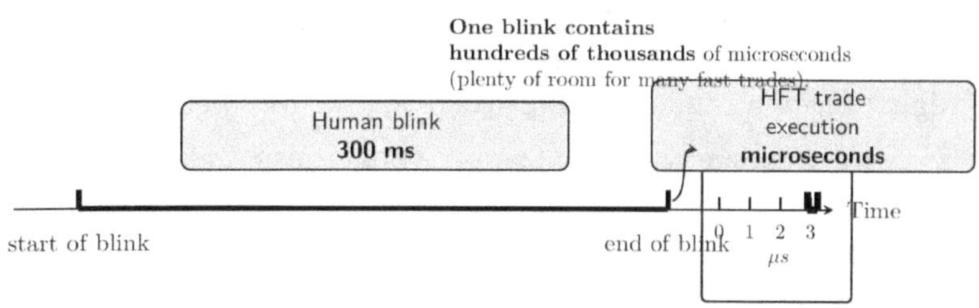

A practical definition: what makes HFT "high-frequency"?

In everyday conversation, people often use "HFT" as a catch-all term for any trading done by computers. That is understandable—many trades *are* automated—but it blurs an important line. Most computerized trading is not high-frequency in the strict sense.

For the purposes of this book, use this **working definition**:

> **High-Frequency Trading (HFT)** is automated trading characterized by (1) **very short holding periods** and (2)

very high order and trade activity, where speed and rapid response to market data are central to the edge.

Two parts of that definition matter.

1) Holding period: how long is the position kept?

A holding period is simply the time between buying and selling (or selling short and buying back). In traditional investing, the holding period is long enough that *business news* (earnings, products, economic cycles) dominates outcomes. In HFT, the holding period is so short that *market mechanics* (quote updates, queue position, tiny price differences, the arrival of other orders) dominates outcomes.

That shift is subtle but crucial. It changes the relevant "skill" from forecasting a company's future to forecasting the next few instants of trading.

2) Turnover: how often does the strategy trade?

Turnover is the pace of buying and selling. An HFT system might trade the same instrument repeatedly throughout the day, potentially submitting, canceling, and replacing orders many times per second.

This is why "frequency" is in the name: not because each trade is huge, but because the *count* is huge.

Algorithmic trading versus HFT: the same tool, different purpose

Think of a computer as a power tool. A power tool can build a house or it can carve a tiny, precise notch. Both use electricity; the difference is the *job*.

Algorithmic trading is a broad category: it means a rule-based process for placing orders. The algorithm could be slow (e.g., buy $500 of an index fund every Monday), medium-speed (e.g., rebalance a portfolio at the close), or fast (e.g., update quotes continuously). In other words, algorithmic trading is about **automation**.

HFT is narrower: it is algorithmic trading where **speed itself is an input to profitability**. The algorithm is designed to react to the market faster than humans and (often) faster than slower systems. The edge may come from:

- seeing price changes first (or reacting first),
- gaining priority in the order queue (getting filled before others at the same price),
- updating quotes quickly to avoid being "picked off" when prices move,
- exploiting tiny and short-lived price differences across related instruments.

The key is not whether a computer is involved; it is whether **micro-timing** is the strategy's core advantage.

Why the word "trading" matters: HFT is not investing

It helps to separate three mindsets:

- 1. **Investing:** owning an asset because you believe its value will rise over time.
- 2. **Trading:** taking positions primarily to profit from price changes (up or down), often with shorter horizons.
- 3. **Market microstructure competition:** competing over *how* trades happen (who gets filled first, at what price, with what information, and with what transaction costs).

HFT lives mostly in the third category. That does not automatically make it "bad" or "manipulative." It does mean HFT firms are playing a different game than most casual market participants. Their profits are often tied to the *process* of trading rather than the *long-run direction* of a company.

Not all fast trading is predatory: two broad roles

Because HFT is a *method*, not a single plan, it includes a spectrum of behaviors. For our purposes, it is useful to separate two broad roles.

Benign (often helpful): fast market making and price competition

Some HFT firms act like ultra-fast liquidity providers: they continuously quote buy and sell prices and try to earn the spread (the small gap between bid and ask) while managing risk tightly. When many firms compete to provide quotes, spreads can shrink and trading can become cheaper for everyone.

In this role, speed is a defensive tool: the market maker updates quotes rapidly to avoid being stuck offering a stale price when the market moves.

Potentially harmful: aggressive, opportunistic strategies

Other behaviors are more aggressive. They may attempt to detect and react to slower orders, exploit temporary dislocations, or pressure the order book in ways that disadvantage slower participants. Some of these behaviors are legal but unfriendly; some cross the line into manipulation (topics we will address later in the book, such as spoofing).

For now, the main point is this: **"HFT" does not automatically mean "crime."** It means the participant is competing in a market where milliseconds and microseconds matter.

A simple mental model: the market as a queue

To make HFT intuitive, picture the market as a busy coffee shop with a single counter:

- The **order book** is the line of customers waiting (buy and sell orders waiting to be matched).
- The **best bid and best ask** are the front of the line on each side (best available prices).
- **Queue priority** is like being first in line: if two people offer

to pay the same price, the one who arrived earlier usually gets served first.

HFT firms invest heavily in being the customer who can step into (or out of) the line at exactly the right moment. If you can join the front of the line a fraction of a second earlier, you may get filled at a desirable price before it disappears. If you can leave the line a fraction of a second earlier, you may avoid selling too cheaply or buying too expensively as prices move.

This "queue" way of thinking is not perfect, but it captures the essence: **HFT is often a competition for timing, position, and immediacy.**

What you should take forward

Before we get into money-making models and infrastructure, lock in these takeaways:

- **HFT is defined by holding period and turnover, not by a single strategy name.**

- **Algorithmic trading is the umbrella; HFT is the speed-dependent subset.**

- **Speed changes the battleground** from long-term value to short-term mechanics: quotes, queues, and micro-price movements.

- **HFT can be liquidity-providing or aggressive.** The label alone does not tell you which.

With that definition in place, the next step is to understand *why* anyone would care about making a fraction of a cent at high speed—and why "thin margins + huge volume" can still become a serious business.

4.2 The Economics of Speed and Scale

In the previous section we defined high-frequency trading (HFT) as a *method*: extremely short holding periods paired with extremely high turnover. That definition answers *what* HFT is. This section answers the more practical question most readers have next:

> **Why would anyone build a business around holding a position for milliseconds? Where does the profit come from?**

The core idea is simple, even if the machinery behind it can be complex:

> **HFT economics are built on thin margins and huge volume.** Instead of trying to make dollars per share a few times, many HFT strategies try to make *fractions of a cent* per share *millions of times*.

From "one big bet" to "many tiny edges"

Most everyday investing stories sound like this: *"I bought a good company and it went up."* The economic logic is long-horizon. You are paid for taking the risk of owning something that can rise or fall over time.

Many HFT strategies live in a different universe. The goal is not to correctly predict where a company will be next quarter. The goal is to repeatedly capture a small, short-lived advantage embedded in the trading process itself—an advantage that may exist for only a moment and may be too small to matter unless you can repeat it at scale.

A useful analogy is retail versus wholesale:

- A traditional trader might look for a **large price move** (a "deal") and try to profit from it.
- An HFT system more often looks for **tiny, repeatable price discrepancies** and tries to profit from them *many times*.

This is why speed matters: the opportunities are small and often vanish quickly. If you are late by even a small amount of time, the edge may be gone—or worse, the trade may flip from a small gain into a small loss.

The arithmetic of "thin margin + huge volume"

The easiest way to understand the model is to do the arithmetic in plain numbers. Consider a strategy that, after all wins and losses are netted together, averages:

> **0.002 dollars per share** (two-tenths of one cent) in profit.

That is $0.002. Many readers correctly react: *"That is basically nothing."* And it *is* basically nothing per share. But now multiply:

$$\text{Daily profit} \approx (\$0.002) \times (\text{shares traded per day})$$

If the strategy trades 50,000,000 shares per day (a scale that requires automation), then:

$$(\$0.002) \times (50{,}000{,}000) = \$100{,}000 \text{ per day}$$

This example is not meant to imply every day is profitable, or that profits are stable, or that every firm can achieve these numbers. It is meant to show why the business model is *possible*. When the edge is tiny, volume is not a luxury; it is the entire business.

Where do micro-profits come from?

HFT is not one strategy, so there is no single source of profit. But most micro-profits fall into a few broad buckets that are worth understanding at a non-technical level.

Capturing the bid–ask spread (fast market making)

Most markets have a **bid** (highest standing buy price) and an **ask** (lowest standing sell price). The difference is the **spread**. If you buy at the bid and sell at the ask, you earn that spread—in principle.

This is the most intuitive "small but repeatable" profit source. It resembles the role of a shopkeeper:

- The shopkeeper buys inventory at a wholesale price.
- The shopkeeper sells at a slightly higher retail price.
- The difference is the gross margin.

A fast market maker tries to do a similar thing with prices instead of physical goods: quote a buy price and a sell price, hoping to buy on one side and sell on the other. If it can repeat this all day long, tiny spreads can add up.

But why does speed matter for market making?

Because the market maker is always vulnerable to being **stuck with a stale quote**. Imagine you are offering to buy at $100.00 and then new information arrives—the true value is now $99.95. If you cannot adjust quickly, someone can sell to you at $100.00 just before your quote updates. That is not a win; that is a loss disguised as a trade.

So speed is partly *offense* (more opportunities to capture spread) and partly *defense* (avoid being picked off when prices change).

Rebates, fees, and the "plumbing" of exchanges

Many exchanges charge and pay fees depending on how an order interacts with the market. A simple high-level idea is:

- Some orders **provide liquidity** (they rest on the book as a bid or ask).
- Some orders **take liquidity** (they immediately hit an existing bid or ask).

Exchanges may encourage liquidity provision by offering **rebates** to the liquidity provider and charging **fees** to the liquidity taker (exact schedules vary by venue and time). For some strategies, these small per-share incentives can meaningfully affect profitability.

For a casual reader, the main takeaway is not the specific fee schedule. The takeaway is that at very high volume, **small per-trade mechanics that most investors never notice can become economically significant**.

Very short-lived price differences across related instruments

Sometimes two closely related instruments temporarily diverge by a tiny amount. For example:

- an ETF versus the basket of stocks it represents,
- a stock versus its options-implied price relationships,
- futures versus the cash market.

When a divergence appears, it may be corrected quickly by competition. Speed matters because the "gap" can close in milliseconds. An HFT strategy may attempt to capture that tiny gap before it disappears.

You do *not* need to learn the math of arbitrage to understand the economic point: HFT firms look for **small mismatches** that are **short-lived**, then attempt to **repeat**.

Why you cannot do this manually (even if you understand it)

A natural question is: *"If the edge is real, why can't a human trader just do it more slowly?"* The answer is that this business is constrained by three realities:

Attention and reaction time

Even if you are skilled, you cannot monitor dozens of instruments, track rapid quote changes, manage a queue position, and update orders continuously by hand. Human reaction time is simply not in the same unit of measurement.

Costs and friction dominate at small edges

When your expected profit per trade is tiny, **friction matters more**. Friction includes:

- fees and commissions,
- the bid–ask spread you must cross,
- slippage (getting a worse price than you expected),
- missed fills (not getting executed when you thought you would).

If your average edge is a fraction of a cent, then paying a fraction of a cent more than expected can erase it. This is why HFT firms obsess over speed, routing, and execution quality: small leaks sink small-margin ships.

Inventory risk scales with time

If a market maker buys shares and intends to sell them back quickly, the risk of a large adverse price move is limited by time. But if the position lingers, the chance that news hits or a broader market wave arrives increases.

So ultra-short holding periods are not only about profit; they are also a way of keeping certain risks small and measurable. (This does *not* eliminate risk. It changes the risk.)

The central trade-off: "being paid" versus "being exposed"

HFT profits often come from providing immediacy—being ready to trade right now. But being ready to trade right now means you sometimes trade with someone who has a reason to be urgent:

- a large institution rebalancing,
- a fund reacting to news,
- a trader using a market order in a fast move.

That urgency can be costly to the liquidity provider. So HFT systems are constantly balancing two forces:

- **Earn** micro-profits for being available (spreads, rebates, tiny discrepancies).
- **Avoid** being the "last person quoting the old price" when the market shifts.

This tension is the economic engine behind much of the technology arms race we will discuss next. If you can update and cancel faster, you can quote more aggressively (tighter prices) *without* taking as much adverse selection risk.

A small table of contrasts: slow-edge vs fast-edge businesses

To keep the logic crisp, here is a compact contrast between the typical economics of longer-horizon trading and HFT-style trading.

Dimension	Longer-horizon trading / investing	HFT economics
Primary goal	Profit from meaningful price moves over time	Profit from tiny edges repeated at scale
Typical holding period	Days to years	Microseconds to seconds (sometimes longer, but still short)
Key advantage	Research, patience, risk budgeting	Speed, execution quality, queue position, microstructure awareness
What kills performance	Being wrong about fundamentals or regime changes	Friction (fees/spread/slippage), stale quotes, adverse selection
How profits scale	Bigger thesis → bigger move	More opportunities → more volume

What you should take forward

The economic intuition of HFT can be summarized in one sentence:

> **HFT turns the market's tiny, fleeting price mechanics into a high-volume business.**

That leads directly to the next question: *What must you build—physically and technologically—to compete in a business where microseconds are valuable?* The next section answers that by introducing latency, co-location, and why the "real estate" of the exchange data center can matter as much as the trading idea itself.

4.3 Latency and Co-Location: The Real Estate of Speed

In the previous section we explained why HFT economics depend on *thin margins* multiplied by *huge volume*. That business model immediately raises a practical constraint: if your average edge is measured in fractions of a cent, you cannot afford to be late.

Latency is the time it takes for information to travel and for your order to reach the market.

If your trading decision depends on the most recent quote, then every microsecond of delay increases the risk that the quote you act on is already outdated by the time your order arrives. In HFT, the world is not "fast" because people are impatient; it is "fast" because **the relevant opportunities and risks disappear on the timescale of electronics and light-speed communication**.

The market is not one place: it is a place *plus a network*

Many casual traders picture "the market" as a single screen. In reality, an exchange is a physical facility (a data center) running matching engines (computers that pair buyers and sellers). Everyone who trades must send information *to* that facility and receive information *from* it.

So every order has a travel itinerary:

Your device → your broker → networks → exchange data center → matching engine

And every price update has the reverse itinerary:

matching engine → networks → your broker → your device

The critical point is that distance and routing are not abstract. They are made of:

- fiber-optic cable length,
- network switches and routers (each adds processing delay),
- congestion (your data may wait in queues),
- software layers (each adds handling time).

HFT firms work to shorten and simplify this itinerary as much as possible.

Co-location: renting a seat inside the building

Co-location (often shortened to *co-lo*) is the practice of placing your trading servers *inside the exchange's data center* or in a facility physically adjacent to it. The idea is as straightforward as it sounds:

Shorter cable → less travel time → faster market data and faster order delivery.

If you are a home trader, your order and your data travel over public and private networks, across cities (sometimes across states), through many devices you do not control. If you are co-located, your order travels a much shorter, more controlled path—often essentially from one rack of servers to another within the same building.

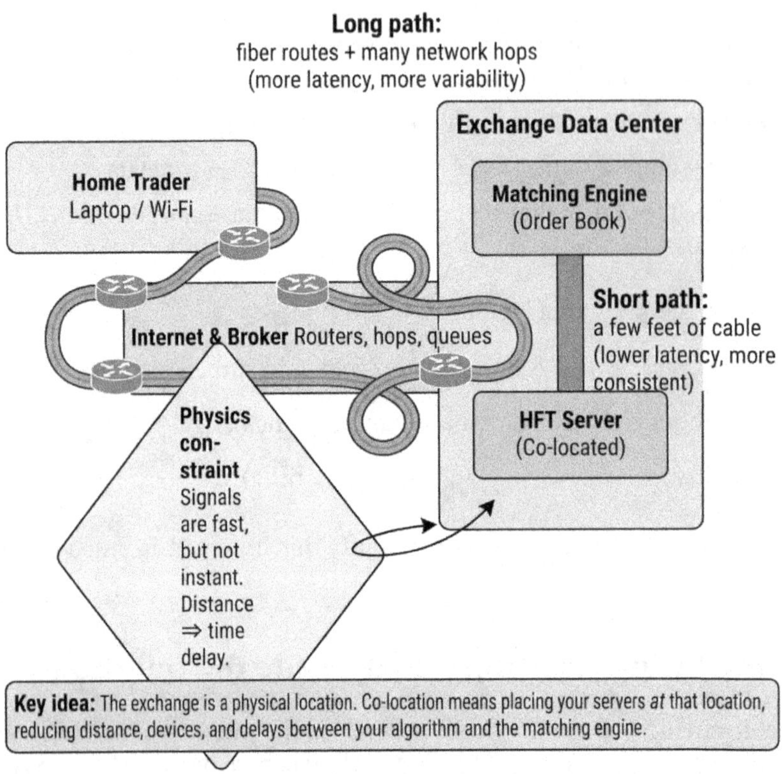

Why "a little distance" becomes a big disadvantage

It is tempting to think: "Surely the internet is already fast enough. What does a small delay change?"

The answer is that in a market measured in micro-movements, small delays change *which state of the market you are trading in*. A simplified timeline illustrates the problem:

- 1. The exchange updates the best bid/ask.
- 2. Co-located participants receive the update almost immediately and react.
- 3. Your platform receives the update after additional network travel and processing.
- 4. You send an order based on what you saw.
- 5. Your order arrives to find the best price already taken, or the queue already long, or the market already moved.

This is not a story about someone "reading your mind." It is a story about the fact that **markets move while your information is traveling**. The slower you are, the more you interact with a market that has already changed.

Latency has two parts: speed *and* consistency

People talk about latency as if it is one number. In practice, two different qualities matter:

- **Low latency:** small average delay.
- **Low jitter:** small variability in delay (more consistency).

For non-professionals, jitter is easy to recognize: it is the difference between *"my order usually fills quickly"* and *"sometimes my order is instant, sometimes it feels stuck"*.

Co-location and specialized network links do not only reduce average delay; they often reduce jitter by controlling routing, minimizing hops, and avoiding the most congested parts of the public network.

The "arms race" is partly an arms race in *real estate*

Co-location is sometimes described as a technology advantage, but it is also a **real estate** advantage:

- Exchange data centers have limited space.
- Rack placement, cable runs, and network architecture can affect timing.
- Firms pay for proximity because proximity can be monetized through execution quality.

Speed advantages are structural. They come from physical placement and infrastructure, not merely from being smart or hardworking.

That structural unevenness does not mean every retail trader is "doomed." It does mean retail traders should be realistic about what kind of competition they are in whenever they demand immediacy (for example, when using market orders during fast conditions).

A non-technical intuition: why microseconds can affect price

Consider a crowded doorway where people enter in single file. If two people reach the doorway at the same time, the one slightly closer goes first. Markets often behave similarly at a given price level: **orders are prioritized**, and being earlier can mean being filled while later orders remain waiting.

If you are late by even a tiny amount of time, three practical consequences follow:

- 1. **You may lose queue position.** Even at the same price, you are behind faster orders.
- 2. **You may get a worse price.** The best quote may vanish before you arrive.

- 3. **You may experience more slippage.** Your expected fill price differs from your realized fill price.

HFT firms invest in co-location because those three outcomes determine whether thin-margin strategies are profitable or not.

Where everyday traders most often feel this (without realizing it)

Retail participants rarely think in microseconds, but they do feel the *symptoms* of speed competition in moments such as:

- **Fast markets:** price moves quickly and you receive fills worse than expected.
- **News releases:** the quote you saw is no longer available by the time you act.
- **Open and close:** heavy traffic increases delays and widens uncertainty about execution.

4.4 The Debate: Liquidity vs. Fragility

We have now built the basic chain: HFT is defined by ultra-short holding periods and high turnover; it often earns thin margins by trading at enormous scale; and it invests in infrastructure—especially low-latency connectivity and co-location—because microseconds affect execution.

That background sets up the central debate that follows HFT everywhere:

> Does HFT **improve** markets by making trading cheaper and more liquid, or does it **weaken** markets by making liquidity more fragile when conditions get stressful?

The honest answer is that both claims have supporting evidence in different contexts. What matters for a casual trader is not picking a side as a matter of identity; it is understanding the *mechanics* behind each claim so you can recognize when you are likely to benefit and when you are likely to be exposed.

First, define the terms: liquidity is not a feeling

In everyday speech, "liquid" can mean "easy to trade." In market terms, liquidity has several related meanings:

- **Tight spreads:** the gap between the best bid and best ask is small.
- **Depth:** there is meaningful size available at or near the best prices.
- **Resilience:** after a trade or a shock, prices and quotes return to normal quickly.

A common mistake is to treat liquidity as a single number. A market can look liquid in one sense (tight spreads) but be illiquid in another (low depth, poor resilience). HFT can improve some dimensions while worsening others, depending on the moment.

The pro-HFT argument: spread compression and "more competition at the top of the book"

Start with the most intuitive benefit. If many fast firms are competing to post the best bid and the best ask, they have an incentive to inch those prices closer together.

Why competition can tighten spreads

Imagine you want to buy a stock right now. You must pay the ask. If the ask is far above the bid, the cost of immediacy is high. When multiple liquidity providers compete, they may:

- quote a slightly higher bid (better for sellers),
- quote a slightly lower ask (better for buyers),

- update quickly so they can afford to quote aggressively without being picked off.

This is the "spread compression" story: faster and more automated quoting can reduce the cost of trading for everyone, especially in normal conditions.

Why speed and co-location matter to this benefit

Recall the previous section: a fast market maker must defend itself against stale quotes. Low latency makes it safer to quote tightly because the firm can cancel or adjust quotes quickly when information changes. In that sense, speed can have a public-facing benefit: it enables tighter prices *when markets are stable enough for quote updates to keep up with risk.*

What a retail trader experiences when this is true

When the pro-HFT story is dominant, you usually notice:

- small bid–ask spreads (especially in highly traded stocks and major ETFs),
- quick fills for modest-sized limit orders near the top of book,
- less "give" required to trade immediately (lower implicit transaction cost).

Importantly, this benefit is often most visible in the most heavily traded names, where competition is fiercest.

The skeptical argument: liquidity withdrawal and "fair weather" quotes

Now the other side of the coin. A key feature of many HFT liquidity providers is that they manage risk by staying very close to flat (not holding inventory for long) and by continuously updating or canceling quotes. That same design has a consequence:

> **If the environment becomes too uncertain too quickly, the safest quote may be no quote at all.**

This is the "liquidity withdrawal" story. It does not necessarily require bad intent. It can happen because the economics change abruptly.

Why liquidity can evaporate exactly when you want it most

When markets become volatile, several things happen at once:

1. **Adverse selection risk spikes.** In calm conditions, getting filled on a quote is often a routine trade. In a fast move, getting filled may mean you are trading with someone who knows (or is reacting to) bad news faster than you can. The probability that a fill is "toxic" increases.
2. **Quote update speed hits limits.** Even the fastest systems are not instantaneous. When prices jump, a market maker can be hit before it has time to cancel. The expected loss per fill rises.
3. **Inventory risk becomes harder to manage.** If you accumulate inventory during a rapid move, you may not be able to unwind without taking losses. HFT firms often try to keep inventory small, so they may reduce quoting size or step back.
4. **Crowding effects appear.** Many firms respond to the same volatility signals. If many pull back together, the book can thin dramatically.

The result can be a market that *looked* liquid a moment ago (tight spreads at the top of book) but becomes illiquid in depth and resilience when conditions deteriorate.

Fair weather liquidity: what the phrase really means

You will sometimes hear the phrase *fair weather liquidity*. It is a blunt phrase, but it captures a real phenomenon:

> **Some liquidity is plentiful when it is safe to provide, but scarce when providing it becomes dangerous.**

This is not unique to HFT. Human market makers can also retreat in stress. The difference is *speed and synchronization*: automated systems can widen spreads or cancel quotes across many instruments in fractions of a second, making the change feel sudden.

A practical reconciliation: spreads can be tight while depth is thin

One way to reconcile the debate is to separate **the top of book** from **the rest of the book**.

- In calm conditions, HFT competition can make the best bid/ask very attractive.
- But the displayed size at those prices may be small, and the next levels may be far away.

For a small retail order, top-of-book liquidity may be enough most of the time. For a large order, or for any order during a sudden shock, shallow depth becomes a problem. When depth is thin, the market can move more for each trade, and slippage becomes more severe.

This is why people can truthfully say, at the same time:

- "Spreads are tighter than they used to be,"
- "The market feels jumpier during stress."

They are talking about different dimensions of liquidity.

What this means for everyday traders: your main vulnerability is urgency

The debate matters because it affects how you should think about **urgency**. The more urgently you demand execution, the more you are exposed to a market that can change while your order is being processed, routed, and matched.

A useful mental model is:

Calm market: you are mostly paying the spread.
Stressed market: you may pay the spread *plus* slippage caused by rapidly changing liquidity.

This does not mean you should never trade during volatility. It means you should recognize that the implicit cost of immediacy is not constant. In fast conditions, the "price" of demanding immediate execution can rise sharply.

A checklist of signs: when you are in "liquidity" mode vs "fragility" mode

The goal of this book is practical awareness. Here are observable symptoms that can help you distinguish the regimes without needing professional tools:

Signs of liquidity (HFT helps you)

- Spreads are consistently tight from moment to moment.
- Small limit orders near the inside prices fill reasonably often.
- Quotes update smoothly rather than jumping.
- Your fills are close to the price you expected.

Signs of fragility (HFT may not be there for you)

- Spreads widen suddenly or flicker (tight one moment, wide the next).
- Prices gap through levels rather than moving in small increments.
- Your market orders (or aggressive orders) fill worse than expected.
- The book feels "thin": small trades move the price more than usual.

These are not proofs of manipulation. They are clues about changing liquidity conditions—which, in turn, tells you how risky urgency has become.

The key takeaway: HFT can lower everyday costs and still increase stress-time uncertainty

Putting it together, the debate is not a simple verdict. A fair summary is:

> **HFT often improves day-to-day trading costs through competition and faster quoting, but the liquidity it provides can be highly conditional. In volatility, it may shrink, widen, or disappear quickly, making markets feel fragile.**

4.5 Separating Myth from Reality

So far in this chapter we have built a grounded picture of what HFT is and why it exists. We defined HFT as a *method* characterized by ultra-short holding periods and high turnover; we explained the economics of thin margins multiplied by huge volume; and we showed how latency and co-location make speed a structural advantage. Finally, we weighed the liquidity debate: HFT can tighten spreads in calm markets, but liquidity can become fragile in stress.

That set of facts is enough to create a healthy skepticism—and it is also enough to trigger a common trap: the belief that *every* bad fill, *every* sudden price move, or *every* losing trade is proof of a rigged game.

This section is a reality check in both directions. It does two things at once:

- It **validates the structural unevenness** of modern markets (some players are objectively faster and better positioned).
- It **rejects the idea that markets are an all-powerful conspiracy** in which outcomes are pre-written.

Your goal as a non-professional participant is not to win a philosophical debate about HFT. Your goal is to learn to tell the difference between:

normal market outcomes you should expect versus **conditions that raise the probability of predatory behavior or structural disadvantage.**

Myth #1: "HFT is one strategy"

Reality: HFT is a *time horizon and an infrastructure choice*, not a single playbook.

In earlier sections we emphasized that "HFT" is like saying "power tools." A power tool can be used to build, to repair, or to vandalize. Similarly, fast automation can be used to:

- provide liquidity (quote bids and asks),
- arbitrage small price differences,
- manage risk quickly,
- or, in some cases, engage in aggressive behaviors that exploit slower participants.

Conflating all of this into one villain makes your mental model less accurate and your defenses less effective. If you treat every fast participant as a criminal, you will misdiagnose ordinary liquidity dynamics as manipulation.

Myth #2: "They can see my order and hunt me personally"

Reality: Most of what feels like "being hunted" can be explained by **market mechanics, not mind-reading.**

There *are* predatory strategies in markets, and we will cover them later in this book. But the default explanation for a disappointing outcome is usually one of these:

- **You crossed the spread.** A market order (or an aggressively priced limit order) pays for immediacy. That cost is not a trick; it is the fee embedded in the bid–ask spread.

- **You arrived late to a moving quote.** In fast conditions, the quote you see may not be the quote that exists at the matching engine when your order arrives. Latency means you sometimes trade in the "past."
- **The book was thinner than it looked.** A tight top-of-book spread does not guarantee deep liquidity behind it. If depth is shallow, modest urgency can cause slippage.
- **Other participants responded faster than you.** This is structural. Co-location and low latency allow some firms to react to price changes before slower routes update.

None of those require that someone identified *you*. They only require that you behaved like a slower participant demanding immediacy in a fast system.

A useful rule of thumb is:

If a pattern happens to you across many different stocks and many different days, it is more likely to be structural microstructure than a personal hunt.

Myth #3: "If I used a limit order, I'm safe"

Reality: Limit orders are often safer than market orders, but they are not a magic shield.

A limit order primarily protects you from one thing: **paying a worse price than you intended**. It does not guarantee:

- that you will be filled,
- that you will be filled quickly,
- or that you will get queue priority.

In an HFT-dominated environment, queue position can change rapidly. A limit order can sit behind faster orders at the same price. And in fast markets, your limit price may become stale and never trade.

So the truth is more nuanced:

A limit order controls price. It does not control *time* or *priority*.

This matters because many conspiracy narratives are built around the emotional frustration of "I did the safe thing and still got a bad outcome." Understanding what a limit order actually guarantees keeps you from attributing every non-fill or partial fill to foul play.

Myth #4: "If markets were fair, speed wouldn't matter"

Reality: Speed matters because markets are **coordination mechanisms** operating in real time.

Earlier we described the market as a queue. In any queue system, timing determines position, and position determines outcomes. That is not inherently unfair; it is simply how order-driven systems work.

The fairness question is not "Does speed matter?" It is:

- **Who can buy speed?**
- **How transparently is access sold?**
- **Do rules constrain abusive behaviors?**
- **Are protections in place during stress?**

Those are institutional questions. They matter, but they are different from assuming every loss is evidence of manipulation.

Myth #5: "HFT always improves liquidity" or "HFT always destroys liquidity"

Reality: HFT can do both, and the sign flips with market conditions.

We have already built the core reconciliation:

- In calm markets, competition among fast liquidity providers can tighten spreads.

- In stressed markets, the same participants may reduce size, widen quotes, or step back to avoid adverse selection.

A practical way to keep this straight is to separate two questions:

- **1. How cheap is it to trade right now?** (spreads)
- **2. How much can you trade without moving the price?** (depth and resilience)

A market can look cheap in the first sense while being brittle in the second sense. Many misunderstandings about "rigged" markets come from treating these as the same thing.

A reality-based filter: five questions before blaming "the algos"

When something feels wrong, use this quick diagnostic before concluding you were targeted. These questions do not prove innocence or guilt; they help you classify what happened.

- **1. Was I urgent?** Did I use a market order or an aggressively priced limit order? Urgency is expensive, especially in fast markets.
- **2. Was the market volatile right then?** If spreads were widening or prices were jumping, liquidity fragility (not manipulation) is often the simplest explanation.
- **3. Was the instrument naturally thin?** Smaller stocks, certain options, and off-peak times often have less depth. Thin markets produce slippage that feels personal but is mechanical.
- **4. Did I trade around a known "event moment"?** Opens, closes, economic announcements, earnings releases, and breaking news compress time and increase adverse selection risk.
- **5. Is the pattern repeatable and specific?** If you can describe a consistent pattern with specific conditions (same order

type, same time of day, same kind of price response), you are moving from story to evidence. If the explanation is "it just happens," you may be seeing normal noise.

This filter does not dismiss the possibility of predatory tactics. It simply forces you to separate the three most common categories of bad outcomes:

(1) Paying for immediacy, (2) trading in a fragile moment, (3) being slower in a speed race.

Only after those are considered should you lean toward the fourth category:

(4) interacting with manipulative or predatory behavior.

What this chapter does *not* claim

To keep the rest of this book intellectually honest, it helps to state what we are *not* claiming:

- We are not claiming HFT is inherently illegal or inherently unethical.
- We are not claiming retail traders can (or should) compete on raw speed.
- We are not claiming that every sharp move is caused by HFT.

And we are also not pretending the playing field is level:

- Latency and co-location create real structural advantages.
- Some strategies are designed to exploit predictable behavior from slower participants.
- Liquidity can be conditional and can vanish quickly in stress.

Holding both truths at the same time is the foundation of good "shark tank" survival: realistic, not paranoid.

Bridge to the rest of the book: from opinions to detection

By this point, you should be able to describe HFT without slogans:

- what HFT *is* (speed + turnover),
- how it *makes money* (thin edges at scale),
- how it *buys speed* (latency engineering and co-location),
- and why it can *help and hurt* depending on market conditions.

That understanding sets the stage for the next chapters, which shift from big-picture debate to practical awareness:

If some aggressive behaviors exist, what can an everyday participant actually notice?
What patterns suggest normal volatility, and what patterns suggest predatory tactics such as spoofing?

In other words, we move from *"Is the ocean dangerous?"* to *"How do I recognize a shark-shaped shadow?"*

Chapter 5

How Sharks Hunt: Predatory Strategies

Imagine sitting at a poker table where your opponent can see your cards before you bet, or running a race where the winner starts three steps ahead of the gun. This chapter strips away the complex jargon of high-frequency finance to reveal the playbook of predatory traders. We will explore how 'sharks' utilize speed, deception, and brute force to create market mirages, trigger panic, and siphon profits from unsuspecting investors.

5.1 The Taxonomy of Manipulation

Modern markets are electronic ecosystems. Orders are messages, prices are the result of message traffic, and *time* is a competitive weapon. In earlier sections of this chapter, we built a basic mental model of how trades happen: buyers and sellers meet through an order book, liquidity is not a guarantee, and your result (the price you actually get) depends on what was available *at the moment your order arrived.*

This section gives you a simple vocabulary for a complicated topic:

predatory trading. The goal is not to turn you into a detective who can prove wrongdoing (that is the job of regulators and exchanges). The goal is to help you recognize the *ways* an unfair advantage can be created, so you can think defensively and avoid the most common traps.

We will group predatory behavior into three pillars:

- **Deception (Fooling the eye):** creating *false signals* of supply and demand.
- **Speed advantages (Beating the clock):** acting on information or price changes *before* others can respond.
- **Information leakage (Stealing the playbook):** inferring what a slower or larger trader is trying to do, then exploiting it.

These pillars are not three separate worlds. In practice they often combine: deception creates a misleading picture, speed makes it exploitable, and information leakage tells the predator *where* to apply pressure.

Why a taxonomy helps (and why names alone don't)

If you read about market abuse, you will quickly encounter a long list of terms: spoofing, layering, quote stuffing, stop hunting, momentum ignition, latency arbitrage, cross-venue pickoffs, order anticipation, signaling, and more. The problem for a casual reader is that the list feels like memorizing species in a jungle without understanding the food chain.

A taxonomy gives you a short set of questions you can ask whenever you see strange price behavior:

- **Is the market showing me something that might be intentionally misleading?** (Deception)
- **Is someone profiting mainly because they are faster, not because they are "right" about value?** (Speed)

- **Is my order (or someone else's big order) leaving footprints that others can track?** (Information leakage)

If you can classify a suspicious episode into one of these three pillars, you are already ahead of most participants. You may not know the exact tactic, but you can respond appropriately: slow down, reduce urgency, improve order placement, and avoid broadcasting your intentions.

Pillar 1: Deception — fooling the eye with phantom liquidity

Deception is the family of behaviors that try to make the order book *look* more bullish or bearish than it truly is. The key idea is simple:

> *If other traders believe there is heavy buying or selling pressure, they may move first.*

In an order-driven market, many traders (and algorithms) react to visible cues:

- large orders near the best bid or best ask,
- sudden increases in displayed depth ("a wall" of orders),
- rapid changes in quotes that imply urgency,
- apparent imbalance (more size on one side than the other).

Deception tries to exploit a basic fact of microstructure: **the order book is not a promise; it is a collection of intentions that can be changed.** Some orders are genuine. Some are strategic. Some exist primarily to provoke a reaction and then disappear.

The core mechanism: moving others without taking risk. A predator would prefer to profit *without* holding a large position through uncertainty. Deceptive tactics aim to *cause others to move the price* while the deceiver keeps risk low by canceling or reversing quickly.

This is the intuition you should keep in mind throughout the chapter:

- **Real liquidity** is willing to trade if reached.
- **Phantom liquidity** is there to influence behavior, not to be executed.

What this looks like to a casual trader. Deception often feels like the market is "playing games":

- You see a large buy wall supporting the price, so you buy.
- The wall vanishes, the price drops, and suddenly liquidity is thin when you want out.

Later sections will name and dissect the common forms (spoofing, layering, quote stuffing). For now, focus on the pillar-level lesson: **the visible book can be engineered to trigger your impatience.**

Pillar 2: Speed advantages — beating the clock

Speed advantages describe strategies where profit comes from reacting faster than other participants to the *same* information. This is not necessarily illegal by itself; modern market design *does* reward speed. But speed becomes predatory when it is used to systematically extract value from slower participants who are behaving reasonably.

To make this concrete, separate two different meanings of "being right":

- **Economic correctness:** you buy because you believe the asset is undervalued, or you sell because it is overvalued.
- **Microstructural correctness:** you profit because you are faster at updating quotes, detecting price changes elsewhere, or positioning in the queue.

High-frequency trading often lives in the second category. A fast trader may hold positions for seconds (or less) and still make money consistently, not by forecasting fundamentals, but by capturing tiny, repeated microstructure edges.

The basic speed game: stale prices and queue position. Electronic markets operate through messages. Messages take time to travel, be processed, and be displayed. Even if that time is measured in milliseconds, it matters. When prices move quickly, some quotes become temporarily *stale*:

- One venue updates first.
- Another venue is a fraction of a second behind.
- A fast trader can trade against the stale quote before it updates.

Separately, even on a single venue, **queue position** matters. If many traders want to buy at the same price, the earliest orders get filled first. Speed and technology help a participant:

- enter the queue ahead of others,
- cancel and replace quickly to maintain position,
- react to incoming information before slower participants can adjust.

What this looks like to a casual trader. Speed-driven predation often feels like:

- **"I clicked buy and got a worse price than I expected."** (slippage)
- **"The quote changed the instant I tried to hit it."** (fading liquidity)
- **"My order never gets filled unless price moves against me."** (adverse selection)

A crucial point: these experiences do not prove misconduct. They do, however, signal that you are competing in a time-sensitive arena where the fastest participant may be earning a small toll from the slower participant.

Pillar 3: Information leakage — stealing the playbook

Information leakage is the family of behaviors where other participants infer what you (or a large institution) are trying to do and exploit it. This is not about reading your mind; it is about reading your *footprints*.

Here is the uncomfortable reality of electronic trading:

> *To trade, you must communicate. Communication creates patterns. Patterns can be learned.*

When a large fund wants to buy a meaningful amount, it rarely buys all at once. It breaks the order into smaller pieces. This is rational: buying too aggressively can push price up. But the act of slicing creates repeated behavior:

- similar-sized child orders,
- repeated activity at similar times,
- consistent response to price changes (e.g., always buying when price dips slightly),
- recurring interactions with the same venues.

Predatory algorithms hunt for these patterns because they reveal something valuable: **a predictable stream of future demand or supply.**

The core mechanism: trade ahead of the predictable flow. If an algorithm detects that a large buyer is steadily accumulating, it can:

- buy first (raising the price the large buyer must pay),
- sell back later at a slightly higher price,
- repeat this many times while the large order continues.

This is often called *order anticipation* in the microstructure literature and in market commentary. The key intuition is simple enough for any reader:

> *If someone must keep buying, they are forced to accept worse prices over time. Predators try to be the ones selling those worse prices to them.*

What this looks like to a casual trader. Retail traders are usually too small to be "hunted" in the same way as a pension fund, but leakage can still matter:

- repeating the same behavior (same time each day, same instrument, same size),
- placing visible orders that telegraph urgency,
- using obvious stop-loss placement that clusters with other traders' stops.

Even if no one is targeting *you specifically*, you can still be swept up in behaviors that target the *crowd*, because crowds create predictable footprints.

How the three pillars interact (a practical mental model)

In real markets, predatory episodes often combine the three pillars in a sequence. One common pattern looks like this:

- **Information leakage identifies a target:** a large buyer is active, or stops are clustered near a round number.
- **Deception shapes the screen:** the order book shows a wall of selling (or buying) that pressures others psychologically.
- **Speed captures the edge:** the predator cancels, flips, or routes across venues faster than slower participants can respond.

This interaction matters because it explains why these events feel so frustrating. The casual trader often responds to what is visible *now*, but the predator is acting on:

- what others *will* do (behavioral predictability),

- what the market *will* show (engineered signals),
- and what can be done *faster than you can react.*

A plain-language diagnostic checklist

When you suspect the market is "hunting," you can use the taxonomy as a checklist. Table summarizes the pillars, what they attempt to achieve, and the everyday symptoms they produce.

Pillar	What the predator is trying to do	What it feels like to you
Deception	Make supply/demand look stronger or weaker than it is; trigger your reaction without taking much risk	"A wall appeared, I acted, and then it vanished"; sudden reversals after you commit
Speed advantages	Exploit delays (even tiny ones) across venues or in your reaction time; trade against stale quotes; win queue position	"The quote moved as I clicked"; frequent slippage; fills only when price moves against you
Information leakage	Infer a predictable buyer/seller (often a large order); trade ahead of it; make the target pay worse prices	"Price walks away from me" when I try to scale in/out; round-number levels feel "magnetic" and then snap back

What this taxonomy is (and is not) claiming

It is important to be precise. This taxonomy does *not* claim that:

- every fast strategy is manipulation,
- every sharp move is a "stop hunt,"
- every vanished order was illegal spoofing.

Markets are dynamic, and legitimate participants cancel orders constantly as prices change. The point is more modest and more useful for survival:

> *If you trade as if the screen is always honest, the fastest and most strategic players will collect a toll from you.*

In the sections that follow, we will take each pillar and study representative tactics in a step-by-step way: first the deceptive methods (spoofing and its variants), then tactics that exploit forced reactions (momentum ignition and stop cascades), and finally speed-based cross-venue pickoffs and order anticipation. Throughout, keep returning to the same question: **what advantage is being used here—deception, speed, or information leakage?**

5.2 Spoofing: The Art of Fake Orders

In the taxonomy from the previous section, **spoofing** sits squarely inside the **Deception** pillar. It is the clearest example of a market behavior that tries to *change what you believe* about supply and demand without actually committing to trade.

Definition in plain language

Spoofing is the act of placing *non-bona-fide* orders—orders that look real on the screen but are not meant to be executed—in order to create a false impression of buying or selling pressure. The spoofer then tries to profit from the price movement that other traders create in response to that illusion.

Two details are essential:

- Spoofing is not simply "canceling an order." Legitimate traders cancel orders constantly as markets change. Spoofing involves *strategic* order placement and cancellation designed to *mislead.*

- Spoofing works because many participants treat the visible order book as a kind of truth serum: "If there is a huge wall of buyers, price must be supported" or "If there is a massive seller, price must be about to fall." Spoofing exploits that reflex.

Why fake orders can move real prices

To understand spoofing, you need one microstructure idea: the market price is not set by a committee; it is set by **the next trade that actually happens**. That next trade often depends on what traders *think* liquidity looks like.

Most casual traders and many algorithms respond to visible cues in the order book:

- **Depth (size) near the best bid/ask:** A large displayed order can feel like a "wall."
- **Imbalance:** More size on the bid than the ask (or vice versa) can look like pressure.
- **Queue dynamics:** If a huge order is at the front of a price level, it may seem hard to push through.

A spoofer tries to insert a *prop* into this stage set: a large order that makes the crowd believe something is about to happen. Then the crowd does the heavy lifting by adjusting quotes, submitting market orders, or pulling their own liquidity.

In short, *Spoofing is a psychological trade expressed through electronics: it manipulates beliefs about supply and demand, and then harvests the reaction.*

The three-step mechanics (trap, reaction, cancel)

A typical spoofing episode can be explained as a three-act play. The details vary across markets and timeframes, but the logic is remarkably consistent.

Step 1: The Trap - "paint the tape" with phantom pressure. The spoofer places a large order (or several large orders) on one side of the book—often near the current price so it is highly visible. The goal is not to get filled. The goal is to be *seen*.

Examples:

- A large **sell** order appears just above the current price, suggesting heavy supply overhead.
- A large **buy** order appears just below the current price, suggesting strong support.

Step 2: The Reaction - others move the market. Other participants respond in predictable ways:

- Liquidity providers may widen spreads or step back, because the displayed "wall" suggests higher risk.
- Short-term traders may front-run the apparent pressure, selling ahead of a sell wall or buying ahead of a buy wall.
- Casual traders may chase the move, fearing they will miss the next leg.

This reaction can change the real tradable prices: bids drop, asks rise, the mid-price shifts, and trades print at new levels.

Step 3: The Cancel - the ghost vanishes and the spoofer profits elsewhere. Once the market has moved, the spoofer cancels the large displayed order (the one that created the illusion). Often, the spoofer has already traded *on the opposite side* with smaller, real orders:

- While displaying a large sell wall (fake), the spoofer may be **buying** with real orders at slightly better prices.
- While displaying a large buy wall (fake), the spoofer may be **selling** with real orders at slightly better prices.

The central idea is that the fake order is a steering wheel, not an engine.

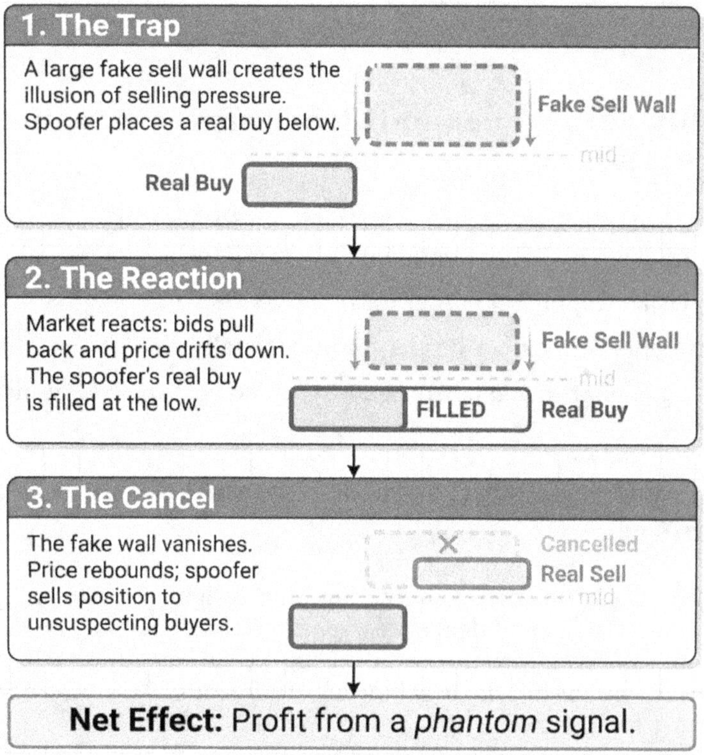

What makes spoofing so effective (and so hard to "see")

Spoofing thrives on three everyday realities of electronic markets.

Reality #1: Cancellation is normal

Order cancellation, by itself, is not suspicious. Many legitimate strategies update quotes continuously to manage risk, especially in fast markets. This normal background noise gives spoofers cover: a misleading order can be explained away as "just a canceled quote" unless you look at *pattern, size, and intent.*

Reality #2: People (and algorithms) are trained to respect size

A large order at a visible price level can influence behavior even if it never trades. This is not irrational; it is a reasonable heuristic:

Large visible supply => harder for price to rise

Large visible demand => harder for price to fall

Spoofing exploits the gap between *visible* and *committed* liquidity.

Reality #3: In thin liquidity, small pushes create big moves

Spoofing is easiest when genuine liquidity is light. In a deep, stable market, it takes a great deal of real money to move price. In a thinner moment (off-hours, around news, during a volatility burst), even modest reactions can shift the best bid/ask. That makes deception cheaper and more tempting.

Common forms: bid-side spoofing vs. ask-side spoofing

Although the details differ across products, most spoofing episodes are variations on two mirror-image patterns.

Ask-side spoofing (fake selling pressure).

- A large fake **sell** order appears above the market.
- Traders infer "overhead supply" and hesitate to buy; some sell.
- Price drifts downward.

- The spoofer (who may have been buying quietly) benefits from lower purchase prices and/or a subsequent rebound after cancellation.

Bid-side spoofing (fake buying pressure).

- A large fake **buy** order appears below the market.
- Traders infer "strong support" and buy more aggressively; some sellers hold out for higher prices.
- Price drifts upward.
- The spoofer (who may have been selling quietly) benefits from higher sale prices and/or a drop after cancellation.

This is why spoofing is sometimes described as a "bait-and-switch" in the order book: the bait is the visible size; the switch is that the spoofer's real trading interest is elsewhere.

Spoofing versus legitimate behavior: the key distinctions

Because honest traders cancel orders, a fair question is: *how is spoofing different from normal quote updates?* You do not need to become a legal expert, but you should understand the intuitive boundary.

Legitimate cancellation typically follows risk and information. A market maker may cancel because:

- the price moved and the quote is now risky,
- new information arrived (news, correlated move, volatility spike),
- inventory limits require adjusting exposure.

Spoofing cancellation typically follows its own impact. A spoofer cancels because:

- the market began to move in the intended direction due to the displayed order,
- other participants reacted (quotes shifted, liquidity pulled, momentum started),
- the deception has done its job and continuing to display increases the chance of being filled.

A practical way to remember the difference is: *Legitimate orders are primarily about trading. Spoof orders are primarily about influencing.*

How spoofing harms everyday traders

Spoofing is not just "unfair in theory." It can translate into concrete costs for casual participants.

Cost #1: Worse execution (slippage)

If the order book is manipulated into looking heavy on one side, you may:

- cross the spread urgently when you did not need to,
- accept a worse price because you fear missing the move,
- get filled right before the market snaps back.

Cost #2: False confidence in support/resistance

Many retail traders use visible depth as a clue for support and resistance. Spoofing can manufacture those "levels" temporarily, causing you to anchor to prices that were never truly defended by real liquidity.

Cost #3: Being induced to reveal urgency

If you react impulsively to a wall, you broadcast that you are a price-taker. Predators generally prefer to trade against urgency because urgency is predictable: it pays the spread and tolerates slippage.

Defensive thinking: what you can do without fancy tools

This book is not about building an HFT system, and you do not need one to reduce your exposure. The most robust defenses are behavioral and procedural—they reduce the number of situations where spoofing can pressure you.

Defense 1: Treat displayed size as "soft information." Use the order book as a hint, not a fact. If your decision depends critically on a single large displayed order, you are vulnerable to anyone who can place and cancel quickly.

Defense 2: Reduce urgency. Spoofing profits from rushed reactions. When appropriate for your strategy:

- prefer **limit** orders over **market** orders,
- avoid chasing sudden one-tick moves that coincide with dramatic depth changes,
- consider breaking your own order into smaller pieces if liquidity is thin.

Defense 3: Look for "vanish on touch" behavior. A common red flag (not proof, but a warning sign) is a large order that repeatedly disappears when price approaches it. If the market repeatedly fails to trade with what appears to be substantial liquidity, discount what you are seeing.

Defense 4: Be cautious around thin moments. Spoofing is easier when the book is thin and participants are jumpy:

- right after major economic announcements,

- around the open and close,
- during sudden volatility bursts,
- in less liquid names or off-peak hours.

In these moments, it is often rational to trade smaller, be more patient, or wait for conditions to normalize.

The bridge to the next tactics

Spoofing is the foundational deceptive tactic because it teaches a broader lesson: **not everything you see in the order book is meant to trade.** In the next section, we extend this idea to more elaborate forms—*layering* (stacking multiple fake orders to build a "wall") and *quote stuffing* (flooding the market with messages). Both amplify the same core trick: overwhelming your perception so that you move first, and pay the cost.

5.3 Layering and Quote Stuffing

The previous section explained spoofing as a three-step deception: a large order appears (the trap), other traders react (the real price moves), and the large order vanishes (the cancel). In practice, predators rarely stop at a single fake order. Once you understand that *displayed liquidity can influence behavior*, the next question becomes: *How can that illusion be made stronger, more credible, and harder to ignore?*

Two common extensions answer that question:

- **Layering:** stacking multiple non-bona-fide orders across several price levels to create the impression of an overwhelming "wall."
- **Quote stuffing:** rapidly flooding the market with quotes (orders and cancellations) to overload message traffic, degrade competitors' ability to react, and create a momentary fog of war.

Both belong to the same Deception pillar as spoofing, but they add two extra ingredients:

- **Scale:** the illusion is no longer a single block; it becomes a structure.
- **Friction:** the opponent is not only misled; they may also be slowed down.

Layering: building a fake "wall" across the book

What layering is

Layering is a spoofing variation in which the manipulator places multiple orders at different prices ("layers") on one side of the order book. The orders are typically large enough to be noticed and are positioned close enough to the current price to feel relevant.

If simple spoofing is one cardboard cutout in a store window, layering is a full fake storefront.

Why multiple layers are more persuasive than one

A single large order can be dismissed as an outlier:

- it might be a genuine trader,
- it might be a hedge,
- it might be quickly canceled for normal reasons.

But *several* large orders arranged neatly at successive prices send a stronger narrative: *"It's not just one seller. It's a whole line of sellers. Price probably can't get through that."*

This narrative matters because markets are not only driven by valuation; they are also driven by **short-term risk management**. When traders believe there is a thick wall, they behave defensively:

- buyers may hesitate or lower bids,

- sellers may become more aggressive ("sell before it drops"),
- liquidity providers may widen spreads or step back.

Layering aims to trigger these responses *without* paying the cost of actually trading those large sizes.

A concrete, intuitive example

Imagine a stock trading around $50.00.

- The best ask is $50.01 (people willing to sell right now).
- The best bid is $49.99 (people willing to buy right now).

A layerer who wants the price to drift down might place a sequence of large sell orders like: $50.02, $50.03, $50.04, ...

When you look at the book, you see what appears to be a deep supply overhang. You might think, "Even if price ticks up, it will run into a wall. Why buy now?" Others reach the same conclusion, bids weaken, and the market can slide down—even though those sell orders were never meant to trade.

How layering is typically "managed" in real time

Layering is rarely static. The layers may be:

- **repositioned** as the price moves (the wall follows the market),
- **scaled** up or down to keep the illusion believable,
- **pulled** quickly if the market threatens to trade into them.

This last point matters. A manipulator does not want the fake orders executed. If the market moves toward the wall too quickly, the wall often disappears or "walks away" by being canceled and reposted farther out.

What layering feels like to everyday traders

Layering produces a distinctive set of frustrations:

- **Phantom resistance/support:** price seems pinned by depth that later vanishes.
- **The market "won't go" until it suddenly does:** after repeated failures at a level, price breaks through instantly once the wall is pulled.
- **You are induced to act early:** the wall pressures you to sell sooner (or buy sooner) than you planned, often resulting in worse execution.

Keep the taxonomy in mind: layering is still fundamentally **deception**. Its power comes from shaping what you infer about near-term supply and demand.

Quote stuffing: flooding the pipes

What quote stuffing is (in plain language)

Quote stuffing is the rapid placement and cancellation of a large number of orders (or order updates) intended to overwhelm the market's messaging system. The goal is not primarily to create a single visible wall, but to create **noise and delay**.

If layering is about building a convincing illusion, quote stuffing is about making it harder for others to see clearly *and* react quickly.

Why flooding messages can create an advantage

Electronic markets operate through continuous streams of data:

- new bids and asks,
- cancellations,
- modifications,

- trades (executions).

Every participant has to:

- **receive** the data,
- **process** it (update internal models of the book),
- **decide** what to do,
- **send** their own orders back.

If the message stream spikes dramatically, slower systems may fall behind. In that brief window, a predator with superior infrastructure can operate in a cleaner, more current picture of the market, while others are effectively looking at a slightly outdated snapshot.

This is where the deception and speed pillars blend:

- The **deception** is that the torrent of quotes may not represent meaningful trading interest.
- The **speed advantage** is that the stuffer can keep up with the torrent better than others can.

What quote stuffing is trying to accomplish

Quote stuffing can support several objectives:

Objective 1: Create a temporary "fog" around the true state of liquidity. When the book is changing faster than many participants can track, displayed depth becomes harder to interpret. A casual trader may see:

- flickering quotes,
- sudden gaps,
- spreads widening unexpectedly.

Objective 2: Increase the chance that others trade on stale information. If someone cannot update quickly, they may:

- hit a quote that no longer exists,
- place a limit order at a price that has already been overtaken,
- fail to cancel a vulnerable order in time.

This is closely related to the "pickoff" concept we will study later under latency arbitrage, but quote stuffing can intensify the conditions that make pickoffs easier.

Objective 3: Mask other manipulative actions. A noisy quote environment can hide a simpler deception (like spoofing or layering). When everything is flickering, it becomes harder to notice the one large order that is strategically appearing and disappearing.

What quote stuffing feels like to everyday traders

From the outside, quote stuffing often feels like the market "glitches," but the effects are real:

- **Your order doesn't behave as expected:** you submit a limit order and it sits unfilled even though the screen seemed to show your price was reachable.
- **Spreads suddenly widen:** liquidity providers protect themselves by stepping back when the environment becomes too noisy.
- **Fast whipsaws:** prices jump a few ticks and snap back, sometimes without obvious news.

Again, none of these symptoms alone prove quote stuffing; markets can become chaotic for many reasons. The practical lesson is defensive: **when the tape becomes noisy and the book flickers, your uncertainty increases and your execution quality often deteriorates.**

Layering vs. quote stuffing: same family, different tools

It helps to compare them directly.

	Layering	Quote Stuffing
Primary aim	Create a visible illusion of heavy supply/demand	Create noise and delay; degrade others' processing
What you see	A structured "wall" across price levels	Flickering quotes, rapid updates, sudden gaps
How it pressures you	You act early because you fear the wall	You act poorly because the environment is unstable
Taxonomy pillar	Deception (primarily)	Deception + Speed (often intertwined)

Why these tactics matter even if you never trade "fast"

A common misconception is that these issues only matter to day traders staring at Level II screens. In reality, the impact can reach ordinary investors because microstructure affects **execution quality**:

- If spreads widen or liquidity becomes unreliable, you may pay more when you buy and receive less when you sell.
- If the market is pushed temporarily, stop orders and conditional orders can trigger at worse moments (a bridge to the next section on stop hunting).
- If your broker routes orders to venues experiencing turbulence, your fills may deteriorate even if you are not watching the book.

Defensive thinking: practical ways to reduce exposure

You do not need to detect layering or quote stuffing perfectly. You need a playbook that reduces how often you are forced to react to them.

Defense 1: Avoid trading "in the noise." If you notice sudden, sustained quote flickering or spreads widening, consider:

- trading smaller,
- using limit orders with patience,
- waiting for conditions to normalize if the trade is not time-critical.

Defense 2: Be skeptical of walls that "walk away." If a large depth wall repeatedly stays just out of reach (moving as price moves), treat it as less informative. Real liquidity is often willing to be hit; phantom liquidity is designed to remain safely unexecuted.

Defense 3: Reduce the market impact of your own urgency. The more urgently you trade (especially with market orders), the more you pay in environments where the book is being manipulated or destabilized. A patient limit order is not a guarantee, but it is often a better default when the market is behaving erratically.

5.4 Momentum Ignition and Stop Hunting

The previous sections focused on **deception through the order book**: spoofing (a single fake order), layering (a structured wall), and quote stuffing (noise that makes the book harder to interpret). In all of those tactics, the "shark" tries to move other people by changing what they *see*.

This section moves from manipulating the *picture* to manipulating the *reaction*. Instead of merely suggesting that the market should go up or down, some predatory strategies try to **force** buying or selling by triggering a chain of automatic behavior. Two related ideas dominate this category:

- **Momentum ignition:** creating (or amplifying) a short, sharp move so that others pile in, extending the move.
- **Stop hunting:** driving price into areas where many stop-loss orders are likely to be clustered, triggering forced market orders that accelerate the move.

These tactics are easiest to understand if you keep one principle in mind:

Stops and other automatic orders turn intentions *into* forced trades. *Predators try to harvest those forced trades.*

A quick refresher: what a stop-loss really does

A stop-loss is often spoken about as if it is a protective floor: "If price hits $X, I'm out at $X." In most markets, that is *not* what happens.

- A **stop-market** order becomes a **market order** once the stop price is touched. You are guaranteed an exit, but *not* a specific price.
- A **stop-limit** order becomes a **limit order** once the stop price is touched. You control the worst acceptable price, but you are *not* guaranteed an exit.

From a predator's point of view, the most important feature of stop-market orders is that they represent **latent urgency**. They are dormant until triggered, and then they demand immediacy. That immediacy is costly in thin liquidity because urgent orders pay the spread and can suffer slippage.

Why stops cluster (and why clustering matters)

Stop hunting is not about targeting *your* stop personally. It is about targeting **where stops tend to concentrate**. Stops cluster for human reasons:

- **Round numbers:** $50.00, $100.00, etc.
- **Obvious chart points:** the last swing low/high, "support/resistance," yesterday's low, the day's low, etc.
- **Common rules of thumb:** "Put the stop just below the recent low," or "just under a moving average."

When many traders use similar logic, they create a **stop-loss zone**: a price region where a large number of stop orders are likely to trigger within a narrow band. The market does not display these stops publicly in a simple, labeled way, but their presence can be inferred from patterns in how prices behave near obvious levels.

The reason clustering matters is mechanical:

Stop triggers $\Rightarrow$ market orders $\Rightarrow$ liquidity gets consumed quickly $\Rightarrow$ price jumps further

That is the cascade predators try to initiate.

Stop hunting: the "spike and snap-back" pattern

Stop hunting: The basic idea

Stop hunting is a strategy where aggressive trading pushes the price into a stop-loss zone to trigger stops, creating forced selling (or forced buying) that briefly exaggerates the move. After the stops have been triggered and the forced orders are absorbed, the price often **snaps back** toward its previous level.

This snap-back is not magic. It is a consequence of supply and demand normalizing after a temporary wave of forced orders.

Stop hunting: The three-step logic

You can think of a classic stop hunt as another three-act sequence (different from spoofing, but similar in structure):

- **The push:** aggressive orders drive price toward a known or suspected stop-loss zone.
- **The cascade:** stops trigger and become market orders, accelerating the move and sweeping liquidity.
- **The absorption and rebound:** the predator (and other liquidity providers) buy from panic sellers (or sell to panic buyers), and price rebounds once the forced flow is exhausted.

Stop hunting: What it feels like to a casual trader

If you have ever said, "My stop got hit and then it immediately reversed," you have experienced the pattern that stop hunting tries to exploit. This does not prove manipulation—sometimes stops are triggered because genuine news or genuine selling pressure arrives. But the *shape* is memorable:

- a sudden, sharp spike into a level,
- a brief trade-through (worse fills than expected),
- and a quick return to the prior range.

The key lesson is that the worst moment to be a forced seller is often *the exact moment stops are triggering*, because that is when liquidity is being consumed fastest.

Momentum ignition: creating a self-fulfilling move

Stop hunting focuses on a specific target zone (where stops live). **Momentum ignition** is broader: it tries to create a burst of price movement that causes other traders and algorithms to *join* the move, turning a small push into a larger wave.

Why momentum can be "ignited"

Many participants are conditional:

- momentum strategies buy when price rises quickly and sell when it falls quickly,
- breakout traders buy when a level breaks,
- liquidity providers may pull back during sudden volatility, widening spreads and making it easier for price to jump.

If a predator can create a short burst that looks like a breakout or a new trend, they may cause:

- trend-following algorithms to chase,

- stops to trigger (if the burst crosses key levels),
- and human traders to react emotionally (fear of missing out or fear of loss).

In other words, **momentum ignition can recruit other traders as unwilling accomplices.**

The predatory profit concept (without technical details)

Predators who ignite momentum typically aim to:

- buy before the crowd buys and sell to the crowd once it is chasing, or
- sell before the crowd sells and buy from the crowd once it panics.

You do not need to know the exact micro-timing to understand the economic point: **the predator profits from the price impact created by others.**

Why thin liquidity makes both tactics easier

Both stop hunting and momentum ignition exploit a vulnerability that appears in many markets, especially during turbulent moments:

When liquidity is thin, it takes less force to move price, and forced orders do more damage.

Thin liquidity can occur:

- in less liquid stocks or contracts,
- during off-hours,
- around the open/close,
- during volatility bursts or news events,

- when market makers widen spreads and reduce displayed size for safety.

In thin conditions, a cascade is easier to start, and the snap-back can be sharper because the initial move was not supported by a lasting shift in fundamental valuation.

Stop hunting in one picture

The following chart illustrates the classic "hunt" shape: price trades in a stable range, plunges suddenly into a **Stop Loss Zone**, and then rebounds quickly after the forced selling is absorbed.

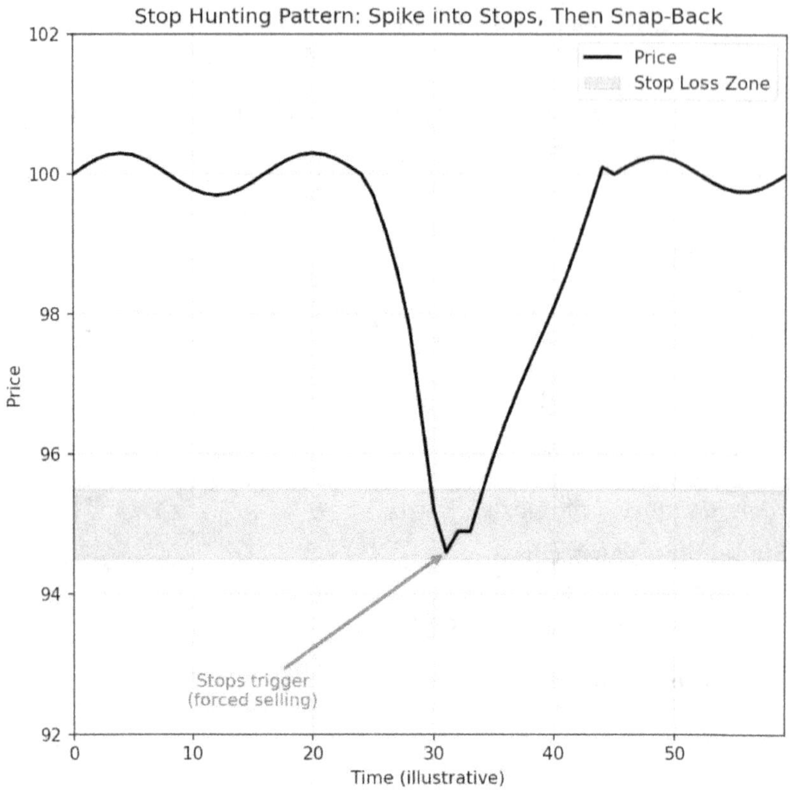

Defensive thinking: using stops without becoming predictable prey

Stops are not "bad." They are a risk-management tool. The vulnerability is not the existence of a stop; it is the combination of **clustering**, **urgency**, and **thin liquidity**. The aim of defense is to reduce those three factors where you reasonably can.

Defense 1: Understand the difference between stop-market and stop-limit.

A stop-market order prioritizes certainty of exit, but it can fill far worse than expected during a cascade. A stop-limit can control slippage, but it can fail to execute if the market gaps through your limit. There is no perfect choice; the point is to choose consciously rather than assuming a stop guarantees a specific price.

Defense 2: Avoid "obvious" stop placement when possible.

If you place stops exactly at the most visible chart point (round numbers, exact prior low), you are joining a crowd. Crowds create stop-loss zones. Slightly less obvious placement can reduce the chance of being swept out by a brief spike. (This is a principle, not a prescription; your risk tolerance and strategy come first.)

Defense 3: Be cautious with stops in very thin or very noisy moments.

The worst stop fills tend to occur during liquidity vacuums. If you must hold risk through such periods, consider whether your position size and stop logic match the reality that the market can trade *through* your level quickly.

Defense 4: Don't confuse a stop-trigger with new information.

A stop cascade can create a dramatic print that looks like "something happened." Sometimes something did. Other times, the move itself *was* the event. Training yourself to pause—even briefly—before reacting to a sudden spike can prevent you from turning a forced exit into a second, voluntary mistake (such as immediately re-entering out of anger or fear).

Transition: from forced reactions to speed-based pickoffs

Stop hunting and momentum ignition exploit predictability in human behavior and automatic order logic: they turn clusters of conditional orders into fuel for a short-lived move. In the next section, we shift to a different weapon: **speed**. We will examine latency arbitrage and cross-venue pickoffs, where the advantage is not triggering your stops directly, but seeing and acting on price changes milliseconds before slower participants can adjust.

5.5 Latency Arbitrage and Cross-Venue Pickoffs

The prior sections focused on tactics that **push** the market by manipulating perception (spoofing, layering, quote stuffing) or by triggering forced reactions (momentum ignition and stop cascades). This section shifts to a different pillar in our taxonomy: **speed advantages**.

Here, the "shark" does not need to fake orders or manufacture panic. Instead, it profits from a simpler edge:

> If you can see a price change *first* and act on it *first*, you can trade against people who are still living in the market's recent past.

Two closely related ideas dominate this part of modern market structure:

- **Latency arbitrage:** earning small, repeated profits by exploiting tiny time delays (latency) in how prices update across venues or across participants.
- **Cross-venue pickoffs:** trading against quotes on one venue that have become *stale* because another venue moved first.

The core concept: "stale quotes" exist because time exists

It is tempting to think of markets as a single, unified place. In reality, modern trading is fragmented:

- the same stock (or related products) may trade on multiple exchanges and alternative venues,
- each venue has its own order book,
- information travels between venues at finite speed,
- and each participant processes that information at finite speed.

A **quote** (a displayed bid or ask) is "stale" when it does not yet reflect the new reality that has already become true elsewhere.

A plain-language example

Suppose you are watching a stock quoted at:

Bid \$99.99 Ask \$100.01

Now imagine that on Exchange A, new buying pressure arrives and the best ask becomes \$100.05. That change may not be reflected instantly on Exchange B. For a brief instant, Exchange B may still show an ask of \$100.01—a price that is now "too cheap" relative to the updated market.

A very fast trader can exploit that window by buying at \$100.01 on Exchange B *before* the quote updates, then either:

- immediately selling at the higher price on Exchange A, or
- selling moments later once the rest of the market reprices.

Latency arbitrage: the market's "micro-time" toll-booth

What latency arbitrage is

Latency arbitrage is the practice of profiting from short-lived price discrepancies caused by delays in information and order processing. The profits per trade can be tiny, but the strategy can be repeated many times.

The important point for a casual reader is not the technology details; it is the economic pattern:

> The latency-arbitrageur is not predicting the future of the company; they are predicting the next few milliseconds of the *market's updating process*.

Where the "arbitrage" comes from

The word *arbitrage* suggests riskless profit. In practice, nothing is perfectly riskless. But the edge comes from being able to do the following sequence more reliably than others:

1. detect a price change first (or detect it on a venue that updates first),
2. route orders fast enough to trade on a venue that is still stale,
3. exit quickly once the market catches up.

Even though the window is small, the logic is durable: **if the market is updating unevenly, speed creates a temporary informational monopoly.**

Why this matters to everyday traders

Retail traders rarely compete directly in microseconds, but latency arbitrage can still affect them through execution quality:

- displayed quotes can be less reliable (they "disappear" when you try to trade),
- spreads can widen in fast conditions because liquidity providers fear being picked off,
- market orders can experience extra slippage because the best quotes are quickly consumed by faster traders.

You may experience this as: "The price was there, but I couldn't get it." The market was not necessarily lying; it was simply moving faster than your path to the exchange.

Cross-venue pickoffs: catching the slowest book

Cross-venue pickoffs are a practical expression of latency arbitrage. The idea is straightforward:

> When one venue moves first, the fastest traders race to trade against any other venue that has not updated yet.

How pickoffs happen (step-by-step)

A typical pickoff episode looks like this:

1. **Trigger:** a price-relevant event occurs (news, a large market order, a correlated asset move).
2. **First mover venue:** one exchange's best bid/ask updates quickly.
3. **Stale venue:** another exchange still shows old quotes for a brief moment.
4. **Pickoff:** a fast trader hits those stale quotes (buying too cheap or selling too expensive).
5. **Aftermath:** the stale venue updates; slower traders see the new price only after the opportunity is gone.

This is not a moral story; it is a structural story. Fragmentation plus finite communication speed creates the opportunity.

Why "being picked off" changes everyone's behavior

If you are a market maker posting bids and asks, being picked off is costly. It means you sold too cheaply or bought too expensively relative to the new information.

So liquidity providers respond defensively:

- they may **widen** spreads (charging more for immediacy),
- they may **reduce** displayed size (show less to avoid being targeted),
- they may **cancel** faster when volatility rises.

This links back to earlier sections: what looks like deception or vanishing liquidity is sometimes simply risk management in a market where pickoffs are a constant threat.

Speed as "traveling into the future" (a mental model)

Because the time differences are tiny, it can be hard to take them seriously. But the market's micro-time is like traffic: if you are even a little late, the best route is gone.

A helpful mental model is to imagine two participants receiving the same signal at different times. The faster trader is not smarter about value; they are simply *earlier*.

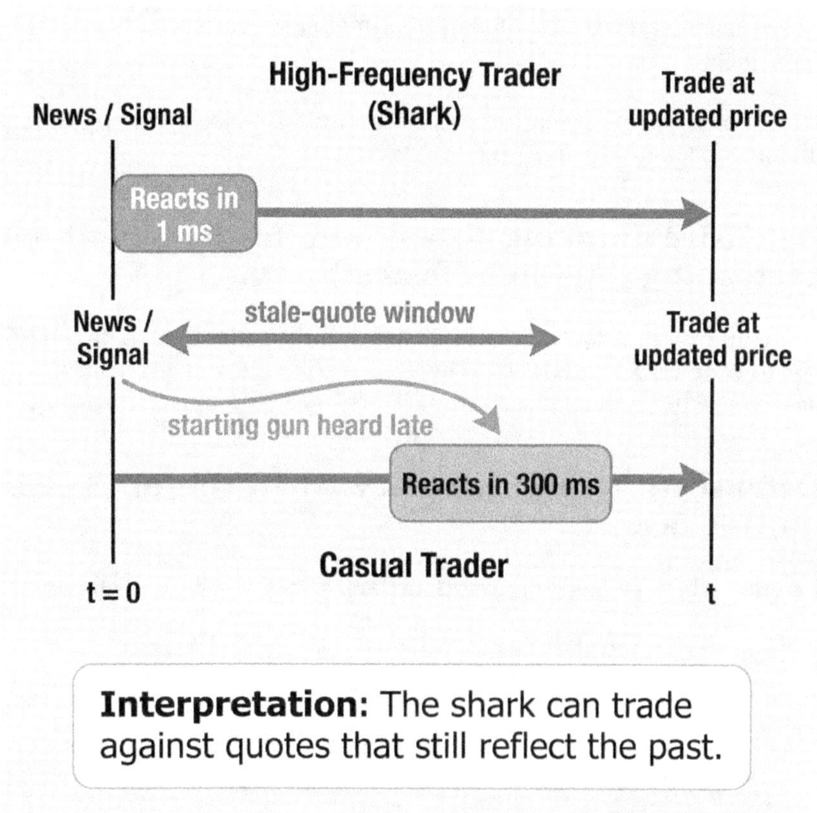

How speed edges translate into your real-world costs

Even if you never look at an order book, speed-based predation can influence the price you receive. The mechanism is indirect but powerful:

1. Fast traders pick off stale quotes.
2. Liquidity providers protect themselves by widening spreads and canceling faster.
3. The market becomes more fragile during bursts of volatility.

4. Casual traders pay more for immediacy (via spreads and slippage).

This is one reason execution can deteriorate precisely when you feel the most pressure to act.

Defensive thinking for slower traders (without pretending you can be fastest)

You cannot win a footrace against firms built to be fast. The goal is not to "out-HFT the HFTs." The goal is to avoid putting yourself in positions where speed disadvantages are most expensive.

Defense 1: Reduce urgency when the market is moving fast

Latency arbitrage feeds on urgent orders. When conditions allow:

- prefer limit orders (with patience) over market orders,
- consider scaling into positions rather than entering all at once,
- avoid chasing quotes during sudden bursts.

Defense 2: Be careful with trades around known volatility events

Around scheduled announcements or major openings/closings, the market's updating process becomes more uneven. This is when stale quotes and pickoffs are more likely, and when spreads can widen sharply.

Defense 3: Watch for "false liquidity" symptoms even when nobody is spoofing

Vanishing quotes are not always deception; they are often self-protection by liquidity providers who fear being picked off. Either way, the practical response is similar: trade smaller, use limits, and accept that displayed liquidity may be fleeting.

Transition: from speed to information leakage

Latency arbitrage and cross-venue pickoffs show how speed turns time into money. In the next section, we move to the third pillar: **information leakage**. Instead of exploiting stale quotes, predators try to detect the footprints of large or predictable orders (often institutional) and trade ahead of them—not because they are faster at receiving news, but because they are better at reading the market's behavioral signals.

5.6 Order Anticipation and Signaling

The previous section showed how speed advantages can feel like "time travel": a fast trader reacts to a price change before slower traders even see it, and profits from stale quotes. In this final section of the chapter, we move to the third pillar of our taxonomy: **information leakage**.

Information leakage is not about reading secret news. It is about reading *footprints*. The market is a stream of messages, and repeated behavior leaves patterns. Predatory algorithms specialize in detecting those patterns and turning them into a trading edge.

Plain-language definition: what is order anticipation?

Order anticipation is a strategy that attempts to infer the presence of a large buyer or seller—often an institution executing a big order in pieces—and then trade in a way that forces that large trader to pay worse prices.

The key idea is deceptively simple:

> If someone *must* keep buying (or selling), their future behavior is predictable. Predictability can be monetized.

In market conversation, you may hear this described loosely as "front-running." In a strict legal sense, front-running often implies misuse of confidential client order information. Here we focus on the broader, market-structure concept: **anticipating** large order flow from publicly observable patterns and then trading ahead of it.

Why large investors leave footprints

Most large investors (mutual funds, pension funds, insurance companies, ETFs, and other institutions) cannot simply place one enormous market order without paying a heavy cost. A giant, urgent order tends to:

- move the price against itself,
- advertise its presence to other market participants,
- and create a worse average execution.

So institutions typically break large orders into smaller **child orders** and execute them over time. This is often done through execution algorithms (sometimes called "algos"), such as time-weighted or volume-weighted approaches, or other schedule-based and liquidity-seeking methods.

This is rational behavior. But it has a side effect:

> Slicing an order reduces immediate impact, but increases *pattern visibility*.

Patterns are the footprints predators hunt.

The footprints: what algorithms can detect (without mind-reading)

Predatory models do not need your identity. They do not need insider information. They look for **statistical regularities** that suggest a persistent buyer or seller. Common footprints include:

Footprint 1: repeated small trades with similar size

If a market sees a sequence like:

$$\underbrace{200,\ 200,\ 200,\ 200,\ 200}_{shares}$$

every few seconds/minutes, it may suggest algorithmic slicing rather than independent, random retail activity.

Footprint 2: one-sided persistence

A genuine, balanced market has two-sided activity. A persistent pattern of aggressive buying (repeatedly lifting the ask) can indicate a buyer who is not price-sensitive in the short run.

Footprint 3: predictable timing

Some execution styles trade on a clock (e.g., "do a little each minute"). If trading intensity appears at regular intervals, it can be a clue that a schedule-based execution algorithm is active.

Footprint 4: venue and routing behavior

Large traders may route orders in a consistent way: same venues, same order types, same interaction patterns with liquidity. Consistency makes behavior easier to classify.

Footprint 5: response to micro price changes

Some execution algorithms become more aggressive when price dips slightly ("buy the dip" mechanically) or pause when price rises quickly. That conditional behavior can be learned by an observer.

None of these footprints are proof of an institution. But combined, they can raise the probability that a large, predictable order is in progress.

How order anticipation makes money: the "forced buyer" problem

Once a predator believes a large buyer is active, the predator's goal is to position so that the buyer's continued demand pushes price in a favorable direction for the predator.

A simple version of the logic looks like this:

- 1. A large buyer is identified (or hypothesized).
- 2. The predator buys first, before the buyer completes the order.
- 3. The large buyer keeps buying, nudging price upward.
- 4. The predator sells back at a slightly higher price.

This is sometimes described informally as "getting in the way" of the institution. The institution is not necessarily doing anything wrong; it is simply large enough that its needed activity becomes a source of predictability.

Why this harms the institution (and can spill over to you)

Order anticipation is costly because it transfers value from the large order to faster or more opportunistic traders:

- the institution pays a higher average price when buying (or receives a lower average price when selling),
- liquidity becomes thinner as others step in front of the flow,
- and the market may move more than it would have otherwise, creating additional volatility.

Retail traders can be affected in two ways:

- **Indirectly:** wider spreads and noisier price action when large flows are being "worked" and contested.
- **Directly:** if you happen to trade in the same name at the same time, your execution price can be worsened by the tug-of-war.

Signaling: when the market accidentally broadcasts your intent

Signaling refers to the unintentional information you reveal through your order placement and execution behavior. In everyday life, signaling is like leaving a trail: not because you want to be followed, but because your behavior is consistent and therefore informative.

There are two main channels of signaling in trading:

Channel 1: price-impact signaling

If your activity repeatedly moves the market (even by a little), others can infer that you are a price-insensitive participant. For example:

- repeatedly buying at the ask can signal urgency,
- repeatedly selling at the bid can signal urgency,
- repeatedly trading through thin liquidity can signal that size remains to be done.

Channel 2: pattern signaling

Even if each individual trade is small, the *pattern* can reveal intent:

- consistent order sizes,
- consistent timing,
- consistent reaction to price changes,
- consistent placement relative to the spread.

From the predator's viewpoint, the best targets are not necessarily the biggest orders. The best targets are the **most predictable** ones.

How this relates to earlier predatory tactics

Information leakage is the bridge that connects all the earlier topics:

- **Deception (spoofing/layering):** can be aimed at places where a large buyer is likely to be vulnerable–for example, creating fake selling pressure to slow the buyer down, then buying ahead of them.
- **Forced reactions (stop cascades):** can be triggered near zones where a predictable participant is likely to have risk controls or conditional orders.
- **Speed (latency arbitrage):** helps execute the anticipation quickly and avoid being caught when the market updates.

A useful synthesis is:

> Deception shapes what people see, speed shapes who moves first, and information leakage shapes where the predator aims.

A practical example: the "walking price" problem

Consider a stock that seems to drift upward all afternoon in small steps. A casual trader might think, "Someone must be buying." That intuition is often correct in a broad sense: persistent one-sided flow can create a slow trend.

Now imagine an institutional buyer executing a large order over several hours. Predatory traders detect the persistence and begin to:

- buy slightly ahead of the buyer,
- offer the buyer liquidity at incrementally higher prices,
- repeat this cycle many times.

The institution's execution becomes more expensive. To an outside observer, the price looks like it is "walking away" from anyone trying to buy. This is a hallmark experience of trading in the presence of predictable flow: the market seems to anticipate you, not because it knows you personally, but because predictable demand is visible in aggregate.

Defensive thinking: what casual traders can do

Retail traders are usually not the primary prey of order anticipation; institutions are. Still, the same defensive mindset helps everyone: **reduce predictability and reduce urgency**. The following are practical, non-technical habits.

Defense 1: avoid broadcasting urgency with market orders in thin conditions

Market orders are sometimes appropriate, but they are the clearest form of urgency. When liquidity is thin or the tape is jumpy, consider using limit orders and accepting that not every trade must happen immediately.

Defense 2: vary behavior when you are trading multiple pieces

If you are scaling in or out over time, repeating the same size at the same interval can make your behavior more legible than you intend. Small variations (timing and size) can reduce the clarity of your footprint. The goal is not to be clever; it is to avoid being mechanically predictable.

Defense 3: be careful with obvious conditional orders

Just as stops cluster at obvious chart points, many conditional behaviors cluster around obvious times and levels. If you rely heavily on automation, remember that automation is predictable by design.

Defense 4: accept that some "bad fills" are structural

Sometimes you will feel as if the market is stepping ahead of you. That can be a sign of information leakage around larger flows. The defensive response is often not to fight harder, but to trade smaller, trade more patiently, and avoid turning execution friction into emotional decision-making.

Closing the chapter: the three pillars as a survival toolkit

This chapter's goal was to replace a confusing list of tactics with a coherent map.

- **Deception** (spoofing, layering, quote stuffing) manipulates what you think the market is.
- **Speed advantages** (latency arbitrage, cross-venue pickoffs) exploit the fact that markets update unevenly in time.
- **Information leakage** (order anticipation and signaling) exploits the footprints you and large institutions leave behind.

In the next chapter, we will turn this map into a more explicit defensive playbook: what everyday traders can notice, what they should stop doing, and which simple habits can reduce the "toll" paid to faster and more predatory participants.

Chapter 6

Spotting the Fin: Detection and Red Flags

You don't need a PhD in marine biology to know that a shark fin slicing through the water signals danger. Similarly, you don't need a supercomputer to spot when the market is behaving like a predator. This chapter moves beyond theory to practice, teaching you to tune your senses to the subtle ripples-vanishing orders, inexplicable bursts of speed, and prices that run away from you-that indicate you are swimming in infested waters. We will build a 'mental dashboard' of red flags that help you decide when to step back before the bite happens.

6.1 Developing Market Awareness

If you have ever watched a price chart and felt like the market was "moving differently today," you were already doing the first step of detection: sensing the *environment*, not just the last traded price.

This book has emphasized a central reality of modern markets: you cannot out-react professional, automated traders on speed. High-frequency systems can observe and respond to order flow in microseconds. Retail and casual participants live on a very different time scale - seconds and minutes - where *the edge is not speed*, but *awareness*. The goal of this section is to re-train your attention away from passive price-watching (staring at candles) and toward **active environment scanning**: noticing the market's "texture"—how it *behaves* while moving.

That may sound abstract, so we will make it concrete. Think of a chart as the *scoreboard*. Market awareness is watching the *game*.

From "Where Is Price?" to "What Kind of Place Is This Market Right Now?"

Most beginners ask one question repeatedly: "Is price going up or down?" That question is not wrong, but it is incomplete. A more useful question—especially in markets influenced by fast, aggressive strategies—is: "Is this a market where my orders are likely to be treated fairly and predictably, or a market where liquidity and behavior change the moment I interact?"

In other words, you are not only trading a symbol. You are trading an **environment**.

In calm conditions, many markets behave like a well-lit grocery store: the aisles are clear, prices are posted, and you can take your time. In stressed or predatory-feeling conditions, the same market can feel like a crowded street market: prices jump, the crowd surges, and the best deals vanish as soon as you reach for them. The product is the same, but the *experience of transacting* changes.

Your job is not to accuse the market of wrongdoing. Your job is to notice when the environment has changed enough that your usual assumptions about execution quality no longer hold.

The Core Idea: Build a Baseline, Then Notice Deviations

Detection is not a single "spoofing alarm." It is a practical habit:

1. Learn what "normal" looks and feels like *for the product you*

trade.

2. Notice departures from that normal.
3. Treat departures as *risk signals*—even if you cannot prove manipulation.

The emphasis on *baseline* is critical. The same behavior can be normal in one product and suspicious in another. A thinly traded small-cap stock and a mega-cap index ETF will have different "natural" textures. Even the same symbol can change texture across:

- time of day (open, lunch, close),
- scheduled events (economic releases, earnings),
- volatility regimes (quiet weeks vs. panic days),
- venue conditions (halts, auctions, rebalances).

So rather than memorizing one universal pattern, you will learn to ask: *Is what I am seeing typical for this instrument at this time, or is it abnormal?*

Market "Texture": The Four Things You Can Observe at Human Speed

You do not need co-located servers to build useful market awareness. You need a short checklist you can apply in real time. The simplest version is four categories of observation:

1. **Ease of movement:** Does price move smoothly, or does it jump in gaps?
2. **Thickness:** Does the market feel "deep" (able to absorb trades) or "thin" (easily pushed)?
3. **Responsiveness:** Does the market respond to trades in a stable way, or does it overreact and snap back?

4. **Stability of displayed liquidity:** Do visible bids/offers seem to persist, or do they "flicker" and vanish when approached?

None of these require you to identify a specific algorithm. They are about *conditions*. Conditions determine whether common retail behaviors—market orders, chasing, tight stops, impatient cancels—become expensive.

1) Ease of Movement (Smooth vs. "Jumping")

A chart can rise in a straight line for two very different reasons:

- Natural buying pressure steadily lifts offers.
- Liquidity repeatedly disappears, so price must jump to find the next available seller.

At a human scale, both can look like "uptrend." But the second case is a more fragile environment. If price is moving by *gaps* (skipping levels), it is telling you: "there isn't much standing in the way." That can be great if you are already in the right direction—but it is dangerous if you are trying to enter calmly or exit precisely.

Practical signs of "jumping" you can notice without advanced tools:

- candles with long bodies and relatively little overlap,
- frequent single-print moves (price appears at a new level without much trading in between),
- sudden, brief spikes that immediately retrace (a sign that price is searching for liquidity).

2) Thickness (Deep vs. Thin)

Thickness is the market's ability to absorb orders without moving much. A thick market is like a deep pool: you can throw in a bucket of water and the level barely changes. A thin market is like a shallow tray: the same bucket sloshes water everywhere.

Thickness is not just volume. You can see high volume on the day and still experience thin *moment-to-moment* liquidity—especially around news, at the open, or when market makers pull back.

A useful mental model: **Thickness is what you feel when you try to trade.** Volume is what you read later.

Even before you open a Level II screen, you can infer thickness from behavior:

- In thick conditions, price tends to "lean" on levels (it tests them repeatedly).
- In thin conditions, price tends to "teleport" between levels (it does not spend time negotiating).

3) Responsiveness (Stable vs. Overreact-and-Snap)

A healthy market can respond to buying with an upward drift, and to selling with a downward drift. But in more toxic conditions, you often see a pattern that feels like: "Every time something trades, the quotes flinch."

This is a key intuition to develop: **quotes are not the same as trades**. Quotes can change because someone updates a model, hedges elsewhere, or removes exposure. Trades are the only thing that proves someone actually exchanged risk.

When responsiveness becomes unstable, you may see:

- price moves quickly on small prints (suggesting fragility),
- price fails to move despite heavy prints (suggesting absorption or hidden liquidity),
- spread widens unexpectedly during otherwise quiet moments (suggesting liquidity providers are backing away).

You do not need to label the cause. You only need to register that your execution assumptions should change.

Natural-feeling conditions (steady flow)	Predatory-feeling conditions (gaps and erratic jumps)
Price moves in overlapping steps; levels get tested repeatedly.	Price leaps between levels; frequent spikes and fast retraces.
Displayed liquidity tends to persist long enough to interact.	Visible size appears and disappears as price approaches ("flicker").
Spreads behave predictably for time of day and volatility.	Spreads widen suddenly or oscillate; fills feel inconsistent.
Small orders typically fill as expected near displayed prices.	Small orders get partial fills, worse prices, or repeated "misses."
Market feels "negotiated" (back-and-forth).	Market feels "slippery" (quotes move away from contact).

4) Stability of Displayed Liquidity (Persistent vs. Flickering)

Displayed liquidity is what you *see* available to trade (bids and offers). In a "natural-feeling" market, displayed liquidity tends to stay in place long enough that you can interact with it. In a predatory-feeling market, displayed liquidity can appear generous—until price approaches, and it evaporates.

This is one reason retail traders feel "tricked" by the screen: "There was size there a second ago—why did it disappear right when I tried to hit it?"

Treat flickering liquidity as an environmental warning sign: it indicates that at least some participants are not posting quotes primarily to trade with you, but to *probe* or *influence* behavior, or to provide liquidity only when it is safe for them.

A Simple Two-Column Lens: Natural Market vs. Predatory-Feeling Market

The point is not that one column is "good" and the other is "illegal." The point is that the second column increases the probability that casual execution will be worse than expected.

This lens is intentionally behavioral. You are training yourself to notice *how the market transacts*, not just where the last candle closed.

Operational Habit: The 10-Second "Scan" Before You Trade

Market awareness is most valuable *before* you click. A good routine is a brief scan that forces you to look at context.

Here is a simple, practical pre-trade scan you can do in about 10 seconds:

1. **Regime check:** Is this a known "fast" moment (open, close, news window)?
2. **Spread check:** Is the spread normal for this symbol right now?
3. **Motion check:** Are recent moves smooth or gappy?
4. **Patience check:** If I place a limit order, does it have a reasonable chance to sit and get filled, or will I likely have to chase?

If the scan says "gappy, flickery, widening spreads," the defensive conclusion is not necessarily "don't trade." The conclusion is: **trade like the environment is hostile**. That usually means reducing urgency and reducing size, and preferring controlled entry (limits) over blind entry (markets). Later in this chapter, we will connect those choices directly to the red flags you can observe in the order book and the tape.

Why This Works Even Against Fast Traders

It is reasonable to ask: *If the other side is automated and fast, why does my awareness matter at all?*

Because many predatory effects are not subtle at human time scales. They leave **footprints**:

- Price jumping because liquidity is thin or being pulled,
- spreads widening because market makers fear "toxic" flow,
- visible size flashing and vanishing because quotes are being updated aggressively,

- repeated "almost fills" because displayed liquidity is not meant to be interacted with.

You cannot win the speed race, but you can refuse to play the game the way the environment wants you to play it—impatient, urgent, and predictable.

Putting It Together: Awareness as a Defensive Skill

Developing market awareness is not about becoming cynical. It is about upgrading your mental model from: "If the chart looks good, my trade will work." to: "If the environment supports fair execution, then a chart-based idea has a chance to express itself."

In the next section, we will move from this broad environmental scan to specific, visual red flags in Level II / depth-of-market data—where the market's "texture" becomes easier to see in real time.

6.2 Red Flags in the Order Book

In the previous section, you learned to scan for *market texture*: whether price moves smoothly or in jumps, whether conditions feel thick or thin, and whether displayed liquidity appears stable or "flickery." Now we zoom in on the most direct window into that texture: the **order book**.

Most retail platforms present the order book through **Level II** quotes or a **DOM** (Depth of Market) ladder. Regardless of layout, you are looking at the same basic idea: *who is advertising willingness to buy or sell, at what prices, and in what displayed size.*

A grounding reminder: Level II shows *advertised* intent, not guaranteed liquidity

Before we hunt for red flags, you need one protective mental model:

Level II is a list of invitations, not promises.

Quotes can be posted, changed, and canceled rapidly. Some quotes are sincere attempts to trade. Others are part of inventory management, hedging, or risk controls. And some quotes are posted in ways that *influence* other traders' behavior without intending to trade at that displayed size.

This section is not a legal guide. We are not trying to "prove spoofing" in the courtroom sense. We are trying to build a **visual checklist** for when the order book is behaving in ways that historically correlate with:

- unstable liquidity,
- predatory reactions to retail urgency,
- worse-than-expected execution.

How to look at a ladder without getting hypnotized

A common beginner mistake is to treat the ladder like an oracle: "The bid is big, so price must go up." That is not how it works. The ladder is a *living surface* that can be re-shaped instantly.

A better approach is to ask three simple questions as you watch:

- **Persistence:** Does size *stay* long enough to be interacted with?
- **Reaction:** When price approaches, does the displayed size *hold*, *fill*, or *vanish*?
- **Consistency:** Is the behavior consistent across a few seconds, or does it change depending on what traders do?

If you train your eye on these three questions, most of the meaningful red flags become easier to spot.

Red Flag Checklist (with plain-language interpretations)

The following list is written for the way retail traders actually encounter the book: visually, in real time, while trying to place or manage an order. You do not need to see every red flag for the environment to be problematic. One or two, repeated consistently, is often enough to justify defensive behavior.

Red Flag 1: Large size that appears and cancels quickly ("flicker size")

What it looks like:

- A very large bid (or offer) suddenly appears close to the current price.
- Other traders react; price begins to move toward that side.
- The large order disappears before it trades in any meaningful amount.

Why it matters: This is a classic pattern associated with *spoof-like* behavior as a *visual phenomenon*: displayed size is used to create the *impression* of strong support or resistance, encouraging others to step in. When the crowd responds and price moves, the displayed size is withdrawn.

Retail impact: You can be lured into entering on the assumption that liquidity will "catch" the price—only to discover the safety net was removed. Even if no laws are broken, the functional result for you is the same: *you traded on information that was not stable.*

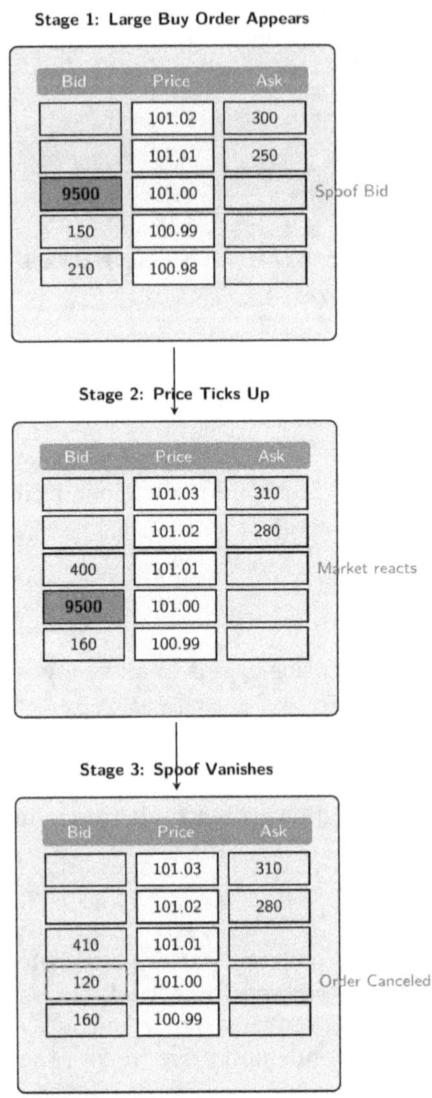
Stage 1: Large Buy Order Appears
Bid
Price
Ask
101.02
300
101.01
250
9500
101.00
Spoof Bid
150
100.99
210
100.98
Stage 2: Price Ticks Up
Bid
Price
Ask
101.03
310
101.02
280
400
101.01
Market reacts
9500
101.00
160
100.99
Stage 3: Spoof Vanishes
Bid
Price
Ask
101.03
310
101.02
280
410
101.01
120
101.00
Order Canceled
160
100.99

Red Flag 2: "Cliff" liquidity at a round number that evaporates on contact

What it looks like:

- A huge wall of size sits at a psychologically important price (e.g., \$50.00, \$100.00, \$4,000.00).
- As price approaches, the wall repeatedly refreshes or shifts.
- The moment price touches the level (or gets within a tick), the wall disappears and price slips through.

Why it matters: Round numbers attract attention, stops, and naive limit orders. That makes them ideal "theaters" for deceptive liquidity. The book can appear thick right where traders feel safest.

Retail impact: You place a stop just beyond the level or you buy because "support is massive," only to experience a quick flush. Whether the cause is predatory signaling, legitimate re-quoting, or risk limits, the conclusion is the same: **do not outsource your risk control to a wall you have not seen actually trade.**

Red Flag 3: The book "runs away" from your limit order (price improvement that never arrives)

What it looks like:

- You place a buy limit at (or near) the bid expecting a fill.
- The inside market shifts away—often by a tick—so you remain unfilled.
- When you cancel and move your order up, the market shifts again.

Why it matters: In a fast market, your order can become a *signal.* Some algorithms attempt to infer whether incoming interest is informed or urgent. When liquidity providers detect risk, they may step back, effectively forcing you to "pay up" if you insist on immediate entry.

Retail impact: This is where traders start chasing. Chasing converts a controlled plan (a limit) into an uncontrolled one (a series of concessions). If you notice this pattern repeatedly, treat it as a message: *your urgency is being priced.*

Red Flag 4: Best bid/offer size looks large, but prints don't match (phantom liquidity)

What it looks like:

- Level II shows meaningful size at the inside price.
- Time-and-sales prints go by, but the displayed size does not decrease in a believable way (or refreshes instantly).
- The market is "busy," yet the queue never seems to get smaller.

Why it matters: Sometimes this is benign (multiple venues, refresh, hidden orders, aggregated feeds). But from a practical standpoint, it warns you that **the displayed queue is not a reliable map of what must trade before you get filled.**

Retail impact: You may think, "I'm next in line," when in reality you are far back—or the line is not even the line you think it is.

Red Flag 5: Spread widens and the book thins *exactly* when activity increases

What it looks like:

- As volatility picks up, the inside spread suddenly widens.
- Depth near the inside price is pulled, leaving a hollow book.
- Price begins to jump between levels.

Why it matters: Liquidity providers widen spreads and reduce size when they perceive adverse selection risk (trading against someone informed). This is not automatically manipulative; it is often rational self-protection. But it is a critical signal for you: **the cost of immediacy just increased.**

Retail impact: Market orders become expensive. Stops become more likely to slip. Entries that worked fine in calm conditions begin to produce surprise fills.

Red Flag 6: One side repeatedly "stacks" in perfect increments (mechanical layering)

What it looks like:

- Multiple price levels on one side populate at once (e.g., five levels of offers appear simultaneously).
- Sizes are oddly uniform or follow a suspiciously neat pattern (e.g., 500, 500, 500, 500).
- The stack shifts together as price moves, like a sliding wall.

Why it matters: Humans do not usually place five perfectly patterned orders at multiple ticks with identical timing. A layered look suggests a mechanical strategy—sometimes genuine liquidity provisioning, sometimes a signaling tactic.

Retail impact: The stack can create the *feeling* of inevitability ("no way it gets through that") or panic ("it's over, huge sell pressure"). Either way, it pushes you toward emotional, urgent orders—the exact behavior that tends to be punished in hostile microstructure.

Red Flag 7: Sudden size appears behind price, not at price ("crowd herding")

What it looks like:

- Price starts to move up, and then large bid size appears *below* the market (not at the inside bid).

- Or price starts to move down, and large offer size appears *above* the market.

Why it matters: Size placed *behind* price can provide psychological comfort without taking immediate trading risk. It can encourage late entrants to chase, while the large displayed orders remain safely out of reach.

Retail impact: You feel supported (or capped), but the support/resistance is not actually being tested. Your decision becomes anchored to a picture rather than to executed trades.

What to do when you see red flags (the defensive interpretation)

This chapter focuses on detection rather than tactics, but detection without a practical takeaway is just anxiety. The simplest defensive interpretation is:

The more the book behaves like a mirage, the more you should reduce urgency.

In concrete terms, red flags in the order book generally argue for:

- **Patience over immediacy:** avoid reflexive market orders in flickery conditions.
- **Smaller sizing:** if liquidity is unstable, your effective slippage risk per share/contract rises.
- **Less reliance on single snapshots:** one frame of Level II can mislead; watch behavior over several seconds.

A final reality check before we move on

Not every cancellation is manipulation. Not every wall is fake. Market makers and liquidity providers *must* update quotes quickly to manage risk—especially when correlated markets move or when volatility rises. Data feeds are also imperfect: what you see may be aggregated, delayed, or missing hidden liquidity.

So the goal is not to point a finger at every fast-moving quote. The goal is to recognize a specific, repeatable feeling:

"The book looks thick until I try to trade, and then it behaves differently."

That feeling—when it occurs consistently—is a meaningful detection signal.

6.3 Reading the Tape for Clues

In the previous section, we treated the order book (Level II / DOM) as the market's *advertised intent*. You learned to look for red flags like flickering size, vanishing walls, and depth that seems to "run away" from your order.

Now we add the second half of the picture: the **tape**, usually shown as **Time and Sales**. If Level II is what traders *say* they are willing to do, the tape is what they *actually did*.

This section teaches you a simple but powerful habit:

> **Watch the disagreement between quotes and prints.**

When markets are calm, the book and the tape generally make intuitive sense together. When fast, aggressive strategies dominate the interaction, they often leave a recognizable mismatch: lots of quote activity with little real trading, bursts of prints that do not move price, or spreads that widen in ways that feel disconnected from the chart.

Tape basics: three columns that matter more than you think

Most Time and Sales windows show some version of:

- **Time** (sometimes down to milliseconds),
- **Price** (the executed trade price),

- **Size** (shares/contracts traded),
- sometimes a **side indicator** (at bid/at ask/within spread) and the **venue**.

For retail detection, you do not need to decode every symbol. You need to internalize one foundational distinction:

> **Quotes are potential. Prints are proof.**

A quote can be posted and canceled without risk changing hands. A print means someone bought and someone sold, and both sides accepted the price. That makes the tape a reality check.

The "Two-Lens" method: link book behavior to tape behavior

Here is the practical workflow that keeps tape-reading from becoming random screen-staring:

1. **First lens (book):** Identify what the book is *claiming* (thick bid, heavy offer, stable inside market, etc.).
2. **Second lens (tape):** Verify whether trades are *confirming* that claim (fills that reduce size, price progress that matches aggression, etc.).
3. **Decision:** If the book's claim is not confirmed by prints, assume the displayed liquidity is less trustworthy and treat execution as higher risk.

A simple example: if you see a "huge bid" on Level II (claimed support), you should expect one of two honest outcomes:

- sellers hit into it and you see prints at/near that price while the bid size decreases (support is real), or
- price cannot trade down to it because buyers are lifting offers and price rises away (support is not even needed).

A suspicious-feeling outcome is different: price drifts up *because the bid intimidated sellers*, but when selling finally appears, the bid evaporates and there is no meaningful printing into it. The book "talked" loudly; the tape stayed quiet.

Red flags on the tape: what algorithmic aggression looks like at human speed

Tape reading is not about recognizing a specific firm. It is about recognizing **signature behaviors** that are difficult for human discretionary traders to produce consistently.

Red Flag 1: "Machine-gun" bursts of tiny prints

What it looks like:

- Many trades in the same second (or within a few milliseconds),
- sizes are unusually small and repetitive (e.g., 1, 5, 10, 20 shares; or 1-lot futures),
- the price often barely moves while the prints accumulate.

How to interpret it: Bursts of tiny prints can be a sign of very short-horizon strategies competing for queue position, slicing orders, or rapidly interacting with liquidity across venues. In some contexts, it can also indicate *sniffing*: sending small trades to test whether hidden liquidity exists or whether someone large is passively absorbing.

Retail impact: This is a warning that the market is being "worked" at a time scale below human reaction. Your order is more likely to be detected as slow-moving interest, and the displayed book may change faster than your platform updates.

Red Flag 2: Heavy volume that fails to move price (absorption / iceberg risk)

What it looks like:

- The tape shows many prints (sometimes large total volume) at roughly the same price,
- the price level does not break despite repeated attempts,
- Level II may not show enough size to explain the amount of trading.

How to interpret it: When a large amount of volume trades without moving price, two broad explanations are common:

1. **Absorption:** a participant is willing to take the other side repeatedly (e.g., a large seller hitting bids is being absorbed by a strong buyer).
2. **Hidden/iceberg liquidity:** more size exists than is displayed; the tape reveals it because trades keep occurring without visible depletion.

Retail impact: This can be a trap for simplistic logic like "big volume means breakout." Heavy volume can also mean *a fight* is happening and one side is quietly holding the line. In those conditions, stops clustered just beyond the level can be vulnerable, and quick breakouts can turn into sharp reversals once the absorbing side finishes.

A practical tape-reading rule:

> **Volume is not directional by itself. Direction comes from what price does *after* the volume prints.**

Red Flag 3: Price moves on surprisingly little printing (air pockets)

What it looks like:

- Price jumps several ticks/cents,
- the tape shows relatively few trades during the jump,

- prints appear at the new level without much "in-between" activity.

How to interpret it: This often means the market is thin nearby. Liquidity may have been pulled (for benign reasons like risk control, or for more strategic reasons). Either way, the tape is telling you there was not much actual trading required to move price. That is fragility.

Retail impact: Fragility increases slippage risk. It is the tape-based version of the "gappy" feel discussed in Developing Market Awareness: you are seeing an environment where price searches for liquidity rather than negotiating smoothly.

Red Flag 4: Repeated "at-ask" buying that does not lift price (or "at-bid" selling that does not drop it)

What it looks like:

- Many trades are flagged/colored as lifting the offer (aggressive buying),
- yet the best offer does not rise and price does not advance,
- or the mirror image: repeated hitting of the bid without price falling.

How to interpret it: This can signal a strong passive counterparty replenishing liquidity, or the presence of hidden size. It can also occur during quote flicker where the inside market is refreshed quickly.

Retail impact: Many retail traders assume aggressive trades must push price. When they do not, it suggests someone is prepared for that aggression-and that your "obvious" read may be too late. It also means that chasing based on tape color alone can be costly.

Red Flag 5: Spread widening during quiet prints (liquidity providers backing away)

What it looks like:

- The tape slows down (few trades),
- but the inside bid/ask spread widens or becomes jumpy,
- small trades cause outsized quote adjustments.

How to interpret it: Liquidity providers widen spreads when they do not want to be picked off. They might be reacting to correlated markets, volatility forecasts, or order flow that looks informed. You may not see the cause, but you can see the effect: the market is charging more for immediacy.

Retail impact: In this state, "just get me in" orders are punished. Even if you are correct on direction, entry and exit can cost more than expected. This is an environment signal, not a prediction signal.

A practical decoding guide: what to look for in each column

To keep tape reading actionable, use this quick guide:

Column	What to notice	What it can imply (non-exhaustive)
Time	Clustering: many prints in the same second vs. a slow drip	Bursts suggest automation/-competition; slow tape with wide spreads suggests cautious liquidity
Price	Does price advance/decline smoothly, or jump? Does it "stick" to a level?	Jumps suggest thin liquidity; sticking with heavy prints suggests absorption or hidden size
Size	Many tiny repetitive sizes vs. occasional large blocks	Tiny repetitive prints suggest slicing/queue competition; large blocks can mark rebalancing or institutional flow
(If shown) Side	Are prints mostly at bid, at ask, or mid? Do they change regime suddenly?	At-ask without progress suggests replenishment/absorption; regime shifts can signal a change in liquidity conditions

The key is to combine columns. A single data point is rarely conclusive. A *pattern* across time, price, and size is what creates a reliable clue.

Common mistakes: how retail traders misread the tape

Because Time and Sales feels "raw," people often over-trust it. Avoid these frequent errors:

Mistake 1: Treating every large print as a directional bet

A large print can be the end of a move (profit-taking), a hedge, or a cross. Without context, a big trade is not automatically bullish or bearish.

Mistake 2: Ignoring price response

Tape reading must always end with: *What did price do after the prints?* If aggressive buying prints do not lift price, that is information. If a small amount of selling knocks price down hard, that is also information.

Mistake 3: Confusing "busy" with "safe"

A busy tape can feel liquid. But some of the busiest tapes occur in the most hostile conditions, where spreads, slippage, and adverse selection are highest. Activity alone is not safety.

Turning tape clues into a defensive posture

This chapter's theme is defensive thinking. The tape helps you decide whether to be patient or urgent.

When you see multiple tape red flags together-machine-gun bursts, heavy volume with no progress, air-pocket jumps, or widening spreads-treat it as a clear environment message:

> **The market is being controlled at a faster time scale than you can comfortably manage.**

A sensible retail response is not panic. It is *de-risking your interaction*:

- reduce order urgency (avoid "must-fill-now" behavior),
- reduce size (so a bad fill is survivable),
- demand clearer confirmation (wait for price to prove it can move *after* volume, not during).

Where we go next: from clues to symptoms

So far, you have learned to detect red flags from two external screens:

- the order book (what is advertised),
- the tape (what is executed).

Next we bring it home to the most personal evidence of all: **your fills**. In the next section, we will diagnose execution symptoms-slippage, partial fills, and the feeling of "chasing"-and show how they often reflect a predatory-feeling environment rather than mere bad luck.

6.4 Diagnosing Execution Symptoms

So far, you have learned to read two external screens:

- the **order book** (what the market is advertising),
- the **tape** (what the market is actually printing).

Now we turn to a third source of evidence that is often more emotionally intense than either of those: **your fills**.

Most casual traders treat bad fills as personal failure or bad luck: "I'm always a tick late" or "My broker is out to get me." That reaction is understandable but it misses the point. In many cases, poor fill quality is not a moral issue and not a conspiracy. It is a **symptom** of the microstructure environment you are trying to trade in.

This section gives you a diagnostic framework: how to recognize when slippage, partial fills, and "price running away" are telling you something systematic about the market's behavior, especially when faster participants are reacting to your urgency.

Execution 101: the price you see is not the price you get

A trade has two prices:

1. the **displayed price** (what you see on the quote),
2. the **execution price** (what you actually receive).

The difference between the two is not always wrongdoing. It comes from three mechanical facts of modern markets:

- **Competition for priority:** At a given price, orders are generally filled by time priority (first in line gets filled first), but that line can change fast.
- **Fragmentation:** Liquidity is spread across venues. Your platform shows an aggregate picture that may update with small delays.
- **Adaptive liquidity:** Many liquidity providers update quotes quickly when they detect risk.

When these features interact with high-speed strategies, the retail experience can feel like the floor is moving. The important step is to convert that feeling into a diagnosis.

The difference between a "bad trade" and a "bad environment"

A **bad trade** is a correct execution of a flawed idea: you got in and out where you intended, but the market moved against you.

A **bad environment** is when the mechanics of trading are degraded:

- you cannot get filled where you reasonably should,
- you pay unexpected spread and slippage,
- your stops and entries behave unpredictably relative to what you saw on screen.

This distinction matters because the correct response differs:

- Bad trade → improve analysis, sizing, or discipline.
- Bad environment → reduce urgency, reduce size, or avoid trading at that moment.

Symptom checklist: what poor fills are trying to tell you

Below are common execution symptoms retail traders encounter. The goal is not to complain about them; the goal is to interpret them as environmental signals that can keep you from compounding risk.

Symptom 1: Slippage that is too frequent to be random

Definition (practical): Slippage is the gap between your intended price and your actual fill, typically worse than expected.

What it feels like:

- You click buy and get filled higher than the ask you just saw.
- You click sell and get filled lower than the bid you just saw.
- It happens repeatedly even with small size.

When it is likely "just market conditions":

- the spread is wide,
- the tape is moving fast,

- the market is jumping levels (thin liquidity),
- there is news or a fast open/close.

When it is an environment red flag: Slippage is not one bad fill. It is a pattern. If you notice that you are consistently paying the "worst end" of the spread during moments that look calm on the chart, it often indicates that liquidity providers are selectively stepping away from trades that look risky. In plain language: **the market is charging you more because your order is arriving as "urgent flow."**

Symptom 2: The "I have to chase" loop

What it looks like (common retail sequence):

1. You place a limit buy at the bid (patient).
2. Price ticks up; you are not filled.
3. You cancel and re-place higher.
4. Price ticks up again.
5. After a few repeats, you give up and use a market order (urgent).

Why this is diagnostic: A single missed limit fill is normal. The diagnostic symptom is **repeated non-fills combined with immediate adverse movement after you show interest**. That experience frequently occurs in environments where:

- the displayed book is not stable (flicker),
- faster participants update quotes to avoid being "picked off,"
- your order placement itself becomes information to the market.

Retail impact: Chasing is more than psychological frustration; it is a measurable cost. Each chase tends to:

- move you closer to the ask (pay more spread),

- increase the chance of buying just as short-term liquidity pulls,
- convert your plan into a sequence of reactive decisions.

If the market repeatedly makes you upgrade your price to get filled, the environment is telling you that patience is being punished and urgency is being monetized.

Symptom 3: Partial fills on small orders (the "why didn't I get all of it?" problem)

What it feels like:

- You place a modest limit order (not huge),
- you receive a partial fill,
- then the rest sits unfilled as price moves away.

Benign explanations exist: queue priority, limited displayed size, and fragmented execution across venues.

Why it can still be a red flag: When partial fills happen repeatedly in a short time window, it often indicates shallow, unstable liquidity at the touch. In a stable environment, small orders at the inside price frequently fill quickly. In a hostile-feeling environment, liquidity is there until you touch it then it either cancels or you discover you were never truly near the front of the queue.

Retail impact: Partial fills are not just annoying. They create position management risk:

- You intended one position size but end up with another.
- You may pay the spread twice (once on the partial, once on the remainder).
- Your stop/target logic can become inconsistent.

Symptom 4: You get filled "right at the turning point" (adverse selection)

What it feels like:

- Your buy fills, and within seconds price drops.
- Your sell fills, and within seconds price rises.
- It happens more often than seems plausible.

Key concept (plain language): Adverse selection means that the market tends to trade with you when it is beneficial for the other side. Think of it like this: if a shopkeeper only sells to you when they know the item is about to go on sale elsewhere, you are being selected as the counterparty at the worst times.

In market microstructure terms, when liquidity providers suspect that incoming orders are informed (or simply urgent during fast conditions), they may protect themselves by widening spreads, pulling quotes, or trading selectively. That can make retail orders disproportionately likely to be filled right before short-term reversals.

Diagnostic clue: Adverse selection often correlates with what you learned earlier:

- a flickery book,
- bursts on the tape,
- price moving in air pockets.

Symptom 5: Stop orders that slip badly or trigger on a "needle"

What it feels like:

- A quick spike hits your stop and immediately reverses (a "needle"),
- your stop executes at a worse price than expected,

- the move seems out of proportion to the chart's normal behavior.

Important reality: A stop order is not a magical exit price. It is typically an instruction that becomes a **market order** (or a marketable order) once triggered. In thin or jumpy conditions, that can produce ugly fills.

Why it is diagnostic: Stops slipping badly often indicates a sudden disappearance of nearby liquidity. This can happen for legitimate reasons (volatility spike, correlated market move), but it is still an environmental warning: if liquidity can vanish fast enough to gap your stop, it can also gap your entry and your profit-taking.

Symptom 6: "I never get the good fills" (asymmetric execution)

What it feels like:

- When you place a market order, you get the worst end immediately.
- When price moves favorably by a tick, you mysteriously do not get price improvement.

How to interpret it: Asymmetric execution is often a sign that you are paying for immediacy without capturing the benefits of patience. This can result from your broker's routing, from queue position realities, and from fast quote updates that remove favorable liquidity before your order reaches it.

Diagnostic takeaway: If you experience systematic asymmetry, the environment is effectively telling you:

Your trading style is donating edge to faster participants.

Again, this is not an accusation. It is a warning to adjust behavior.

A simple scoring approach: when is it "just noise" vs. a consistent problem?

To avoid paranoia, use a structured filter. Ask:

1. **Is the symptom repeatable?** (One bad fill is normal. Five in a row is information.)

2. **Is the symptom concentrated in certain times?** (Open, news, illiquid hours.)

3. **Does it align with book/tape red flags?** (Flicker size + machine-gun tape + slippage is a coherent story.)

4. **Does it improve when you reduce urgency?** (If patient limits behave better than markets, the diagnosis is confirmed.)

If your experience checks multiple boxes, you are likely dealing with an environment problem, not personal bad luck.

Turning symptoms into defensive decisions (without "fighting the market")

The purpose of diagnosing execution symptoms is not to become angry at the screen. It is to make safer choices that fit your time scale.

When fills start to degrade, the simplest defensive responses are:

- **Reduce urgency:** prefer limit orders, accept the possibility of no fill.

- **Reduce size:** in unstable liquidity, size magnifies execution risk more than you expect.

- **Increase selectivity:** fewer trades, only when the environment feels stable.

- **Treat "no fill" as a gift:** in a hostile environment, not trading can be the best execution.

These are not tactics to "beat HFT." They are tactics to avoid being harvested by your own urgency.

Where we go next: avoiding false positives

You now have three lenses:

- **texture** (broad conditions),
- **book** (advertised intent),
- **tape** (executed reality),
- and a fourth, personal lens: **your own fills**.

That is powerful but it also creates a risk: seeing predators everywhere. In the next section, we will ground these ideas with a reality check. We will review legitimate, benign reasons for fast cancellations, volatility, and wide spreads, and build a mindset that is skeptical without becoming conspiratorial.

6.5 The Danger of False Positives

By now, you have built a practical detection toolkit:

- **Market awareness:** noticing texture (smooth vs. gappy, thick vs. thin).
- **Order book red flags:** flickering size, vanishing walls, and depth that seems to retreat from contact.
- **Tape clues:** machine-gun bursts, volume that does not move price, and air-pocket jumps.
- **Execution symptoms:** slippage, chasing, partial fills, and adverse selection.

This toolkit is powerful-and that creates a new risk.

The risk is **false positives**: mistaking normal market mechanics, data limitations, or routine risk management for predatory behavior. False positives are not just an intellectual error; they are dangerous because they can:

- turn a trader into a victim mentality ("the market is rigged against me, so learning is pointless"),
- cause overtrading (revenge trading against imagined enemies),
- cause undertrading (paralysis-avoiding all participation),
- weaken discipline (breaking rules because you feel "forced").

This section is the reality check that keeps you skeptical without becoming conspiratorial. The goal is not to dismiss predatory tactics. The goal is to maintain a **high standard of evidence** before you label what you see.

A healthy mindset: detection is about *risk*, not blame

A key idea for survival:

You do not need to prove manipulation to protect yourself.

Your job as a casual or non-professional participant is not to prosecute anyone. Your job is to decide whether the current environment deserves:

- normal sizing and normal order types, or
- reduced urgency, reduced size, or no trade.

That means you can treat suspicious patterns as *hazards* even when they have innocent explanations. But you should avoid turning every hazard into a villain.

Why quotes cancel quickly (benign reasons that look "shady")

Fast cancellations are one of the most common triggers for false positives. Many traders see a quote appear and vanish and immediately conclude "spoofing." Sometimes that conclusion is right. Often it is not.

Here are legitimate reasons that liquidity providers cancel and re-post quickly:

Reason 1: Risk updates from correlated markets

Market makers quote thousands of instruments while hedging their overall exposure. If a related product moves (index futures, sector ETF, options-implied volatility, FX rates for ADRs), a market maker may need to update quotes *immediately* to avoid being picked off at stale prices.

What it looks like to you: the book "flickers" even though nothing dramatic is happening on your chart.

Interpretation: not necessarily manipulation; it may be routine risk control.

Reason 2: Inventory management ("I'm already too long/short")

Liquidity providers are not charities; they manage inventory. If they get filled on one side repeatedly, they may pull that side or widen spreads until inventory normalizes.

What it looks like: bids disappear after a burst of selling, or offers disappear after a burst of buying.

Interpretation: inventory pressure can mimic predatory "pulling the rug" behavior.

Reason 3: Quote protection during volatility

In fast markets, quoting tightly can be hazardous. Firms often widen spreads and reduce size to protect against rapid adverse moves.

What it looks like: sudden widening spreads, shallow book, jumpy price.

Interpretation: the environment is hostile, but it may be hostile because volatility rose-not because someone is "messing with you."

Reason 4: Routing and venue dynamics

Displayed liquidity is fragmented across venues. Quotes can change because:

- a venue briefly becomes the best bid/offer and then loses that status,
- an order is re-posted on a different venue for fee/rebate or queue reasons,
- the consolidated display updates with small timing differences.

What it looks like: size appears and disappears in ways that seem coordinated, but you are really seeing *aggregation artifacts*.

Why "big size" may not trade (innocent explanations for phantom liquidity)

Another major source of false positives is the mismatch between what the book shows and what the tape prints.

Reason 1: Hidden and iceberg orders

Some markets allow participants to show only a portion of their true size. The tape may show repeated prints at a level even though displayed size looks small (or never seems to deplete).

What it looks like: "Where is all this volume coming from?"

Interpretation: may be hidden liquidity rather than deception.

Reason 2: Your data feed is not the whole market

Retail platforms often provide:

- aggregated Level II that is incomplete or filtered,
- slower updates than professional feeds,

- limited visibility into certain venues or order types.

What it looks like: the tape prints trades that you did not see coming from the displayed book.

Interpretation: the mismatch may be a *visibility problem* rather than a manipulation problem.

Reason 3: Lots of activity can be internalization or dark execution

Depending on the market and your broker's routing, some trades may be executed away from the lit order book and then reported. This can create the feeling that the tape is doing one thing while the visible book is doing another.

Interpretation: again, the environment may still be unfavorable for you, but the explanation is not always a predatory algorithm targeting your specific trade.

Why price sometimes "needles" your stop (and it isn't always a hit job)

Stop-outs that trigger on a spike and reverse are emotionally memorable. They also produce some of the strongest conspiracy thinking.

Here are benign forces that can create "needle" behavior:

Reason 1: Thin pockets and gap risk

If the book is thin, a relatively small burst of market orders can move price several levels. Once those orders are done, price snaps back to where deeper liquidity exists.

Reason 2: Auctions, openings, and rebalances

At the open and close, and during certain rebalancing events, order flow can be one-sided and discontinuous. Prints may cluster and price may jump, even in large, reputable instruments.

Reason 3: Stops cluster near obvious levels

Retail (and many systematic strategies) place stops at similar, obvious locations: just below yesterday's low, just under a round number, just beyond a recent support line. When price approaches those levels, triggered stops can become a wave of market orders, creating the very spike that triggers more stops.

Important nuance: The market does not need a mastermind for this to happen. Crowded behavior can create self-reinforcing cascades.

A disciplined standard of evidence: three questions before you label something "predatory"

To prevent false positives, use a structured filter. Before you conclude that what you saw was manipulation, ask:

Question 1: Is the pattern repeatable across time?

One event is not a pattern. A repeatable signature is what matters:

- Does the same behavior occur multiple times within a session?
- Does it occur on multiple days in similar conditions?
- Does it cluster around certain times (open, news)?

If it is not repeatable, treat it as noise.

Question 2: Does the tape confirm it?

Many false positives vanish when you apply the quote-versus-print distinction.

- If a wall is "fake," do you see little to no printing into it before it vanishes?

- If pressure looks heavy, do prints show real aggression, or mostly quote motion?

If the tape contradicts the story your eyes tell you on Level II, downgrade confidence.

Question 3: Does your execution improve when you reduce urgency?

This is the most practical test because it uses *you* as the instrument:

- If you switch from market orders to patient limits, do fills become more reasonable?
- If you trade smaller, do partial fills and slippage become manageable?
- If you avoid the most volatile minutes, does the problem largely disappear?

If simple defensive changes improve outcomes, the diagnosis is: **the environment penalizes urgency**. That can be true with or without illegal behavior.

A balanced conclusion: skepticism without paralysis

It is healthy to be skeptical in modern electronic markets. It is unhealthy to assume every frustrating outcome is a coordinated attack.

A robust trading mindset holds two ideas at once:

- **Predatory behaviors exist.** Some participants use speed and order placement strategically to influence others and to avoid trading when it is unfavorable.
- **Benign microstructure noise exists.** Quotes cancel for legitimate reasons; liquidity thins rationally; data feeds are incomplete; volatility changes the rules of engagement.

The practical takeaway is simple:

Treat red flags as risk signals, not as personal insults.

If your screens and your fills suggest a hostile environment, you do not need to prove intent. You only need to respond defensively: reduce urgency, reduce size, and require clearer confirmation before committing capital.

That is how you stay calm in the shark tank-without imagining sharks where there are only waves.

Chapter 7

Building Your Cage: The Defensive Playbook

If the market is a shark tank, this chapter is the blueprint for your steel cage. We move from theory to immediate action, providing a step-by-step defensive protocol designed to protect the casual trader. By adjusting how you enter orders, when you choose to engage, and how you configure your trading platform, you can render yourself invisible-or at least unappetizing-to the predatory algorithms lurking in the data.

7.1 The Defensive Mindset: Survival First

If you have read the earlier chapters of this book, you already have the uncomfortable takeaway: modern markets are not just crowds of humans exchanging opinions. They are also arenas where ultra-fast, highly automated firms compete for microscopic edges—edges that come from reacting faster than you can click, detecting predictable behaviors, and monetizing urgency. That fact leads to a simple but easily misunderstood conclusion:

> For a retail trader, the first job is not to *win*. The first job is to *not die*.

In this section we build the mental framework that makes the rest of the defensive playbook make sense. Everything that follows—order choice, timing, broker settings, and transaction-cost audits—depends on adopting a survival-first philosophy. Without it, a trader naturally drifts into the exact behaviors that predatory algorithms feed on: impatience, urgency, oversized positions, and the belief that speed can be matched with willpower.

Why "survival first" is not pessimism (it is arithmetic)

Many trading books, ads, and social media clips sell a *hunter mentality*: be aggressive, seize opportunity, strike quickly, don't hesitate. That mindset can work for a professional firm with co-location, dedicated execution infrastructure, and a risk desk that can shut down the system after a bad morning.

But retail trading does not take place in that environment. Retail traders operate with:

- **Slower execution** (your order travels farther and is processed later),
- **Less information** (you see simplified quotes, not full microstructure),
- **Fewer controls** (you often rely on default settings),
- **Limited capital** (you cannot "reload" after deep drawdowns),
- **Human emotion** (stress rises as losses grow).

Survival-first is simply accepting that *your edge is not speed*. Your edge is the ability to decide *when not to play*, *how not to be rushed*, and *how not to be forced into bad prices*. That is not pessimism. It is the rational choice when your opponent's weapon is *your urgency*.

The compounding problem: avoiding death matters more than chasing returns

Trading losses hurt more than trading gains help, because losses change the base you are compounding from.

If you start with $10,000:

- A **50% loss** takes you to $5,000.
- To get back to $10,000 from $5,000, you need a **100% gain**.

This is why capital preservation is not a vague motivational slogan—it is a mathematical prerequisite for profitability. Large drawdowns create a recovery problem that becomes psychologically and statistically harder to solve. After a big hit, many traders do not calmly "make it back." They take larger risks, become more urgent, and feed the very mechanisms that caused the damage in the first place (slippage, wide spreads, whipsaws, and adverse selection).

Survival-first means you treat any decision that risks a large drawdown as a *different category* of action, not just a "slightly more aggressive trade." A predator does not need you to lose often; it needs you to lose *big* occasionally. Your defense is to make "big losses" structurally difficult to achieve.

The market's speed advantage creates a retail trap

In a human-to-human bazaar, being bold and fast can create an advantage: you get the good deal before someone else. In an algorithmic marketplace, boldness often converts into **paying for immediacy**.

A large fraction of predatory behavior is not mystical. It is the monetization of a common retail pattern:

> *"I need to get in (or out) right now."*

From the market's perspective, that sentence is valuable information. It signals:

- **You are price-insensitive** (you will accept a worse fill),

- **You are predictable** (your behavior follows emotion and headlines),
- **You can be rushed** (you will cross the spread without negotiation).

That does not mean every fast trader is "out to get you," nor does it mean every bad fill is manipulation. It means something more practical: **when you trade urgently, you volunteer to pay extra.** The defensive mindset is learning to recognize urgency in yourself as a cost signal—like noticing you are shopping at an airport convenience store rather than a normal supermarket. You can still buy the water, but you should *expect* the markup and use it sparingly.

Defensive alpha: the profits you earn by refusing to donate money

Most retail traders think "alpha" means a clever entry signal, a chart pattern, or a secret indicator. In the environment described earlier in this book, a different kind of advantage is often more realistic:

> **Defensive alpha** is money you do *not* lose to avoidable costs: bad fills, slippage, wide spreads, panic clicks, and preventable mistakes.

Defensive alpha has three important properties:

1. It is **available to almost everyone**. You do not need faster servers to avoid a market order during a spike.
2. It is **low variance**. Cutting avoidable costs works in many market regimes.
3. It **compounds quietly**. A few cents saved on many trades can outweigh a "great" trade idea that is executed poorly.

This is why this chapter is called *Building Your Cage*. A cage is not a weapon; it is protection. You are not building a system to hunt sharks at their speed. You are building a set of constraints—rules and settings—that keep you from bleeding when sharks are active.

A practical mental model: trading needs a hierarchy

To keep the survival-first idea concrete, it helps to visualize trading as a hierarchy. If the base is unstable, the top cannot be reliably reached. You cannot pursue consistent profit if your process allows catastrophic mistakes, repeated slippage donations, or emotionally forced trades.

Read the pyramid from bottom to top:

- **Capital preservation** is the base: you must prevent the kinds of losses that permanently shrink your future options.

- **Execution control** comes next: even good ideas can be destroyed by bad order placement and rushed decisions.
- **Process consistency** means your behavior is stable enough that you can learn from it.
- **Profit** is the top: it is the result of the lower levels working, not something you can force directly.

This hierarchy also explains a common retail experience: someone finds a strategy that looks profitable in hindsight, applies it with urgent entries and exits, and then wonders why real results look worse. The missing layer is often *execution control*—the very place where speed and microstructure punish urgency.

The three "survival rules" that govern everything in this chapter

To translate mindset into behavior, keep three rules in front of you as you move through the rest of the defensive playbook.

Rule 1: You do not get paid for being fast

In modern electronic markets, "fast" is already owned. If you try to compete on speed, you are choosing the opponent's battlefield. Your job is to compete on *selectivity*:

- waiting for calmer conditions,
- choosing instruments with healthier liquidity,
- using order types that prevent surprise prices,
- rejecting trades where the spread and volatility are telling you "this is dangerous."

Rule 2: You treat urgency as an alarm

Urgency is not a sign you are about to miss the best trade of your life. Most of the time, urgency is a sign you are about to *pay extra*. When you feel rushed, you should automatically ask:

> *"What is the cost of immediacy right now?"*

If you cannot estimate that cost (spread, recent volatility, likelihood of slippage), you are trading in low visibility.

Rule 3: The goal is not "right"; the goal is "not fragile"

Retail traders often obsess over being correct: predicting the next move. The survival-first approach shifts the goal:

> *Build a trading method that is hard to break.*

A fragile method collapses when spreads widen, when a headline hits, or when you make a single mistake. A resilient method expects friction and plans around it.

How this mindset changes your definition of a "good trade"

A good trade is not simply one that makes money. A good trade is one that was **well-defended**:

- You knew your maximum acceptable price (or minimum acceptable sell price).
- You were not forced by a sudden spike to accept a terrible fill.
- Your position size did not turn a normal fluctuation into a crisis.
- Your decision was calm enough that you could repeat it tomorrow.

Sometimes a well-defended trade will be *unfilled*. From a beginner's point of view, that can feel like failure—"I missed it." From a defensive point of view, an unfilled order can be a success:

> *"I refused to overpay in a dangerous moment."*

This is the psychological pivot that makes the next sections workable. If you believe every missed trade is a loss, you will repeatedly choose marketable urgency over controlled execution. If you accept that avoiding bad prices is a form of profit, you can use tools like limit orders and time-of-day selection without feeling like you are "hesitating."

What to expect next

With the survival-first hierarchy in place, we can now move from philosophy to mechanics. The next section focuses on the most basic and powerful defensive choice available to a retail trader: **how you ask the market for a fill**. In particular, we will contrast market orders (fast, convenient, and often expensive) with limit orders (controlled, disciplined, and protective).

7.2 Smart Order Choice: Limit vs. Market

The previous section argued for a survival-first mindset: your first objective is to avoid the kinds of losses and hidden costs that permanently shrink your account and destabilize your decision-making. This section converts that philosophy into one of the most practical defensive tools you have: **order choice**.

Order choice sounds technical, but the core idea is simple.

A market order says, "Fill me *now*, at almost any price."
A limit order says, "Fill me *only if* you can meet my price."

In a fast, competitive marketplace, that difference is enormous. Market orders are "blood in the water" because they broadcast urgency.

Limit orders are armor because they remove urgency from the instruction you send into a market filled with faster participants.

The two questions every order answers (even if you don't realize it)

Every time you place an order, you are answering two questions:

- **How fast do I need execution?** (urgency)
- **How much price risk will I accept?** (slippage risk)

A market order chooses *speed* over *price control*. A limit order chooses *price control* over *certainty of immediate execution*. Retail traders often choose market orders because they feel "safer" (you get filled), but the hidden truth is that market orders can be the *riskiest* choice when liquidity is thin or prices are moving quickly.

What you are really buying with a market order: immediacy

A market order is not "free." You pay for immediacy in three main ways:

Spread cost (the visible toll)

Most of the time, you buy at the **ask** and sell at the **bid**. The difference is the **spread**. If the spread is $0.02, then crossing it costs about $0.02 per share (ignoring fees and rebates). This is the basic cost of demanding immediate liquidity.

In calm, liquid markets, spreads can be small. In thin or fast markets, spreads widen. When spreads widen, a market order becomes an expensive convenience.

Slippage (the invisible tax)

Slippage is the gap between the price you *thought* you would get and the price you *actually* get. It is most common when:

- price is moving quickly (news, open/close, macro headlines),
- the order book is thin (low volume stocks/ETFs, extended hours),
- your order size is large relative to available liquidity at the top of book,
- volatility spikes temporarily and quotes "flicker."

A key survival principle is this:

Market orders convert uncertainty into your fill price.

If the market moves against you between the moment you click and the moment your order is executed, the fill price adjusts—and you own the difference.

Adverse selection (you get filled when it is worst)

Even without any illegal behavior, fast liquidity providers and other algorithms update quotes rapidly. When conditions change, stale quotes disappear first. A market order arriving a moment later can interact with a worse price level than you expected.

In plain language: when you insist on "now," you increase the chance that your order is executed at the exact moment the market is becoming less favorable.

The defensive alternative: limit orders as a hard boundary

A limit order is a commitment to *not overpay* (when buying) or *not undersell* (when selling). It sets a maximum purchase price or minimum sale price.

- **Buy limit:** "Buy *at or below* $X."

- **Sell limit:** "Sell *at or above* $Y."

This is why limit orders are the default defensive choice for casual traders: they put a fence around the worst-case execution price. You are trading off certainty of immediate fill for certainty about price.

Slippage in one picture: why a market order can "jump" during a spike

The following diagram shows the survival-first logic in visual form. On the left, a market order arrives during a brief volatility spike and gets "walked up" into worse prices. On the right, a limit order refuses to pay up; it may remain unfilled, but it stays safe.

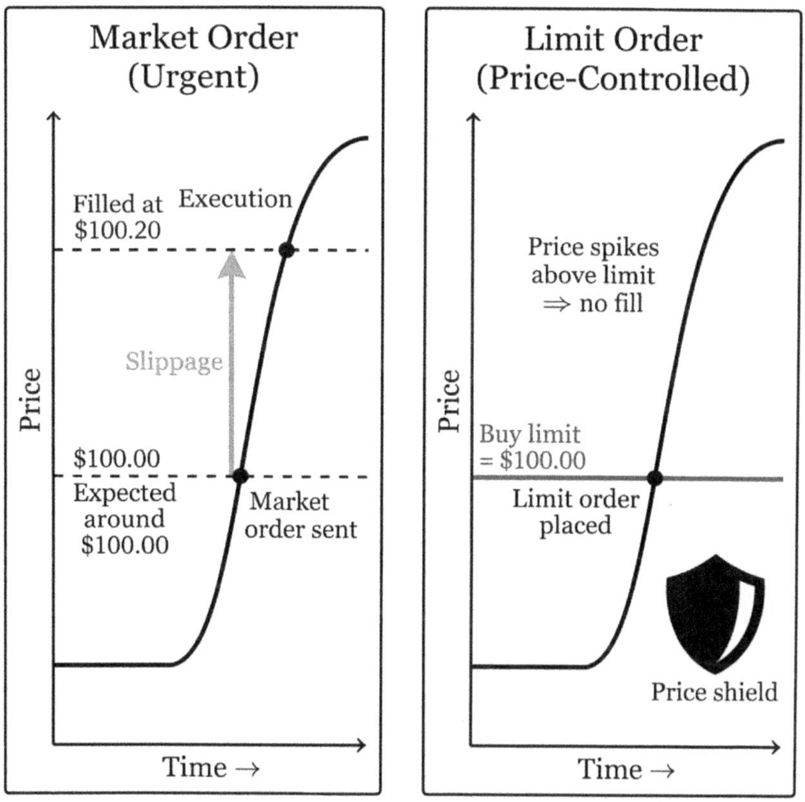

The important lesson is not that limit orders always win. The lesson is that limit orders *define your worst case* on price. A market order does not.

When a limit order is protective (and when it can be frustrating)

Limit orders are not magic; they are a trade-off. Understanding that trade-off is part of becoming "defensive."

What limit orders protect you from

Limit orders directly reduce the two survival threats most relevant to casual traders:

- **Runaway execution prices** during fast moves (you refuse to chase).
- **Accidental overpayment** in wide spreads or thin books (you set the boundary).

They also reduce the chance you will later say, "I don't even recognize the price I got," which is a common symptom of trading during chaotic microstructure moments.

What limit orders do *not* guarantee

A limit order does *not* guarantee:

- that you will get filled,
- that the market will not move away from you,
- that your trade idea is good.

That last point matters. A limit order is execution discipline, not an edge by itself. It is the seatbelt, not the engine.

A practical way to choose a limit price (without pretending you can time the perfect tick)

Casual traders often avoid limit orders because they fear "missing the move." The fix is to stop thinking of the limit price as a perfect forecast. Instead, treat it as a **maximum acceptable deal**.

Here are three simple, defensible approaches:

Method A: Use the current quote as a starting point

If you want to buy, look at the **ask**. If you want to sell, look at the **bid**. Then decide how much you are willing to concede for immediacy.

Example (buy):

- Bid/Ask: $99.98 / $100.00
- You can place a buy limit at $100.00 (likely fill soon), or $99.99 (more protective, may or may not fill).

This forces the right question: *Is a one-cent improvement worth waiting?* Sometimes yes, sometimes no. The point is that you consciously price your urgency instead of donating it automatically.

Method B: Use a "patience band" instead of a single perfect number

Think in ranges, not single points. For example: *"I want this only if I can buy at $100.00 or better. If it runs away, I am fine not owning it."* This is survival-first thinking: you are refusing to convert FOMO into a worse price.

Method C: Scale your entry with multiple small limit orders

Instead of one large order, you can place several smaller limits at slightly different prices. This reduces the emotional pressure of "all or nothing" and makes your execution less fragile.

This is not about being clever; it is about reducing the chance that a single moment of volatility determines your entire outcome.

The most common retail mistake: using a market order because you are afraid

Most "bad fills" are not caused by exotic manipulation. They are caused by a moment of fear:

- fear that the price will run away,
- fear that you will miss the opportunity,
- fear that you will be wrong if you wait.

That fear pushes traders into the most expensive instruction possible: **"Now, whatever it costs."**

The defensive mindset reframes the situation:

If the trade requires urgency to work, it is probably not built for my survival constraints.

This single sentence prevents a large share of retail losses caused by slippage and spread expansion.

A short checklist: choosing between market and limit under pressure

When you feel tempted to use a market order, pause for five seconds and ask:

- **Is the spread currently wide?** If yes, that is a visible warning sign.
- **Did the price just spike?** If yes, market orders are most likely to slip.
- **Is this extended hours or a thin instrument?** If yes, liquidity is often worse than it looks.
- **What is my maximum acceptable price (or minimum acceptable sale)?** If you cannot answer, you should not be sending an "unbounded" order.

If you still decide a market order is necessary (for example, in a genuine emergency exit), at least recognize what you are doing: you are paying for immediacy. In a survival-first framework, that should be the exception, not the default.

Where we go next: choosing safer moments to trade

Order choice is your first line of defense, but it is not the only one. Even a limit order can struggle in the most chaotic parts of the day, when spreads widen and prices whip around.

The next section expands the defensive playbook from *how* you trade to *when* you trade: selecting liquidity-rich, calmer periods and avoiding the market's daily "danger zones."

7.3 Timing the Waters: Liquidity Selection

The previous section introduced the first hard defensive tool: **order choice**. In particular, you saw why market orders advertise urgency and why limit orders are a basic form of price control. Now we extend the same survival-first logic to a broader question:

> **Even a good order type becomes fragile in bad water.**

"Bad water" means periods and places where liquidity is unreliable: spreads widen, prices jump between levels, and fast participants are most active. In those conditions, retail traders pay more for immediacy, experience more slippage, and are more likely to get psychologically pushed into urgent actions.

This section gives you a practical, non-technical way to avoid the market's danger zones by making two selections *before* you click:

1. **Select the time-of-day environment** (when to trade).
2. **Select the liquidity environment** (what to trade).

These are defensive choices. They do not require predicting price direction. They reduce the chance that microstructure frictions—spreads, partial fills, and sudden price gaps—become the dominant driver of your results.

Liquidity in plain language: "How hard is it to get a fair price?"

Liquidity is often described as a technical concept, but for survival purposes you can define it simply:

> **Liquidity is how easily you can trade without moving the price against yourself.**

High liquidity usually means:

- **Tight spreads** (small bid–ask difference),
- **Thick order book** (lots of shares available near the current price),
- **Stable quotes** (prices don't "flicker" or gap as often),
- **Lower slippage risk** (fills are closer to what you expect).

Low liquidity usually means the opposite. The key point is that low liquidity is not merely "annoying." It is *a cost amplifier*. It turns small mistakes into expensive mistakes, and it makes urgent orders far more dangerous.

The daily rhythm: why liquidity and volatility often form a "U-shape"

Most markets have a recognizable intraday pattern:

- **Open:** a burst of activity, news digestion, price discovery.
- **Midday:** calmer trading, more stable spreads.
- **Close:** another burst of activity, portfolio adjustments, index-related flows.

You do not need to memorize microstructure jargon to benefit from this. You only need the defensive inference:

> **The open and close tend to be the most stressful, most expensive times to demand immediacy.**

During the open, the market is processing overnight information. Quotes adjust quickly. Spreads can widen as participants protect themselves from uncertainty. During the close, many institutions rebalance, hedge, and match benchmarks. Volume can be high, but so can speed and short-term price pressure.

Midday often has fewer "forced" flows and a more stable negotiation between buyers and sellers. That tends to make price control easier—which is exactly what a retail trader wants.

Danger zones: open, close, and "headline minutes"

A survival-first trader treats certain windows as **danger zones**. This does not mean you must never trade in them; it means you should assume the environment is more predatory *by default.*

The open (first minutes of regular trading)

Common retail trap at the open:

> *"The stock is moving! I need in now."*

Why this is dangerous:

- Quotes can move several times between your decision and your execution.
- Early spreads can be wider than you expect, especially in less liquid names.
- Stop and market orders are most likely to suffer from poor fills when prices jump levels quickly.

Defensive posture:

- Prefer limit orders if you participate.
- Consider waiting for the first wave of price discovery to settle before committing size.
- If you are new or trading casually, making "do nothing" your default during the open is a legitimate advantage.

The close (last minutes of regular trading)

The close can bring heavy institutional flows (including index-related trading and end-of-day positioning). Even if you see large volume, you may also see:

- sudden bursts of buying/selling pressure,
- spreads that widen briefly,
- more rapid short-term price movement.

Defensive posture:

- Avoid placing urgent orders late in the session unless you have a clear reason.
- If you must trade, again default to limit orders and accept that "no fill" can be a protective outcome.

Headline minutes (economic releases and major announcements)

Certain scheduled events (economic releases, central bank statements, company earnings for the stock you are trading) can create short-lived but extreme microstructure stress:

- spreads widen quickly,
- quotes update rapidly,

- prices can jump multiple levels without trading at intermediate prices.

In these moments, a retail trader can experience the most painful form of slippage: you are filled *far* from your mental expectation, and the fill feels almost "unfair" even though it is simply the market repricing quickly.

Defensive posture:

- If you cannot clearly explain why you need to trade *during* the event, you probably do not.
- Waiting is a position. It is often the best one.

The "safer zone": why calm hours favor retail execution

The survival-first goal is not constant action; it is controlled action. Calmer periods tend to offer:

- more stable spreads,
- less quote flicker,
- a higher chance your limit orders get filled near your intended price,
- less emotional pressure to "hit the button."

In other words, calmer hours allow your main defensive tools—patience and price boundaries—to work as intended. You are not trying to predict where the market goes; you are trying to avoid paying avoidable microstructure tolls.

Instrument selection: not all tickers are equally safe water

Time-of-day selection helps, but it cannot fully compensate for trading in an intrinsically thin product. The second half of liquidity selection is choosing instruments that are structurally harder to "nickel-and-dime" you through spreads and slippage.

A useful rule:

> **A wide spread is a hazard meter.**

When the spread is wide, it is telling you that liquidity providers and other participants demand more compensation for the risk of providing immediacy. That compensation comes from traders who cross the spread—often retail traders using market orders or aggressively priced orders.

Safer liquidity profiles (generally)

While no instrument is perfectly safe, retail traders often find execution is more forgiving in products with:

- **Consistently high volume** (many shares trading throughout the day),
- **Tight typical spreads** (not just sometimes tight),
- **Deep interest across venues** (more competition to provide liquidity),
- **Simple, widely followed structures** (major large-cap stocks, highly traded broad-market ETFs).

These environments tend to reduce the penalty for being slower because there are more resting orders and more competition to trade with you at reasonable prices.

Higher-risk liquidity profiles (generally)

Retail traders should be cautious with:

- **Low-volume stocks (often small caps):** spreads can be wide and the book thin, so small orders can cause disproportionately bad fills.

- **Thin or niche ETFs:** the on-screen spread can look manageable until a volatility burst reveals that depth is limited.
- **Extended-hours trading in almost anything:** even popular names can become "thin" outside regular hours.

The point is not "never trade these." The point is to recognize that these instruments are *execution-sensitive*. If your skill set is still developing, execution sensitivity is the enemy of survival because it increases the role of slippage and reduces the reliability of your defensive tools.

A practical liquidity checklist you can use in seconds

Before trading a symbol, you can do a quick "liquidity sanity check" using information most retail platforms display:

1. **Spread check:** Is the bid–ask spread tiny and stable, or does it jump around?
2. **Volume check:** Is trading volume consistently high relative to the instrument, or is it sporadic?
3. **Quote stability:** Are bid/ask prices flickering rapidly even when the broader market seems calm?
4. **Time-of-day:** Are you near the open, close, or a known news window?

If two or more answers look bad, the survival-first response is simple:

> *Reduce urgency, reduce size, use stricter limits, or do not trade.*

How liquidity selection reinforces limit-order discipline

Liquidity selection and limit orders work together:

- In **healthy liquidity**, limit orders are more likely to fill near your intended price.
- In **poor liquidity**, limit orders often protect you by *not* filling during unstable moments.

This is why "unfilled" should not automatically be interpreted as failure. In dangerous water, an unfilled limit order may be the market telling you: *the only available fills right now are expensive.*

A defensive example: two traders, same idea, different water

Imagine two traders with the same directional opinion on a stock:

- Trader A trades the first minutes after the open with a market order.
- Trader B waits for calmer conditions and uses a limit order near the displayed quote.

Even if both are "right" about direction later, Trader A is more likely to donate value through spread and slippage at entry. Trader B may miss some trades, but the trades they *do* get are more likely to be executed within a controlled cost envelope.

That is defensive alpha in practice: not predicting better, but paying less to participate.

Where we go next: building safety into your platform

By now the pattern should be clear:

- The survival-first mindset tells you to reduce fragility.
- Limit orders help you control price.
- Liquidity selection helps you choose environments where control is possible.

The next step is to make these defenses harder to break in the heat of the moment. In the next section, we turn to **broker and platform settings**—the "armor plating" that prevents fat-finger errors, accidental one-click trades, and risky extended-hours behavior when liquidity dries up and the shark tank gets hungry.

7.4 Armor Plating: Optimizing Broker Settings

So far, the defensive playbook has focused on *decision-level* defenses:

- **Mindset:** survival first (avoid fragility and large drawdowns).
- **Order choice:** prefer limit orders to keep price boundaries.
- **Timing and selection:** avoid dangerous liquidity environments.

This section adds a different layer of protection: **platform-level defenses**. These are the settings and safeguards inside your broker or trading app that reduce two common retail failures:

- 1) **Accidental errors** (fat-finger mistakes, wrong symbol, wrong quantity, wrong order type).
- 2) **Speed traps** (features designed to make trading frictionless, which can also make losses frictionless).

Think of broker settings as *armor plating*. Armor does not make you invincible. It makes it harder for a single mistake, a single impulsive click, or a single chaotic minute of volatility to do serious damage.

Why settings matter in an HFT-dominated environment

In a fast market, the interval between impulse and execution can be extremely short. That is exactly the problem: retail traders often need a *pause* to confirm what they are doing, but many modern platforms are designed to remove pauses.

From a defensive point of view, convenience features often have a hidden cost:

Anything that reduces your friction can also reduce your safety.

Predatory algorithms do not need access to your account settings to benefit from them. If your platform makes it easier for you to send urgent, unbounded orders (or to trade in low-liquidity sessions), the market ecosystem will naturally "charge you" for those choices through spread, slippage, and adverse selection.

The core principle: build a "two-step" process for every trade

Your goal is not to make trading slow for its own sake. Your goal is to make *harmful actions* slower than *thoughtful actions*. A simple way to do this is to enforce two steps:

- 1) **Design:** choose symbol, size, order type, and price boundary.
- 2) **Confirm:** verify the order details before it reaches the market.

Most of the settings in this section support that two-step discipline.

The Safety Checklist: settings that protect retail traders

Not every broker uses the same names, but most provide variants of the controls below. If you cannot find a setting, search the help menu for the keywords in parentheses.

1) Turn Order Confirmation ON ("trade confirmation", "review order")

This is the single highest-impact safety toggle for most casual traders.

What it does. It forces your platform to show a summary screen (symbol, buy/sell, shares, order type, limit price, time-in-force, session) before sending the order.

Why it matters defensively. Order confirmation creates a micro-pause that catches the most expensive errors:

- buying when you meant to sell (or vice versa),
- adding an extra zero to share quantity,
- sending a market order when you intended a limit,
- placing the correct trade in the wrong symbol.

Survival-first framing. A confirmation screen is not a nuisance; it is an anti-impulse circuit breaker.

2) Disable One-Click / One-Tap Trading ("quick trade", "instant trade")

One-click trading is marketed as empowerment. In practice, it is a speed lever. If you are not competing on speed (and you are not), it is usually unnecessary.

Why it matters defensively. One-click trading makes it easier to:

- chase a spike with a marketable order,
- trade during a moment of stress without checking the spread,
- accidentally submit duplicate orders.

Recommendation. For most casual traders: keep one-click trading **off** and trade through the standard ticket with review.

3) Set your default order type to Limit ("default order", "order preferences")

If your platform allows a default, choose the defensive default.

Why it matters. Defaults shape behavior under pressure. In volatile moments, people revert to the path of least resistance.

Defensive benefit. If the ticket opens as a limit order by default, you are less likely to "accidentally" grant the market permission to fill you at a bad price.

4) Use Share size guards and notional warnings ("quantity warning", "order size alert")

Many brokers allow alerts when an order exceeds a threshold number of shares or dollar value.

Why it matters defensively. A large accidental order is one of the fastest ways to create catastrophic loss. It can also trigger margin usage unintentionally.

How to set it. Choose a threshold that would be meaningfully painful if mistaken. For example, if your typical trade is $500–$2,000 notional, set an alert at $2,500 or $3,000 so you must consciously override it.

5) Enable Market order warnings ("market order risk", "price uncertainty warning")

Some platforms show special warnings when you choose a market order.

Why it matters. A warning is a second reminder that you are choosing immediacy over price control. This is particularly valuable after the previous sections, because it reinforces the concept of slippage at the exact moment you are most likely to ignore it.

If your broker has no warning. Make your own rule: any time you select Market, you must verbally state (yes, out loud): *"I am accepting an unknown price within the current liquidity conditions."* If that sentence feels uncomfortable, it is doing its job.

6) Treat Extended Hours as OFF by default ("pre-market", "after-hours")

Extended-hours trading is where many retail traders unknowingly step into thinner liquidity.

Why it matters defensively. Outside regular hours:

- spreads often widen,
- depth is thinner,
- price gaps are more common,
- a small order can move the price more than expected.

This magnifies slippage risk and makes market orders especially hazardous.

Defensive policy. Keep extended-hours trading disabled unless you have a clear, specific reason and you are prepared to use strict limit orders. If your broker allows session selection, confirm you are in the intended session before sending the order.

7) Choose a conservative Time-in-Force default (often Day)

Time-in-force controls how long your order remains active.

Why it matters defensively. A limit order that lingers longer than you intended can fill later under different conditions. Many avoidable surprises happen because a trader forgets an order exists.

Defensive recommendation.

- Default to **Day** orders while learning.
- Use longer durations (e.g., GTC) only when you actively monitor open orders and understand the fill risk.

8) Monitor and manage Open Orders ("working orders", "order status")

This is not a toggle, but it is an essential habit: knowing what orders are currently working in the market.

Why it matters. Open orders are exposure. They represent intentions that can become executions.

Defensive routine. Before placing a new order, glance at your open orders:

- Do you already have an order working in this symbol?
- Could two orders accidentally double your position?
- Is there a stale order from earlier in the day?

9) Turn on Account and margin safety controls ("margin calculator", "buying power alerts")

Even if you do not plan to use margin, your platform may allow trades that create margin exposure.

Why it matters defensively. Margin increases fragility. It can turn a normal adverse move into a forced liquidation at the worst possible time (when spreads are wide and volatility is high).

Defensive approach.

- Enable buying power alerts if available.
- Avoid settings that automatically "upgrade" you to more leverage without deliberate choice.

10) Secure your account (2FA, device approvals)

This is not microstructure-related, but it is still part of survival. A compromised account can create losses that have nothing to do with trading skill.

Recommendation. Enable two-factor authentication and device approvals if offered. Survival-first includes operational safety.

A compact reference table: "Recommended toggles"

The goal is a setup you can trust in stressful moments. The following table summarizes the default posture for most casual traders.

Setting / Feature	Default	Defensive reason
Order confirmation / Review screen	ON	Catches fat-finger errors; forces a pause before sending.
One-click / Instant trading	OFF	Reduces impulse trading and accidental submissions.
Default order type	LIMIT	Keeps price control as the default behavior.
Market order warnings	ON	Reminds you that price is not guaranteed under stress.
Extended-hours trading	OFF	Avoids thin liquidity where spreads and gaps amplify slippage.
Time-in-force default	DAY	Prevents forgotten orders from filling later unexpectedly.
Order size / notional alerts	ON	Blocks catastrophic mistakes (extra zeros, wrong size).
Buying power / margin alerts	ON	Reduces leverage-related fragility and forced exits.
Two-factor authentication	ON	Protects against operational/account risk.

A defensive workflow: "slow is smooth, smooth is fast" (for retail)

You are not trying to be slow. You are trying to be *unforced.* A simple workflow that works well for casual traders is:

- **Check the water:** time-of-day and spread (from the previous section).
- **Choose the boundary:** limit price (from the order-choice section).
- **Confirm the ticket:** symbol, size, session, time-in-force.

- **Send once:** avoid repeated clicks.
- **Verify open orders:** confirm the order is working as intended.

Notice how this workflow is designed to prevent the two retail-killers: impulsive urgency and avoidable mistakes.

What this section deliberately does *not* recommend

Because this book focuses on awareness and defense rather than aggressive tactics, it is worth stating what we are *not* doing here:

- We are not trying to outsmart or outrun professional algorithms.
- We are not adding complex conditional orders as a substitute for understanding.
- We are not turning the platform into an autopilot that trades without oversight.

Armor plating is about reducing the damage from predictable human error and predictable market friction.

Where we go next: measuring your hidden costs

After you set your defenses, you should verify that they are working. The next section is the "after-action report": a practical way to audit your trades for the costs you do not see on the commission line—slippage, spread payments, and systematically poor fills.

In survival-first trading, what you measure is what you can improve.

7.5 The After-Action Report: Auditing Transaction Costs

The earlier sections built your defensive **"cage"** in layers:

- a **survival-first mindset** (avoid fragility and large drawdowns),
- **order choice** that favors price control (limit orders over market orders),
- **liquidity selection** (avoid bad water: open/close, thin instruments),
- **platform armor** (confirmations, warnings, and safety toggles).

Now we add the missing piece that turns defense from a philosophy into a measurable practice: the **after-action report**. In aviation, medicine, and high-reliability engineering, teams do not improve by hoping. They improve by *reviewing what actually happened* and looking for systematic failure modes.

Retail trading is no different. If you do not audit your transaction costs, you will tend to:

- blame your strategy when execution is the real culprit,
- repeat the same avoidable mistakes (because they feel "normal"),
- underestimate how much you are paying for immediacy and chaos.

This section teaches you how to journal trades specifically to identify the hidden costs that most retail traders never compute: **spread payments, slippage, and suspiciously bad fills**. The goal is not paranoia. The goal is **feedback**.

Transaction costs: the part of your P&L you didn't mean to trade

When people hear "transaction costs," they often think only of commissions. But in modern retail trading, commissions are often small or zero. The larger costs are usually *microstructure costs*:

- **Spread:** the cost of crossing from bid to ask (or ask to bid).

- **Slippage:** the gap between your intended price and your fill price.
- **Market impact:** your own order moving the price (more common in thin names).
- **Opportunity cost:** missing a fill because your limit was too strict (a real cost, but often the price of safety).

Defensive trading is not just about choosing better ideas. It is about ensuring that *execution friction* does not silently eat those ideas.

The key mindset shift: audit the process, not the outcome

A single trade can be profitable even with terrible execution, and a single trade can lose money even with excellent execution. If you judge execution quality only by profit, you will learn the wrong lessons.

Your after-action report should ask:

Did I trade well, even if the market outcome was random?

This is why professional traders separate:

- **Decision quality** (your thesis, risk, timing), from
- **Execution quality** (how efficiently the market filled you).

This section focuses on execution quality.

The minimum viable audit: five numbers per trade

You do not need a complex spreadsheet to start. For each order (entry and exit), record these five items:

- 1. **Timestamp** (to the minute is usually enough for retail review)
- 2. **Order type** (market/limit; and any special instructions if used)

- 3. **Your intended price** (the price you were aiming for when you clicked)
- 4. **Your fill price** (what you actually received)
- 5. **The spread at submission** (bid/ask when you sent the order)

That is it. Those five numbers are enough to detect most retail execution problems.

What counts as "intended price"?

Use a definition that is consistent and easy:

- For a **market order**, your intended price can be the **quote you saw** (typically the ask for a buy or the bid for a sell) at the moment you clicked.
- For a **limit order**, your intended price is usually your **limit price**. (If you were trying to get improvement, note that too.)

The point is to create a baseline expectation so you can measure the gap.

Compute slippage the retail way (simple, not perfect)

You can quantify slippage without complex market data.

Per-share slippage

For a buy order:

$$Slippage_{per\_share} = FillPrice - IntendedPrice$$

For a sell order:

$$Slippage_{per\_share} = IntendedPrice - FillPrice$$

Under this convention:

- positive slippage means you did worse than intended (a cost),
- negative slippage means you did better than intended (price improvement).

Dollar slippage

$$DollarSlippage = Slippage_{per\_share} \times Shares$$

This is the number that makes slippage real. A one-cent slippage feels small until you realize you traded 2,000 shares. Your journal should make these costs visible.

Separate "spread cost" from "extra slippage"

Many traders confuse spread with slippage. They are related but not identical.

Spread cost (expected friction)

If you buy immediately, you typically pay the ask, which is above the midprice. If you sell immediately, you typically hit the bid, below the midprice. That difference is the cost of immediacy.

If you record the bid and ask at submission, you can compute the midprice:

$$Mid = \frac{Bid + Ask}{2}$$

Then you can estimate:

- **Buy spread cost per share** $\approx Fill - Mid$
- **Sell spread cost per share** $\approx Mid - Fill$

This is not perfect (quotes move), but it is useful as a discipline tool.

Extra slippage (the "something weird happened" component)

If your fill is far beyond what the spread would suggest, that is when you should pay attention.

Example:

- Bid/Ask at click: $99.98 / $100.00 (spread $0.02)
- You buy with a market order and fill at $100.12

A two-cent spread does not explain a twelve-cent fill above $100.00. That additional ten cents is a warning sign: a volatility burst, a thin book, or a speed trap moment. Your journal is designed to capture these situations so you can stop repeating them.

A journal template you can actually maintain

Use a lightweight table with one row per *order* (not per trade). Entries and exits are separate rows. Keep it short enough that you will fill it in.

Date/Time	Symbol	Side	Shares	Bid	Ask	Fill	Notes

In **Notes**, record just enough context to make later pattern-finding possible:

- order type (market/limit),
- time-in-force,
- whether it was open/close/extended hours,
- "headline hit" or "spike," if applicable,
- whether you changed the order (canceled/replaced).

Pattern recognition: what you are looking for after 20–50 orders

A single bad fill can be random. A repeated pattern is a behavioral or environmental problem you can fix.

After you have a modest sample (even 20–50 orders), look for these patterns:

Pattern 1: "I always pay the spread plus extra"

If your fills are consistently worse than the spread would suggest, you are likely trading in unstable moments (open/close, thin instruments) or using order types that expose you to slippage.

Defensive response:

- reduce market orders,
- tighten your "danger zone" rules,
- trade more liquid instruments,
- reduce size in thin names.

Pattern 2: "My worst fills cluster at the same times"

If your worst slippage occurs repeatedly near the open, near the close, or during extended hours, you have found a time-of-day vulnerability.

Defensive response:

- avoid those windows by default,
- if you must trade, use stricter limits and smaller sizes,
- consider waiting 10–30 minutes for conditions to stabilize (depending on your style).

Pattern 3: "Certain symbols are consistently expensive to trade"

If a particular stock or ETF shows wide spreads, frequent partial fills, or repeated negative slippage, it may simply be a poor fit for casual execution.

Defensive response:

- treat spread as a hazard meter and respect it,
- avoid thin tickers unless you have a specific reason and discipline,
- consider replacing niche instruments with more liquid alternatives.

Pattern 4: "My fills are fine when I'm calm, bad when I'm rushed"

This is the most important pattern because it is directly fixable. Many retail traders discover that slippage is not just a market property; it is an emotion property. Urgency leads to marketable orders and sloppy ticket checking.

Defensive response:

- strengthen platform armor (confirmations on, one-click off),
- impose a "cooldown" rule (e.g., no trades for 5 minutes after a spike),
- pre-write limit prices instead of typing under stress.

Detecting "predatory" fills without becoming conspiratorial

Retail traders sometimes interpret every bad fill as manipulation. That is rarely productive. At the same time, the market does contain strategies that profit from predictable urgency and weak execution discipline.

The after-action report helps you identify *conditions* where you are being consistently charged.

You are not trying to prove intent. You are trying to identify **repeatable vulnerability**.

Here are practical "investigate further" flags:

- **Outlier slippage** that is far larger than the spread and happens repeatedly.
- **Slippage clustering** at specific times (open/close/extended hours) or after specific triggers (headlines).
- **Immediate adverse move after fill** that happens frequently (not once), suggesting you are repeatedly trading at moments when price is about to move against you.

You are trading in water where speed punishes urgency.

The cure is defensive behavior, not anger: better order choice, better timing, better instrument selection, and stronger platform controls.

A simple scoring system: give your execution a grade

To keep the audit actionable, assign each order an execution grade based on slippage relative to the spread.

One practical rubric:

- **Grade A:** price improvement or fill within a small fraction of the spread.
- **Grade B:** fill roughly consistent with paying the spread (expected cost).
- **Grade C:** fill worse than the spread would reasonably explain.
- **Grade F:** extreme outlier slippage (a "never again" event worth diagnosing).

Then ask one question:

What changed on my C and F orders?

If the answer is consistently "I used a market order during a spike" or "I traded at the open," then the market has given you a clean, defensible improvement plan.

Turn the audit into one concrete rule per week

The danger of journaling is collecting data and doing nothing with it. The purpose of the after-action report is to create one small, durable rule at a time.

Examples of rules that come directly from transaction-cost audits:

- "No market orders in the first 15 minutes of regular trading."
- "No extended-hours trades unless spread is under $0.02 and I use a limit."
- "If spread is wider than my typical profit target, I do not trade."
- "If I change an order twice, I step away for five minutes."

These rules do not require prediction. They reduce fragility. Over time, they create **defensive alpha**—profits earned by refusing to donate money through avoidable execution costs.

The bottom line

Your broker statement tells you whether you made money. Your after-action report tells you *how much you paid to play*. In a market shaped by speed and automation, that second question is often the difference between a strategy that looks good on paper and a process that survives in reality.

If you consistently measure intended price versus fill price, record spreads, and hunt for patterns, you will stop treating slippage as "bad luck" and start treating it as what it usually is: **a solvable cost problem**.

Chapter 8

Rules of the Road: Regulation and Integrity

If the market is a shark tank, who is watching the water? This chapter moves beyond the mechanics of trading to explore the philosophy of fair play. We examine why market integrity is essential for trust, why proving 'intent' in an algorithmic world is notoriously difficult for regulators, and why the law often feels like it is moving in slow motion compared to the lightning-fast evolution of predatory code.

8.1 The Philosophy of Market Integrity

Imagine you walk into a busy farmers' market. You see apples at $2 per pound at one stand and $4 at another. You assume those prices mean something real: how many apples are available (supply), how many shoppers want them (demand), and how urgently. You also assume that nobody is shouting fake offers just to lure you toward one stall, then disappearing when you approach.

Financial markets work on the same basic social contract. You and

I cannot personally inspect every company, every share, every other trader's motives. So we rely on the market's central output—*price*—to be an honest summary of genuine buying and selling interest. That summary process is called **price discovery**. When price discovery works, the market is not perfect, but it is *legible*: the price is a usable signal. When price discovery is distorted, the market becomes a hall of mirrors, and ordinary participants start making decisions from *fake reflections*.

This section explains why regulators obsess over **market integrity**. The goal is not to prevent competition or stop fast trading. The goal is to preserve *trust in the meaning of prices*—because once that trust erodes, the market's most basic functions weaken: trading becomes more expensive, long-term investing becomes less attractive, and the market's ability to allocate capital (fund businesses, price risk, and support retirement savings) deteriorates.

Price discovery: the market's "measurement system"

A useful way to think about price discovery is as a measurement device, like a thermometer. If the thermometer reads 72°F, you might decide to open a window. If it reads 95°F, you might turn on the air conditioning. You don't need the thermometer to be *perfect*; you need it to be *honest and reliable enough* that it guides decisions in the right direction.

Markets produce prices through the continuous interaction of:

- **Supply:** how many shares people are willing to sell, and at what prices.
- **Demand:** how many shares people are willing to buy, and at what prices.

In modern electronic markets, that interaction is mediated by the **order book**—the constantly updating list of buy and sell orders. The best available buy price is the **best bid**. The best available sell price is the **best ask**. The gap between them is the **spread**. When people trade, they typically trade at (or near) those best prices, and the last traded price becomes the headline number people see on charts and screens.

Here is the key intuition: *the order book is supposed to be a scoreboard of real intent.* If the scoreboard is polluted with actions that are not true expressions of willingness to trade, the market's displayed "reality" diverges from actual reality. That divergence is where integrity problems begin.

Trust is not a moral add-on; it is a market input

Many people first encounter "market integrity" as a moral phrase—as if regulators are simply saying, "Be fair." But integrity is more practical than that. It is a **functional requirement** for a market to operate at low cost.

When traders and investors *trust* displayed liquidity and prices, several good things happen:

- **More participation.** More people are willing to place limit orders and provide liquidity because they believe the posted prices are meaningful.
- **Tighter spreads.** When liquidity providers feel safe, they quote closer to the current price, reducing the spread.
- **Lower "friction."** With tighter spreads and steadier liquidity, the cost of buying and selling falls for everyone, including long-term investors.
- **Better allocation of capital.** Companies' stock prices more accurately reflect real information and real risk preferences, supporting healthier financing decisions.

When trust erodes, the direction reverses. Participants become more cautious. They widen spreads, reduce displayed size, or avoid placing orders until the last possible moment. Liquidity becomes more "skittish," and trading costs rise.

This is why manipulation is not treated as a private quarrel between two traders. Manipulation is a **pollution problem**. It contaminates the information environment the entire market relies upon.

The three pillars regulators use to think about manipulation

Regulation around manipulation can look like a thicket of rules. But beneath the details, enforcement tends to revolve around three core questions—three pillars you can remember as:

Intent $\rightarrow$ **Deception** $\rightarrow$ **Harm**

Different laws and agencies phrase these elements differently, and not every case requires proving every element in the same way. Still, as a learning tool, this three-part frame is extremely useful, because it mirrors how we evaluate "fake" behavior in everyday life.

Pillar 1: Intent (what was the actor trying to do?)

Intent is the idea that an action is not suspicious merely because it is aggressive or fast. Markets are competitive by design. A trader can legally:

- buy quickly because new information arrived,
- cancel an order because conditions changed,
- place a large order because they genuinely want a large position.

What changes the legal and ethical character is **purpose**. If someone places orders not to trade, but to *create a false impression*—for example, to make it look like there is heavy demand when there isn't—that is a different category of conduct.

For casual readers, the simplest phrasing is: *Honest intent says: "I'm showing you what I'm willing to do." Deceptive intent says: "I'm showing you something so you'll do what I want."*

Pillar 2: Deception (did the conduct create a false signal?)

Deception is about the **signal** the market receives. The central question is whether other participants could reasonably interpret the activity as genuine supply or demand.

In electronic markets, signals are not just headlines and news. Signals are also:

- orders placed at or near the best bid/ask,
- sudden changes in displayed size,
- rapid sequences of updates that make one side of the book appear "stronger,"
- patterns that trigger other algorithms to react.

A crucial point: deception in markets often works without any words. No one has to "lie" in a conversation. The deception is performed through the **structure of orders** and the **timing of cancellations**.

Pillar 3: Harm (who paid for the distortion?)

Harm can be direct or indirect.

Direct harm. A trader buys at a worse price (or sells at a worse price) because the market was momentarily pushed in an artificial direction. For example, someone sees apparent buying pressure, pays up, and then the pressure vanishes.

Indirect harm. Even traders who were not the immediate counterparties can be harmed because repeated distortions degrade liquidity and widen spreads. Over time, that translates into:

- worse execution for retirement accounts,
- higher costs for index funds rebalancing,
- more volatile price moves around thin liquidity,
- less confidence in displayed markets.

This "ecosystem" harm is why regulators care about behavior that, at first glance, might look like a minor trick. A small distortion repeated thousands of times a day becomes a structural problem.

Why "fake prices" are more damaging than they first appear

It is tempting to think: "If I'm not trading at that moment, who cares if the book flickers?" But market prices are not only used for immediate trading decisions. They are reference points used for:

- valuing portfolios,
- computing risk and margin,
- triggering stop orders and algorithmic rebalancing,
- pricing options and other derivatives,
- deciding whether to invest more money (or pull money out) of the market.

So the damage from distorted price discovery is not limited to a single trade. If the price signal becomes noisy in the wrong way—noise that is *strategically manufactured* rather than naturally occurring—people begin to treat the market like an unreliable instrument. They respond by demanding a bigger "safety cushion" in their prices. In plain terms: they raise the fee they require to participate.

A practical takeaway: integrity is about keeping the market's signals usable

For the rest of this book, you will see a recurring theme: many predatory strategies are best understood as attacks on the market's signaling system.

They aim to:

- make demand look stronger than it is,
- make supply look heavier than it is,
- create urgency where none exists,
- bait others into revealing their intentions,

- exploit predictable reactions in other algorithms.

In other words, these strategies try to bend the "scale" of price discovery so that the displayed weight of supply or demand is no longer truthful.

That image captures the philosophy in one glance:

- A functioning market is not "calm"; it is *informative.*
- Price discovery is the process of balancing real supply and real demand.
- Manipulation is an outside force that *distorts the reading* without adding genuine information.

Looking ahead: the hard part is proving the "mind" behind the message

If integrity were only about spotting obvious lies, enforcement would be easy. The problem is that modern markets are built from actions that can look similar on the surface:

- A legitimate trader might place and cancel orders rapidly because information is changing rapidly.
- A deceptive trader might place and cancel orders rapidly because the *cancellation* was always the plan.

The line between "competitive" and "manipulative" is often not the speed of the behavior, but the **purpose** and the **message** it sends.

That takes us naturally to the next section, where we translate this philosophy into the legal hurdle regulators face: **defining manipulation in a way that hinges on intent**, and doing so in markets where the "actor" may be an algorithm executing thousands of decisions per second.

8.2 Defining Manipulation and Intent

In the previous section, we treated market integrity as a practical need: prices are only useful if they reflect genuine supply and demand. That brings us to the uncomfortable question regulators must answer in real cases:

> If fast markets are full of cancellations and rapid-fire orders, how can anyone tell the difference between legitimate competition and illegal manipulation?

The short answer is that regulators rarely prosecute *speed* by itself. They prosecute **deception**, and the hardest part of proving deception is proving **intent**—what the actor meant to do. In legal language, this mental-state requirement is often described as **scienter** (pronounced roughly *SYE-en-ter*): a culpable state of mind, such as intending to mislead or defraud.

This section builds a plain-English framework for understanding what "intent" means in markets, why it is central to spoofing cases, and why it is uniquely difficult when the "actor" is an algorithm.

Canceling orders is normal; placing orders *to cancel* is the problem

A beginner's misconception is that "lots of canceled orders" must be illegal. In modern electronic markets, cancellations are not only common; they are often rational.

Here are examples of **legitimate reasons** to cancel:

- **Information changed.** A news headline hits, a correlated asset moves, or liquidity suddenly appears elsewhere.
- **Risk limits changed.** The trader's inventory is too large, volatility spiked, or a risk system throttles exposure.
- **Execution occurred.** A portion of the order filled, and the trader updates the remainder.

- **Better opportunity appeared.** The trader can now quote at a better price or route to a better venue.

So what turns "normal canceling" into "spoofing"?

> **The difference is not the cancellation. The difference is the plan.** Spoofing is about placing an order that was never meant to trade, but was meant to *change what others believe.*

A useful everyday analogy is a fake "For Sale" sign. Posting a sign is legal. Taking it down is legal. But posting it with the purpose of tricking neighbors into thinking prices are rising (so they overpay you for your house) is deception. The action is the same; the *purpose* is different.

What makes intent so central in manipulation law

Many forms of market manipulation are defined by the idea that the manipulator injected a *false signal* into the price discovery process. A false signal is not an accident; it is a choice. That is why the legal system cares about intent.

From an enforcement perspective, intent matters for two reasons:

- **Fairness:** Markets are competitive. A law that punished every aggressive tactic would chill legitimate trading and market making.

- **Precision:** Regulators need a criterion that separates "smart trading" from "dishonest signaling." Intent is that criterion.

But intent is also the regulator's greatest headache. Unlike a person in a conversation, an order book does not come with footnotes explaining motivation. The market shows you *actions* (orders, cancels, trades), not the trader's internal reasoning.

The core concept: did the order express real willingness to trade?

A simple way to interpret "intent" in this context is to ask whether the order expressed a **bona fide** (good-faith) willingness to trade.

- **Good-faith order:** "If someone hits this, I'm okay trading."
- **Deceptive order:** "I want people to *think* I'm okay trading, but I plan to pull it before it can execute."

That distinction sounds clean in a textbook, but real cases involve gray areas:

- A trader may *prefer* not to be filled but will accept a fill if it happens (many liquidity providers feel this way).
- A trader may quote large size but dynamically manage it as conditions change (common in market making).

So regulators often look for evidence that the order was not merely "unlikely to fill," but was **designed not to fill** while still influencing others.

Strategic bluffing vs. illegal spoofing (a decision-tree)

Markets do involve strategy, and strategy sometimes looks like "bluffing." For example, a large investor might break a big purchase into smaller pieces to avoid moving the price against themselves. That is *concealment*, but it is not necessarily deception. The investor is not required to announce their full intentions to the world.

Spoofing is different because it attempts to manufacture a false appearance of supply or demand *in the public order book.*

The following flowchart captures the basic intuition regulators try to apply: "Is the order there to trade, or is it there to move you?"

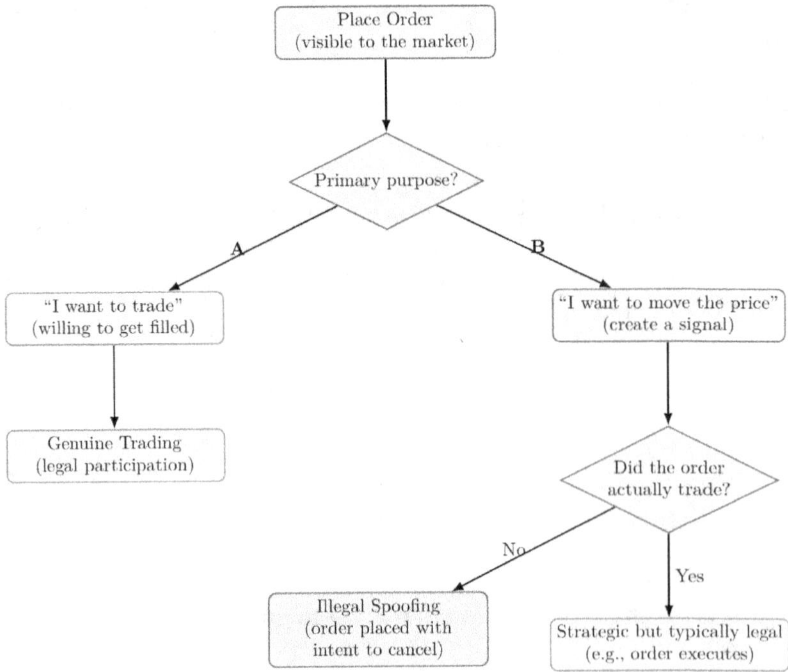

This diagram is deliberately simple. Real enforcement is more nuanced, but the decision-tree gets you to the essence: spoofing is not "placing a big order and canceling it." Spoofing is "placing a big order *because* you intend to cancel it, and you want the market to react before you do."

How do regulators infer intent from data?

No regulator can read a trader's mind. Instead, enforcement teams infer intent from a combination of **order-level data** and **context**.

Think of it like investigating arson. The investigator rarely has a confession. They look for patterns: accelerants, ignition sources, motive, and behavior inconsistent with an accident. Market investigators do something similar with the order book.

Common categories of evidence include:

1) Execution asymmetry: "real trades on one side, cancels on the other"

A classic spoofing pattern is **asymmetry**:

- The trader repeatedly places large visible orders on one side (say, large sell orders),
- those large orders are repeatedly canceled,
- while the trader executes real trades on the opposite side (buying) at better prices that result from the apparent selling pressure.

This is a behavioral "tell": one side looks like theater, the other side is business.

2) Layering and persistence near the best price

Manipulative orders are often placed:

- close enough to the best bid/ask to influence the perceived supply/demand,
- large enough to be noticed by humans and machines,
- in repeated "layers" that build the appearance of depth.

Importantly, this does *not* mean "large orders near the best price are illegal." It means that, in combination with other factors, certain placement patterns can support the inference that the goal was to influence perceptions rather than transact.

3) Timing: canceling when the market gets close

One of the strongest indicators of "never meant to trade" is a repeated pattern where orders are canceled *precisely when they become likely to execute.*

If a trader posts a large sell order and price rises toward it, then cancels right before it would be hit, and does this repeatedly, the behavior looks less like risk management and more like a plan to avoid any chance of execution.

4) Repetition and predictability

One-off odd behavior can happen for many innocent reasons. Regulators often care about:

- repeated sequences,
- consistent outcomes,
- a "signature" that appears across days or instruments.

Repetition is important because it reduces the plausibility of accident. A pattern that reliably produces profit while consistently avoiding execution on the "signal" side looks like design.

5) Communications, design documents, and controls (when available)

Sometimes enforcement includes evidence beyond the tape:

- chat logs or emails,
- algorithm specifications,
- parameter settings (e.g., auto-cancel thresholds),
- supervision and compliance failures.

For casual readers, the key point is simple: **the more the evidence shows the strategy was engineered to send a false message, the easier intent is to prove**.

Why algorithms make the intent question harder (and sometimes easier)

Algorithms complicate intent in two opposing ways.

Harder: "whose intent counts?"

With humans, intent is tied to a person. With algorithms, you can have:

- a programmer writing logic months earlier,
- a trader adjusting parameters today,
- a risk system changing behavior mid-session,
- an algorithm reacting to market conditions in ways nobody predicted.

This creates legal and practical questions:

- Is intent the programmer's original goal, the trader's current settings, or the firm's incentives?
- If the algorithm adapts, does that change culpability?
- If the firm failed to supervise or test the strategy, does that substitute for intent?

Those are not merely philosophical puzzles; they affect real cases and real defenses.

Easier: code leaves footprints

At the same time, algorithms can make intent *easier* to infer because machines are consistent. A human liar forgets details. A program repeats the same logic again and again, leaving a clean statistical footprint in the data.

If a system is effectively designed to:

- place large orders,
- pull them when threatened with execution,
- profit from the reaction,

then the pattern can be unusually crisp.

A simple practical rule for readers: "Was the order meant to be a trade, or a message?"

For everyday market participants, you do not need to prosecute spoofing. But you do need to understand the *regulatory idea* that separates normal microstructure from manipulation.

The most useful mental model is this:

> **A legitimate order is primarily a willingness to trade. A manipulative order is primarily a message designed to move others.**

Everything else—scienter, deception, harm, data analysis—is the system's attempt to make that distinction reliably in a world where trading is fast, noisy, and highly automated.

Why this matters for the rest of the chapter

In the next section, we will address the practical reality that even when the legal theory is clear, detection is not. Regulators face a *needle-in-a-haystack* problem: modern markets generate staggering amounts of order messages, and proving intent requires reconstructing context from that flood of data.

Understanding intent is the conceptual foundation. Understanding surveillance limits is the operational reality.

8.3 Surveillance and Enforcement Limits

The previous section explained the core legal hurdle in manipulation cases: you must show not only that an order was placed and canceled, but that it was placed with deceptive intent—a "message," not a genuine willingness to trade. That idea sounds straightforward until you confront the operational reality regulators face every day.

Modern markets produce an ocean of order messages. Proving intent requires finding a small, meaningful pattern inside that ocean.

This section explains why enforcement is often selective, why "obvious" manipulation can still take years to prosecute, and why the limits are not just about budgets or willpower. They are about a genuine **technology mismatch**: markets generate data at machine speed, while surveillance, legal process, and proof must move at human speed.

The needle-in-a-haystack problem: markets generate mostly *messages*, not trades

When most people picture trading, they picture *trades*—a buy and a sell meeting in the middle. But the modern market is dominated by **quotes and order messages**: new orders, cancellations, modifications, and routes across venues.

A helpful mental model is to think of the market as a crowded room where:

- **Trades** are actual handshakes (commitments).
- **Quotes/messages** are people constantly raising their hands, changing their minds, repositioning, and signaling.

The enforcement challenge is that manipulation often happens *in the signaling layer*—in the messages that shape perception and trigger reactions—even if the manipulator's true profit comes from a smaller number of executions.

For a casual reader, here is the key point: **the suspicious behavior is often the absence of trading.** Spoofing, for example, can be defined by orders that were *not supposed to trade*. That means regulators must analyze what *didn't happen* (fills that were avoided), not just what did happen.

Why surveillance requires order-level detail (not just price charts)

A price chart shows you the outcome: the last traded price over time. But as we discussed earlier, manipulation is often about poisoning price discovery by injecting false supply/demand signals. Those signals live in the order book, not in a simple line chart.

To investigate intent, surveillance needs **order-level data** such as:

- the time each order was entered, modified, and canceled,
- price and size at each moment,
- whether it executed (partially or fully),
- how close it came to execution before being pulled,
- which venue it was on, and whether it was routed elsewhere,
- identifiers that can link activity to a participant (subject to rules and privacy).

This is why regulators emphasize audit trails: they are trying to reconstruct a detailed movie of the order book, not a snapshot of prints on a tape.

From philosophy to proof: what surveillance must establish

Recall the three pillars introduced earlier—**Intent, Deception, Harm**. Surveillance is the bridge between the philosophy ("prices should reflect real supply and demand") and the courtroom ("prove this specific defendant ran a deceptive strategy").

In practice, surveillance must do at least four jobs:

1) Identify the pattern

Detect a repeatable signature consistent with manipulation (for example, large displayed orders that repeatedly disappear when threatened by execution, alongside real trades on the opposite side).

2) Rule out ordinary explanations

Show that the pattern is not better explained by benign market making, risk controls, or routine order management. This matters because aggressive-but-legal trading can look superficially similar to spoofing.

3) Link the pattern to a participant

Connect the behavior to a specific firm, algorithm, trader, or supervisory chain. This step can be complex when activity is fragmented across venues and accounts.

4) Demonstrate impact (harm) in a way a court will accept

This does not always mean proving a single victim lost exactly $X because of one order. It can involve demonstrating artificial price moves, degraded liquidity, or profits earned in a manner consistent with deceptive signaling. But the argument must be concrete enough to survive legal scrutiny.

Each job is hard. Together, they explain why regulators cannot "just look" at the market and instantly see manipulation.

Why the haystack is so big: fragmentation, speed, and adaptive behavior

There are three structural reasons the data problem is enormous.

Fragmentation: the same stock trades in many places

A single stock can trade across multiple exchanges and other venues. Participants route orders dynamically to chase rebates, avoid fees, reduce latency, or access displayed liquidity. As a result:

- the full story of supply and demand is distributed,
- a strategy can be split across venues to be less visible,
- cause-and-effect can occur across markets (an action on Venue A influences behavior on Venue B).

Surveillance must reconstruct cross-venue sequences with accurate timing. That is a non-trivial engineering problem.

Speed: meaningful sequences happen faster than human intuition

Human intuition is comfortable with seconds and minutes. Many algorithmic sequences unfold in milliseconds or microseconds.

At those speeds:

- the difference between "pulled because risk changed" and "pulled to avoid execution" can hinge on tiny time windows,
- thousands of events can occur between two trades,
- a strategy can probe the market repeatedly without leaving obvious traces on a price chart.

This matters because legal claims often depend on careful reconstruction: who acted first, who reacted, what was displayed, and what was withdrawn.

Adaptation: strategies evolve as detection improves

Regulators and exchanges do not stand still, and neither do sophisticated traders. When a detection method becomes known, strategies adapt:

- order sizes vary to avoid "large order" filters,
- timing is randomized to evade simple pattern matching,
- activity is spread across symbols, times, or venues to reduce concentration,
- deceptive actions are mixed with legitimate executions to create ambiguity.

This creates an arms-race dynamic: surveillance is not solving a static puzzle; it is chasing a moving target.

False positives are expensive, so thresholds are high

A crucial and often overlooked constraint is that regulators must avoid accusing legitimate traders based on noisy data. Surveillance systems must handle two kinds of error:

- **False negatives:** missing real manipulation (bad actors slip through).
- **False positives:** flagging innocent behavior as manipulation (harmful to trust, costly, and unfair).

False positives are especially costly because once a case escalates, it triggers:

- intensive data pulls and analysis,
- interviews, legal process, and compliance burdens,

- reputational damage even before a final outcome,
- litigation risk if allegations are mishandled.

So surveillance often uses conservative thresholds. That means some borderline behavior may be monitored but not immediately prosecuted, and some harmful behavior may persist until there is a strong enough evidentiary package.

The computational reality: why "just run an algorithm" isn't a complete answer

It is natural to ask: if manipulation is algorithmic, why can't regulators just use better algorithms to catch it?

They do use sophisticated analytics. But there are practical limits:

Scale

Data volume is massive. Storing it, cleaning it, normalizing it across venues, and querying it quickly is a major undertaking. The work is not only "compute." It is also data engineering and governance: timestamps, identifiers, format differences, missing fields, and quality checks.

Context dependence

A pattern that looks suspicious in one context might be normal in another. For example, rapid cancellations can be consistent with:

- normal market making in a volatile moment,
- a firm pulling quotes because a risk limit was hit,
- a liquidity provider responding to a sudden news shock,
- an execution algorithm adjusting to partial fills.

A detection rule that ignores context will either miss subtle manipulation or generate too many false positives.

Proving intent is not the same as predicting intent

A model might estimate that behavior is "likely manipulative," but a legal case requires something stronger: a coherent narrative supported by evidence, robust to cross-examination. In other words, enforcement is not simply classification; it is **explanation**.

Courts and settlements require demonstrable facts: sequences, timing, profit links, and (when possible) documentary corroboration. This is why surveillance output is often the start of an investigation, not the end.

Deterrence versus certainty: why enforcement is necessarily selective

Even with perfect tools, regulators cannot investigate every anomaly. That forces a trade-off between:

- **Deterrence:** bringing some cases publicly to raise the expected cost of manipulation.
- **Certainty:** only bringing cases that are extremely strong and likely to prevail.

In practice, agencies often prioritize cases with some combination of:

- clear, repeated patterns over long periods,
- significant market impact or profits,
- strong linkability to a responsible party,
- aggravating factors (e.g., weak supervision, prior warnings, explicit communications).

This can feel unsatisfying to retail traders who suspect manipulation in real time. But it reflects a reality of enforcement: **the market moves instantly, while proof must be assembled methodically**.

What this means for everyday participants

This chapter is not asking you to become a surveillance analyst. But understanding surveillance limits helps you adopt a healthier mindset:

- You should not assume that "if it were illegal, it would be stopped immediately."
- You should expect that some harmful behaviors may persist in the gray zone before a pattern is strong enough to prosecute.
- You should focus on defensive thinking: avoid trading decisions that rely heavily on fleeting, easily manipulated signals.

The practical implication is not paranoia; it is humility. The displayed market is an extraordinary information machine, but it is not immune to strategic distortion, and oversight has real constraints.

Looking ahead: why regulation lags innovation

Once you understand the technology mismatch—the flood of messages, the need for order-level reconstruction, the high cost of false positives, and the legal burden of proving intent—the next step becomes intuitive.

Rules are written and enforced by institutions that move carefully for good reasons. Meanwhile, traders and technologists iterate rapidly, test variations, and exploit short-lived edges. That creates a persistent cat-and-mouse loop, which is the focus of the next section: why regulation tends to be reactive, and why everyday traders must navigate the gaps while the rulebook catches up.

8.4 Why Regulation Lags Innovation

In the first section, we established the purpose of market integrity: preserve price discovery so that prices reflect genuine supply and demand rather than manufactured signals. In the second section, we saw why intent is the legal fulcrum: canceling is not illegal, but placing orders *with the plan to cancel* can be. In the third section, we confronted the enforcement bottleneck: surveillance must sift through oceans of messages, reconstruct intent from patterns, and do so with high confidence to avoid false accusations.

Even when a behavior is harmful and even when regulators care, rules and enforcement often arrive after the innovation has already reshaped the playing field.

This section explains why regulation tends to lag trading innovation, why this lag is not simply incompetence or indifference, and how that lag creates a perpetual cat-and-mouse game between lawmakers (and regulators) on one side and coders (and market strategists) on the other.

Two different clocks: code iterates quickly; law moves carefully

At the heart of regulatory lag is a mismatch in operating tempo.

The coder's clock (fast). A trading team can:

- test a new idea in simulation,
- deploy it in small size,
- measure results immediately,
- revise parameters the same day,
- roll it out broadly once it works.

Iteration is cheap, fast, and continuous. If something breaks, it can be patched quickly. If a tactic stops working, it is replaced.

The regulator's clock (slow). A regulator must:

- define the problematic behavior in a way that is not overly broad,
- consult stakeholders (exchanges, brokers, investors, academics, and industry),
- draft rules that can survive legal challenge,

- coordinate across agencies and venues,
- implement, monitor, and enforce consistently.

Iteration is slow because mistakes carry high costs: unintended consequences, chilling effects on legitimate liquidity provision, and the risk of rules being overturned or evaded.

This is why the common saying rings true: markets can evolve at "the speed of light," while formal rulemaking evolves at "the speed of institutions."

Why rules can't simply ban "unfairness"

A natural reaction is: why not just ban strategies that feel predatory?

Because "predatory" is not a precise legal standard. Markets contain behavior that looks aggressive but serves legitimate purposes:

- Market makers update quotes rapidly to manage risk.
- Execution algorithms slice large orders to reduce impact.
- Arbitrageurs move prices across venues to keep them aligned.

A rule that simply bans "rapid cancellations," "large orders," or "fast reactions" would likely harm normal market functions. It could reduce liquidity and widen spreads, making trading more expensive for everyone.

So regulation is forced into a narrow corridor:

The rule must be specific enough to target deception, but flexible enough not to criminalize competition.

That corridor is exactly where coders look for openings.

The loophole principle: when you target a pattern, the pattern changes

Many regulatory responses are necessarily pattern-based:

- identify the signature of a harmful behavior,
- write a rule against that signature,
- enforce it,
- observe changes.

But once a signature becomes known, sophisticated actors ask a simple engineering question:

How can we achieve a similar economic effect without matching the banned signature?

This is not unique to finance. It is the same dynamic you see in cybersecurity (malware evolves), tax policy (avoidance structures evolve), and doping controls in sports (methods evolve).

In trading, this means that if enforcement focuses on one obvious form of spoofing (say, large orders repeatedly canceled near the best price), the next generation may:

- use smaller orders but many of them,
- distribute activity across venues and symbols,
- randomize timing to avoid simple thresholds,
- mix in occasional executions to create ambiguity,
- use short-lived signals that vanish before human review.

The economic goal remains similar—influencing others' perception long enough to profit—but the surface pattern changes.

Why enforcement is reactive by design

Many readers interpret "reactive" as "late." But the deeper point is that enforcement is reactive because it relies on **evidence of harm and intent**.

Regulators are constrained by:

- **Due process:** accusations must be supported by verifiable facts.
- **Proportionality:** the remedy should match the problem.
- **Demonstrability:** the behavior must be identifiable in data in a way that can be explained to a court (or at least defended in a settlement process).

That usually requires that a strategy first *exist in the wild* long enough to generate data, victims, patterns, and investigative leads.

In other words, there is a structural delay between:

Innovation → Widespread Use → Detection → Investigation → Rule/-Case

By the time a public case is brought, the strategy may already be less profitable or replaced—but the case still matters as deterrence and as a boundary-setting event.

The "exploitation window": when gaps in the fence are most dangerous

From the everyday trader's perspective, the most consequential part of the cat-and-mouse cycle is the period when:

- a tactic is profitable,
- it is not yet widely recognized,
- detection tools are immature,
- enforcement theories are untested.

This is the **exploitation window**. It is when the "fence" exists but has gaps large enough for sophisticated players to run through.

Importantly, the exploitation window does not always involve clearly illegal behavior. Much of the time, the window is about operating in gray areas:

- behavior that is harmful but not yet cleanly categorized,

- behavior that resembles legitimate market making,
- behavior where intent is hard to prove,
- behavior that is legal but predatory in spirit.

This is why the earlier sections matter: once you understand how price discovery can be distorted (Section 1), how intent draws the legal line (Section 2), and how hard it is to detect at scale (Section 3), it becomes intuitive that the fence will always be catching up.

Why "more rules" can sometimes create more complexity

It is tempting to think that adding rules always improves integrity. Sometimes it does. But rules can also create new incentives and new complexity:

- Market participants optimize around the rule, not around the spirit.
- Compliance becomes "box-checking," while behavior shifts elsewhere.
- Complexity itself becomes a competitive advantage for sophisticated firms.

This is another reason regulation can lag: the system must balance the desire for clarity with the risk of making the market so rule-heavy that only the most technologically advanced participants can navigate it efficiently.

The feedback loop: markets teach regulators, regulators teach markets

The cat-and-mouse game is not purely adversarial. It is also informational.

Markets teach regulators. New strategies reveal:

- which signals are most easily manipulated,
- which types of data are necessary for surveillance,
- where rules are too vague or too narrow,
- how intent can be disguised.

Regulators teach markets. Each enforcement action communicates:

- what patterns will be scrutinized,
- what explanations will not be accepted,
- what supervisory failures are punishable,
- what kinds of evidence are decisive.

This is why major cases and rule changes often trigger an industry-wide shift. Even firms that never engaged in manipulation adjust behavior because the boundary has moved, the risk calculus has changed, or surveillance has improved.

A grounded takeaway for non-professional traders: defensive thinking fills the gaps

The purpose of this book is not to make you cynical about markets. The purpose is to make you realistic about where protection is strong and where it is inherently imperfect.

Given the cat-and-mouse dynamic, a practical mindset is:

- **Assume displayed signals can be strategic.** Treat sudden, short-lived order book imbalances with caution.
- **Prefer robust execution habits.** Use tools (like patient limit orders) that reduce vulnerability to momentary distortions, especially in thin or fast markets.
- **Avoid "urgency traps."** Many predatory tactics exploit rushed decision-making.

- **Focus on what you can control.** You cannot control the fastest algorithms or the timing of enforcement, but you can control order type, timing, and position sizing.

The deeper lesson is that integrity is not a one-time achievement. It is a continuous maintenance problem. Market structure evolves, strategies evolve, and oversight evolves in response. That is not a failure of the idea of regulation; it is the reality of regulating a machine-speed ecosystem while preserving competition and innovation.

In the trading shark tank, the rules of the road matter—but so does knowing that the road is always under construction.

Chapter 9

Case Studies: Scenarios from the Wild

Theory is clean, but the live market is messy, fast, and unforgiving. In this chapter, we step out of the classroom and into the crossfire, dissecting minute-by-minute autopsies of real trading traps. By witnessing exactly how a spoof lures a crowd or how a stop-loss cascade begins, you will learn to spot the shark fin in the water before the price turns against you.

9.1 Anatomy of a Spoofing Event

In earlier chapters we built the basic vocabulary of market microstructure: the *order book* (resting bids and offers), the *spread* (the gap between best bid and best ask), and the uncomfortable truth that *the price you see is not automatically the price you get.* We also distinguished between a market that is genuinely liquid (lots of real interest to trade) and a market that only *looks* liquid (lots of displayed orders that may vanish).

This section uses a concrete, step-by-step case study to show how spoofing can manufacture that illusion.

The core idea: spoofing is a story told with fake orders

Spoofing is a bait-and-switch maneuver executed through the *displayed* order book:

- **Bait:** A large order (or several large orders) appears in the book, signaling heavy demand or supply.
- **Switch:** The spoofer never intends to trade that displayed size. Instead, the displayed order is canceled or pulled the moment it has served its purpose.
- **Profit mechanism:** The spoofer benefits from the price move the bait helped create, typically by having *real* orders on the other side that do execute.

For a casual trader, the trap is psychological as much as mechanical: humans are pattern-seeking. A very large "wall" of bids feels like safety. A very large "ceiling" of offers feels like resistance. Spoofing exploits that instinct by displaying size that is *persuasive* but not *committed.*

The setup: a "buy wall" that seems to guarantee support

Imagine a liquid stock trading around $100.00. The best bid is $99.99 and the best ask is $100.01. The spread is small; everything feels normal.

Now a massive cluster of bids appears just below the market, concentrated at $99.90–$99.95. Many retail platforms visualize this as a thick bar in the depth chart: a *buy wall.* In plain language, it looks like:

> "If price dips, surely it will bounce there—look at all those buyers waiting."

Here is where the spoof begins: the large bids are not meant to be executed. They are meant to be *seen.* The spoofer is trying to change how others behave *before* any meaningful trade happens.

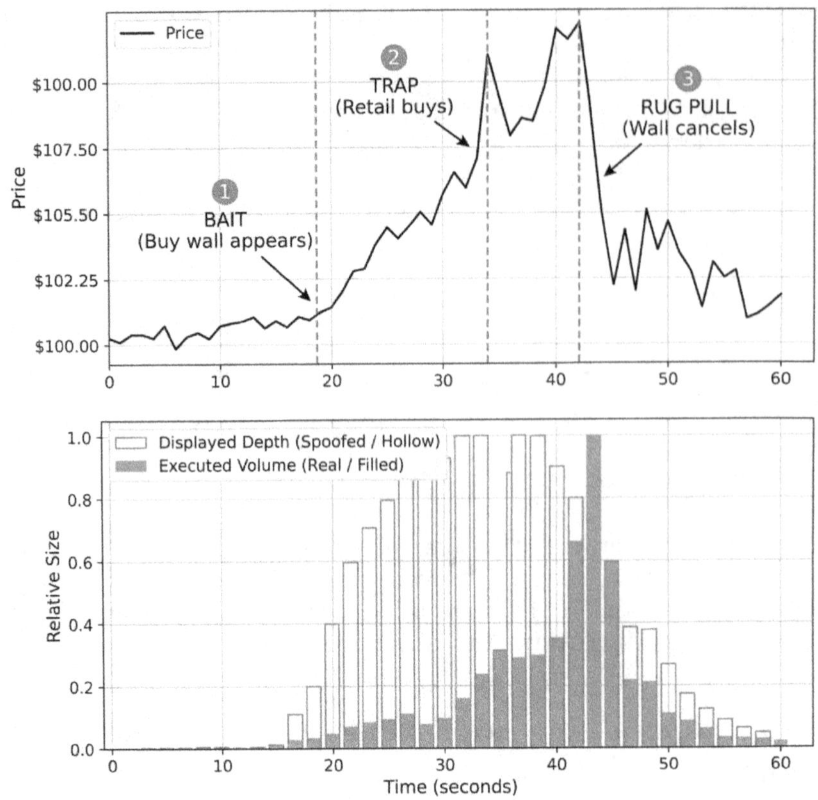

Millisecond logic in human language: what happens next

Once the buy wall is displayed, the spoofing event can unfold very quickly. Think of it as three phases, each with a different goal.

Step 1: The Bait ("Support" appears without commitment)

What you see (retail perspective):

- A huge stack of bids just below the current price.
- The tape may look calm; price does not need to move much yet.
- Commentators (or your own brain) translate it as "strong support."

What is really happening (mechanism):

- The spoofer is trying to influence *beliefs* and *order placement*.
- Crucially, the spoofer is paying almost nothing to display these orders. If they are canceled quickly enough, they may never trade.
- The spoofer can also place smaller, *real* sell orders above (or sell via another venue) to monetize a short-lived upward push.

The key microstructure lesson: *Displayed* liquidity is not the same thing as *available* liquidity. The book is an advertisement board, not a binding promise.

Step 2: The Trap (your "safe" entry becomes their exit)

What you see:

- Price starts to tick up.
- You (and many others) feel "confirmed" by the wall: "The downside looks protected, so buying here seems smart."
- Retail buys often arrive as marketable orders (market orders, or aggressive limits that cross the spread) because nobody wants to "miss the move."

What is really happening:

- Those retail buy orders *consume* the offers at the top of the book, nudging price higher.

- The spoofer's real objective is to use that retail urgency as *counterparty flow*. If the spoofer wants to sell, retail buying provides a convenient audience.
- Importantly, the fake wall does not have to be hit. It only has to be *believed*. The trap works even if price never trades down to those bids.

A telltale behavioral clue: the market begins to move on *confidence*, not on *executed volume*. When the "support" is truly real, you often see meaningful trades *at* or *near* the level. With a spoof, the market reacts to the *presence* of size rather than trades *into* it.

Step 3: The Rug Pull (liquidity vanishes exactly when you need it)

What you see:

- The buy wall disappears (or shrinks dramatically) in an eyeblink.
- Price stalls or snaps lower.
- Your entry, which felt protected, suddenly has no "floor" beneath it.

What is really happening:

- The spoofer cancels the displayed bids once they have served their purpose.
- Without that apparent support, other participants pull their own bids, spreads widen, and the price can drop quickly because the market becomes *thin*.
- If the spoofer has already sold into the rally (or has a short position), the reversal is where the trade gets paid.

The emotional aftershock: many casual traders interpret the drop as "bad luck" or "manipulation I cannot understand." The more useful interpretation is operational:

The market was not as deep as it looked. I paid for urgency in a moment when displayed liquidity was least trustworthy.

The "flicker" heuristic: the practical signature of fake liquidity

Casual traders often focus on the *size* of the wall: "It was huge." Predatory algorithms rely on that. A more defensive focus is the *behavior* of the wall.

A practical heuristic is the **flicker test**:

- **Does the wall persist?** Real interest tends to remain when price approaches it; spoof interest often vanishes.
- **Does it refill after partial hits?** Genuine large buyers often absorb sells and re-post. Spoof orders are often canceled rather than refilled.
- **Does the market trade into it?** Real support leaves a footprint in executed trades near the level. Spoofed support mainly leaves a footprint in *your attention*.

These are not courtroom standards of proof; they are *risk management signals*. You are not trying to prosecute spoofing from your screen. You are trying to avoid being the most predictable source of liquidity when the book is sending unreliable signals.

Why spoofing works so well on non-professionals

Spoofing exploits three vulnerabilities common to everyday traders:

1) Confusing "displayed" with "guaranteed."

A limit order displayed in the book can be canceled. Until it executes, it is not a commitment. Many traders intellectually know this, but emotionally treat a wall as protection.

2) Overweighting a single indicator (the depth chart).

Depth is seductive because it looks concrete. But the most important information is often *dynamic*: what stays, what cancels, and what executes.

3) Paying for immediacy at the worst time.

When you react to a wall by buying aggressively, you are typically crossing the spread and accepting slippage. In a spoofing environment, you are paying extra precisely when the "insurance" (depth) may be fake.

Defensive takeaway (without turning you into a microstructure engineer)

This book is not asking you to fight algorithms at their speed. The goal is to recognize when the environment is *trying to rush you.*

When you see a sudden, persuasive buy wall just below price:

- **1. Pause and watch behavior, not size.** A wall that appears suddenly and then "flickers" is information.
- **2. Refuse urgency by default.** If your trade requires *immediate* execution because a wall "proves" something, treat that as a warning.
- **3. Prefer prices you choose.** A patient limit order (even if it means missing the move) is often a rational response when displayed liquidity looks theatrical.

In the next case study, we will see a related phenomenon where a small initial push can cascade into a large move—not because fundamentals changed, but because the market's own *order mechanics* amplify the motion.

9.2 Surviving a Stop Cascade

The previous case study (spoofing) had one central lesson: *the market can look deep until the moment you actually need that depth.* A stop cascade is the same lesson expressed through a different mechanism.

In a cascade, the liquidity does not necessarily vanish because someone "faked" it. Instead, liquidity becomes overwhelmed because many ordinary, well-intentioned orders are forced to become *urgent market orders* at the same time.

If spoofing is a magician's misdirection with the order book, a stop cascade is a stampede through a narrow doorway.

The ingredients: stops, thin liquidity, and a trigger

A stop cascade typically requires three ingredients.

Ingredient 1: clustered stop-loss orders

Many casual traders learn a simple rule: "always use a stop-loss." That advice is directionally sensible, but it creates a predictable pattern: stops cluster around obvious reference points such as:

- the previous day's low,
- a round number (e.g., $50.00),
- a recent swing low on a chart,
- a widely watched moving average.

These levels are attractive because they are easy to see. Unfortunately, *they are easy for everyone to see*, including fast traders.

Ingredient 2: a thin moment (liquidity is lower than usual)

Stop cascades happen most often when the market is "thin"—not necessarily illiquid in an absolute sense, but *less liquid than traders assume*. Common thin moments include:

- lunchtime lulls,
- just after the open settles,

- late afternoon before the close,
- around minor news events (when some liquidity providers widen spreads or step back),
- in smaller stocks or smaller crypto pairs where depth is always limited.

In thin conditions, the book has fewer resting limit orders to absorb a sudden wave of selling.

Ingredient 3: a trigger that pushes price into the stop zone

The trigger can be natural (a real sell program, a headline, a macro move). But in predatory contexts, it can also be engineered: a fast trader may push the market just far enough to *touch* a level where stops are likely clustered. This is often described as **momentum ignition**: creating a small initial move that provokes other traders' automated responses, turning a spark into a burst of speed.

The critical mechanical detail: what a stop-loss order becomes

A stop-loss is not a special protective shield. Mechanically, it is a conditional instruction: "If the market trades at (or through) my stop price, then send an order." In most retail setups, a stop-loss becomes a **market order** once triggered. That conversion is the heart of the problem:

- A **limit order** is patient: "Sell at $49.90 or better."
- A **market order** is urgent: "Sell now, at whatever bid exists."

When many stops trigger together, you do not get one calm seller. You get a sudden *pile* of urgent sellers all competing for the same limited set of bids.

A stop cascade in slow motion (even though it happens fast)

Consider a stock trading around $50.20 on a quiet midday tape. The visible order book might have decent depth, but not much *close* to the current price. Under the surface, many retail traders have stops around $50.00 (a round number) and $49.95 (just below it).

We can narrate a stop cascade in three stages.

Stage 1: The poke (price is nudged into the trigger level)

A relatively small burst of selling pushes the price from $50.20 down toward $50.00. In a thick market, that move might be absorbed easily. In a thin market, the best bids are fewer and smaller.

Two important things happen as price approaches $50.00:

- Liquidity providers (and cautious traders) may pull bids or widen spreads because short-term risk is rising.
- The probability of hitting stops increases, which encourages some traders to sell *preemptively* to "get out before the flush."

This preemptive selling adds to the downward pressure before the cascade even starts.

Stage 2: The conversion (stops turn into market orders)

Once $50.00 trades, the clustered stop-loss orders begin to trigger. Each one becomes a market sell (or a marketable sell). Those market sells consume the best bids, pushing price down to the next set of bids.

Now the feedback loop begins:

Trigger -> Stop converts to market sell -> Price drops -> Next stops trigger -> ...

This is why cascades can feel like the market "fell through the floor." The market is not choosing a new fair value in a thoughtful way. It is processing a queue of urgent orders.

Stage 3: The air pocket (gaps and ugly prints)

In a cascade, trades may occur at prices that surprise you because the book is being consumed faster than new bids appear. That can produce:

- **slippage:** you sell well below your stop price,
- **gaps:** the tape prints at multiple lower prices quickly, with little trading in between,
- **a wick/reversal:** after the forced selling ends, price snaps back because the "natural" buyers were simply waiting for the panic to finish.

This last point is emotionally brutal: the trader who used a stop to control risk may end up selling near the temporary low, only to watch the price rebound minutes later. The stop did what it was designed to do (exit during a drop), but the *execution* was poor because the exit became urgent at the worst possible time.

Why this is called "momentum ignition"

Momentum ignition describes a strategy (legal or illegal depending on intent and method) that attempts to create a burst of short-term momentum by forcing others to react. Stops provide a particularly powerful reaction mechanism because they automatically generate marketable orders.

The ignition does not require supernatural power. The playbook is simple:

- 1. Identify where stops are likely clustered (obvious technical levels).

- 2. Wait for thin conditions.
- 3. Push price just far enough to trigger the first layer.
- 4. Let the market's own stop-flow provide the fuel.

Notice how the predatory trader is not necessarily "bigger" than the market. They can be *smaller* than the market and still succeed if they can trigger the right chain reaction at the right time.

A practical survival mindset: stop placement is also "crowd placement"

A stop is not only a risk-control tool; it is also a *place where the crowd is likely to be forced to act.* When you place a stop at an obvious level, you are choosing:

- a point where many others will also be forced to sell, and therefore
- a point where liquidity may be worst at the exact moment you need it.

This does not mean "never use stops." It means you should understand that a stop can transform you from a deliberate trader into involuntary fuel for a cascade.

Market stop vs. stop-limit: a trade-off, not a free upgrade

Many traders respond to stop cascades by asking: "Should I use a stop-limit instead of a stop-market?" This is a reasonable question, and the answer is not a slogan. It is a trade-off.

Stop-market (common retail default)

Benefit: You almost always exit once triggered.

Cost: You do not control the price. In a fast cascade, slippage can be severe.

Stop-limit (a conditional limit order)

Benefit: You set a worst acceptable price, which can prevent selling at the very bottom of a momentary spike.

Cost: You might *not* exit at all. If price gaps through your limit, your order can sit unfilled while the market continues to drop.

A stop-limit is best understood as: "I will exit, but only if the market allows me a price I can accept." In calm markets, that may work well. In true panic, it may leave you still holding the position.

Defensive techniques that do not require speed

The goal here is not to out-race algorithms. It is to avoid being a predictable source of forced liquidity.

Defense 1: stop logic over stop location

A stop should be placed where your *reason for the trade* is invalidated, not where it is merely uncomfortable. If you entered because of a thesis (trend, support, catalyst), define the point where that thesis is wrong. Very often, that point is *not* exactly at the most obvious round number or yesterday's low.

Defense 2: widen stops in thin conditions, reduce size instead

Tight stops and thin liquidity are a dangerous combination. If you choose to trade during thin periods:

- consider using a wider stop (less likely to be clipped by noise),
- but reduce position size so the dollar risk stays controlled.

This keeps your risk discipline while reducing the probability of getting swept into the crowd.

Defense 3: treat "obvious levels" as high-risk zones for execution

Obvious technical levels are not only chart markers; they are execution hotspots. If you must use a stop near an obvious level, consider:

- placing it *past* the level (so a mere touch does not trigger you),
- or avoiding initiating a position right above such a level during thin times.

Defense 4: plan your exit type in advance

Before you enter, decide what kind of failure you can live with:

- **"I must be out no matter what"** → stop-market accepts slippage risk.
- **"I refuse to sell into a vacuum"** → stop-limit accepts non-execution risk.

This is not about being "right." It is about aligning the order type with your risk preferences.

Defense 5: watch the tape for cascade signatures

You do not need Level II expertise to notice cascade conditions. Some common signatures:

- multiple rapid prints downward with little pause,
- spreads widening suddenly,
- brief plunges followed by fast partial rebounds ("flush and snap-back").

When these appear, the correct instinct is usually *not* to chase. Cascades often overshoot because they are driven by forced orders, not by a calm reassessment of value.

Key takeaway: cascades are about order urgency, not just direction

A stop cascade is not merely "price went down fast." It is a specific microstructure event where many conditional orders become urgent market orders at once, overwhelming nearby liquidity and creating air pockets.

If you remember one mental model, make it this:

"**Stops concentrate urgency. Thin books punish urgency.**"

In the next scenario, we will expand the same theme to a different dimension: not just *when* liquidity disappears, but *where* it disappears across fragmented venues when fast traders exploit tiny time delays between exchanges.

9.3 The Fragmented Venue Scenario

The first case study (spoofing) taught you to distrust *displayed* liquidity that can vanish. The second (stop cascades) taught you to respect *order urgency* and what happens when many orders become market orders at once.

This third scenario adds a new dimension: **where** trading happens. Modern markets are fragmented across multiple venues (exchanges and other trading centers). Fragmentation is not automatically bad—it can foster competition and narrower spreads—but it creates a race condition: when the same stock trades in many places, *a price change is not delivered everywhere at the same instant.* That tiny delay is the opening latency arbitrage uses.

What "fragmented" really means (without the jargon)

In a simple mental model, there is one marketplace and one best price. In reality, many U.S. stocks can trade simultaneously on multiple exchanges (and off-exchange venues). Each venue has its own order book, its own matching engine, and its own participants.

Here is the key practical implication:

There is no single physical order book. There are many.

When you see the "best bid" and "best ask" on your screen, you are seeing a consolidated view (often called the *NBBO* in U.S. equities). That consolidated view is built from messages traveling across networks. Messages take time to move, even if that time is measured in microseconds or milliseconds.

Retail traders tend to think in seconds. Predatory speed-based strategies live in microseconds. In fragmented markets, that gap matters.

The basic problem: the price you see is already a little old

Suppose you place a buy order because you see:

$$\text{Best Ask} = \$25.10$$

You click "Buy" expecting to pay about $25.10 (or maybe $25.11 with a bit of slippage).

But between:

- the time your platform shows $25.10,
- the time you click,
- the time your broker routes the order, and
- the time your order reaches the venue that actually has the shares,

the market can change.

In a non-fragmented world, that would just be ordinary slippage risk. In a fragmented world, there is an additional risk: **someone else can learn about your buying pressure on Venue A and race to Venue B before your order gets there.**

That is the essence of latency arbitrage in plain language:

See the demand first in one place, then buy the supply elsewhere before the slower trader arrives.

A story: one click, two paths, and one predictable loser

Let's walk through a concrete narrative. We will use simplified numbers and timing, but the logic mirrors real markets.

The cast

- **You (the casual trader):** You send a buy order through a retail broker. Your order may be routed to different venues to find shares.
- **The fast trader (HFT-style):** Co-located (physically close) to exchange matching engines, with extremely fast market data and routing.
- **Two venues: Exchange A** and **Exchange B**. Both trade the same stock.

Initial state (calm market)

At time t_0:

- Exchange A: best ask is \$25.10 for 300 shares.
- Exchange B: best ask is \$25.10 for 500 shares.

The consolidated display shows $25.10 as the best ask. Everything looks consistent.

The event (your buy starts to move the market)

At time t_1 you click "Buy." Your order (say, 400 shares) is routed and a portion reaches Exchange A first. Your order consumes the 300 shares offered at $25.10 on Exchange A. Now the best ask on Exchange A jumps to $25.12.

Here is the important point: *your buy has created information.* Even if you did not intend to signal anything, the act of taking liquidity at the ask is a message to the market: "someone is buying aggressively."

The race (fast trader reacts before your order arrives elsewhere)

A fast trader sees the update from Exchange A essentially immediately (relative to you). The fast trader infers:

"The best ask is likely to rise everywhere once slower orders reach the other venues."

So the fast trader sends an ultra-fast buy order to Exchange B to grab the remaining $25.10 offers *before your routed order reaches B.*

At time t_2 (very shortly after t_1):

- The fast trader buys the 500 shares at $25.10 on Exchange B.
- Exchange B's best ask jumps to $25.13.

At time t_3 your remaining order finally reaches Exchange B expecting $25.10—but $25.10 is gone. You get filled at $25.13 (or higher), or you do not get filled at all if your order was a limit.

The outcome (why it feels like "I never get the price I see")

From your point of view, the market behaved unfairly:

- You saw $25.10.
- You tried to buy at $25.10.
- You got $25.13.

But mechanically, nothing mystical happened. Your buying pressure was detected on one venue and "pre-positioning" happened on other venues.

A fast trader can then turn around and sell those shares back at the new higher price (perhaps on Exchange A, B, or elsewhere). The profit per share may be tiny, but it can be repeated frequently.

Why this is not the same as classic front-running (but feels similar)

Retail traders often describe this experience as "front-running." In strict terms, traditional front-running is a broker trading ahead of a client using confidential knowledge of that client's order. Latency arbitrage more often relies on *public market data* and *speed advantages*:

- The fast trader does not necessarily know it is *you*.
- They do not need your identity.
- They only need to observe *a price-impacting trade* on one venue and predict the next step.

It can still feel predatory because the effect is similar: someone seems to step in front of your demand and make you pay more.

The intuition: fragmented markets create "information lead-lag"

A useful mental model is to think of a price change as a ripple:

- A trade hits Exchange A and moves its local best prices.
- A message about that change is sent out to the rest of the market.

- Other venues adjust as participants react.

In the tiny window between those steps, different venues can temporarily disagree about the "true" best price. That disagreement is what latency strategies attempt to harvest.

Even if the window is small, the advantage can be large if you can:

- 1. detect the first ripple faster than others, and
- 2. route orders to the other venues faster than others.

Why casual traders are disproportionately exposed

Retail traders are exposed for structural reasons, not because they are foolish:

- **Longer path to market:** Your click must travel through your device, internet, broker systems, routing logic, and finally to an exchange.
- **Inferior information timing:** Your displayed quotes are consolidated and subject to update delays; your screen is not a co-located feed.
- **More marketable orders:** Retail often uses market orders (or aggressive limits) when excited, which turns them into liquidity takers—the preferred counterparty for strategies that profit from short-term price impacts.

Defensive thinking: you cannot win the race, so stop racing

You do not need to "beat" latency arbitrage to reduce its impact on your results. The defensive approach is to avoid turning yourself into a predictable liquidity taker at fragile moments.

Defense 1: prefer limit orders when you can tolerate non-execution

A limit order is a statement of price discipline:

> "I will buy at $25.10 or better; otherwise, I do nothing."

This shifts the risk from *price risk* (paying too much) to *execution risk* (not getting filled). For casual traders, that is often a healthy trade-off because the worst retail outcomes come from paying up during short, artificial bursts.

Defense 2: break the "one big urgent order" habit

Large marketable orders create a strong signal. Smaller, staged entries reduce your footprint and reduce the chance that your action alone triggers a race across venues.

This is not about being secretive; it is about not broadcasting urgency.

Defense 3: be wary of chasing sudden quote changes

If the offer just jumped and you feel compelled to hit the new price immediately, pause. In fragmented markets, sudden jumps can reflect:

- a genuine news-driven repricing, *or*
- a brief, technical micro-move where liquidity was swept and is now refilling.

Chasing tends to be worst precisely when the market is transitioning and spreads are unstable.

Defense 4: understand what your broker's "smart routing" can and cannot do

Retail routing can be very sophisticated, but it cannot rewrite physics. "Smart" routing still involves travel time and decision time. It can help search venues for price improvement, but it cannot guarantee you will capture a fleeting quote that disappears when faster traders react.

The healthy expectation is:

Smart routing can reduce friction on average; it cannot eliminate speed disadvantage in the smallest windows.

Connecting the case studies: the unifying pattern

Across spoofing, stop cascades, and fragmented venues, one unifying pattern keeps appearing:

> *The most dangerous moments are the moments when you feel rushed.*

- Spoofing creates a false sense of certainty and urgency to enter.
- Cascades convert many traders into urgent sellers simultaneously.
- Fragmentation punishes urgent buyers and sellers because speed differences decide who gets the old price.

9.4 Applying the Defensive Playbook

The three scenarios in this chapter were deliberately uncomfortable:

- In spoofing, the book *looked* supportive until the support vanished.
- In stop cascades, "good risk management" (stops) became fuel for forced selling.
- In fragmented markets, the price you saw was not the price you got because speed differences played out across venues.

This final section ties those lessons together into a single, realistic "day in the life" narrative. The purpose is not to teach you tricks; it is to teach you *habits*. A defensive trader survives hostile microstructure by being hard to rush, hard to bait, and disciplined about when to demand liquidity versus when to provide it.

The protagonist: a trader who refuses to be hurried

Meet Alex, a casual trader with a normal job and a simple routine:

- Alex trades infrequently.
- Alex uses position sizing to keep any single trade from being emotionally overwhelming.
- Alex prefers **limit orders** (price control) and accepts that sometimes the trade will not happen.

Alex does not attempt to outsmart high-frequency traders. Alex aims for something more realistic: **Make the market come to me, instead of chasing the market.**

Morning: the tempting setup and the first "rush" test

Alex is watching a well-known large-cap stock that has been trending up for weeks. There is no urgent news. The plan is simple: buy a small position on a pullback, not on a spike.

At 10:17 a.m., the stock is trading around $100.20. On the depth display, a large stack of bids appears around $100.00–$100.05. Social media chatter immediately frames it as: "Huge buy wall. Institutions defending $100. Load up."

Alex pauses. The earlier spoofing case study taught a specific lesson: *size is not commitment*. Alex does not ask, "How big is the wall?" Alex asks, "How does it behave?"

Alex's first checklist moment: *Is this liquidity stable or theatrical?*

Alex watches for about 30–60 seconds (a long time in a fast market):

- The wall appears suddenly, not gradually.
- The wall "refreshes" oddly: it shifts price levels and changes size in a flicker-like way.
- The stock ticks upward a few cents even though there is no meaningful increase in executed volume.

Alex's conclusion is not "spoofing proved." Alex's conclusion is simpler and more useful: **I do not trust the book enough to chase.**

Action: Alex refuses the baited entry

Instead of buying at $100.22 with a market order (or an aggressive limit), Alex places a **patient limit order** well below the current price, at a level that would be attractive even if the wall is fake:

Buy limit at $99.80, small size.

This accomplishes two defensive goals:

- It removes urgency (Alex is not paying the spread to "be in now").
- It sets a price where Alex is comfortable *even if a fast reversal happens.*

The order does not fill immediately, and Alex is fine with that. Not trading is a valid outcome.

Midday: the stop cascade arrives (and Alex treats it as weather)

At 12:23 p.m., the market enters a familiar thin period. The stock has drifted sideways near $100.10. Then, in under a minute, it drops sharply toward $100.00, trades through it, and continues lower.

On the tape, you can see classic cascade signatures:

- rapid prints down,
- a sudden widening of the spread,
- very little pause between price levels.

This is the moment where many traders do the worst possible thing: they convert surprise into urgency. They sell with market orders at the bottom, or they chase the breakdown by shorting late, or they smash the buy button on a rebound that is just a reflex.

Alex treats the cascade like a thunderstorm: **I cannot stop it. I can decide where I stand when it passes.**

Alex's second checklist moment: *Do I need to act right now?*

Alex asks two questions:

- **Was this move caused by new information?** There is no headline, no earnings release, no broad-market shock.
- **Is liquidity behaving normally?** No. The speed and gapping suggest forced orders (stops) and temporarily thin bids.

That framing matters because it changes the correct behavior:

- If the move is information-driven, you might need to re-price your thesis.
- If the move is mostly order-mechanics-driven, the worst fills happen to the people who panic.

Action: Alex lets the cascade do the work

As price flushes down, Alex's resting limit at $99.80 fills. The fill is not magical; it is the market finally coming to Alex.

Alex does *not* immediately add more. In a cascade, the first fill can be early. Alex waits to see whether the tape stabilizes:

- Do prints slow down?
- Does the spread stop widening?
- Do bids begin to hold for more than a heartbeat?

After a few minutes, the stock rebounds to $100.00. Many traders feel instant regret: "I should have bought more!" Alex feels something else: **My plan worked. I avoided the worst decision: urgent buying or selling during the air pocket.**

Afternoon: fragmentation and the execution trap Alex avoids

At 2:41 p.m., the stock begins to climb again. The quote is moving quickly. Alex considers adding a second small piece, but the fragmented venue scenario is fresh in mind: fast micro-moves can make displayed prices unreliable for a slower trader.

This is where Alex changes tactics *without changing discipline.*

Alex's third checklist moment: *Am I about to pay for immediacy?*

Alex notices:

- the offer is jumping in small increments,
- fills on the tape are occurring at slightly different prices in quick succession,
- the spread occasionally widens by a cent or two and then snaps back.

This is exactly the type of environment where a market order is an invitation to be "picked off" across venues.

Action: Alex uses a limit order that is designed to *not* chase

Alex chooses a limit price that reflects willingness, not excitement:

Buy limit at $99.95 (near the rebound area), not at the current offer.

Alex is explicitly declining to race. If the stock runs away, that is acceptable; missing a trade is cheaper than paying an unpredictable premium in a fast, fragmented moment.

The order does not fill. The stock continues to $100.30. Alex does nothing.

This is a key psychological milestone for survival: **A defensive trader measures success by decision quality, not by constant participation.**

Putting the playbook into words: what Alex actually did

Alex's day was not heroic. It was disciplined. The playbook can be summarized as a sequence of small, repeatable choices.

1) Alex treated the order book as *suggestive*, not *authoritative*

In the spoofing section, the danger was believing displayed depth. Alex responded by watching behavior (persistence, flicker, execution footprint) and refusing to treat a wall as guaranteed support.

2) Alex refused to become an urgent order during unstable liquidity

In the stop cascade section, the danger was forced urgency (stops turning into market orders) and thin books. Alex responded by placing resting limits *before* the chaos and letting volatility come to the order, rather than sending urgent orders into the chaos.

3) Alex accepted speed disadvantage and adapted through price discipline

In the fragmented venue section, the danger was being slow in a cross-venue race. Alex responded by not racing at all: using limits, waiting for favorable prices, and avoiding the "click-to-chase" reflex.

A practical "never again" list for casual traders

To close the chapter, here are the specific mistakes this playbook is designed to prevent:

- **Buying because a wall looks big** (instead of because it is stable and supported by actual trades).
- **Placing stops in the most obvious locations** without considering crowding and thin-market conditions.
- **Using market orders in fast, jumpy quotes** where fragmentation and speed advantages are most punitive.
- **Turning surprise into urgency**—the most expensive habit in hostile microstructure.

The chapter's bottom line

Predatory strategies thrive on one thing: **your impatience**. They do not need to predict your long-term thesis. They only need to pressure you into becoming a liquidity taker at the worst moments.

A defensively minded trader is not passive in the sense of being uninvolved; they are passive in the most important sense: **They choose their prices, they choose their timing, and they refuse to be rushed by the market's theatrics.** That is what "surviving the shark tank" looks like in practice.